From Slave Ship to Harvard

From Slave Ship to Harvard

Yarrow Mamout and the History of an African American Family

James H. Johnston

Fordham University Press | New York 2012

Library of Congress Cataloging-in-Publication Data

Johnston, James H., 1944–
From slave ship to Harvard : Yarrow Mamout and the history of an African American family / James H. Johnston.
p. cm.
Includes bibliographical references and index.
ISBN 978-0-8232-3950-4 (cloth : alk. paper)
1. Mamout, Yarrow, 1736–1823. 2. Mamout, Yarrow, 1736–1823—Family. 3. Slaves—Maryland—Biography. 4. Free African Americans—Maryland—Biography. 5. African Americans—Maryland—Biography. 6. Slavery—Maryland—History. 7. African American families—Maryland—Biography. I. Title.
E185.93.M2J65 2012
306.3′62092—dc23
[B]

2011047006

Printed in the United States of America
14 13 12 5 4 3 2 1
First edition

For Beth and Meredith

Contents

From Slave Ship to Harvard

Introduction

When the eminent American portrait painter Charles Willson Peale was visiting Georgetown in 1818, he heard of a Negro living there, said to be 140 years of age. Peale wrote in his diary that he proposed "to make a portrait of him should I have the opportunity." The man was Yarrow Mamout.

Almost two hundred years later, I, too, was in Georgetown when I came across Yarrow—his last name—or, I should say, a portrait of him hanging in the library. It was by a different artist, James Alexander Simpson, and done in 1822. Yarrow looks older and poorer. Still, I was captivated, even before I saw a copy of the stunning Peale portrait. Who was this black man, famous enough in his day to sit for two formal portraits, and why had I never heard of him? Thus began the research that uncovered this saga of an extraordinary African American family that went from slave ship to Harvard.

Our mental image of slavery is typically the slavery of cotton plantations in the Deep South at the time of the Civil War. The slavery Yarrow and his family experienced in the border state of Maryland was different. Yarrow came to America more than one hundred years before the Civil War. He knew freedom in Africa, the horrors of a slave ship, slavery in America, and then freedom again. Peale's portrait of Yarrow is one of only two or three formal portraits by a major artist of an American slave who was brought from Africa.

I chose to write this book as a history of race and family, but it could just as easily have been a detective story about my research. For example, I knew that Yarrow was a slave to the prominent Beall family of Maryland, so I went to a historical library and began perusing a folder on the Bealls. I noticed two men talking to the librarian. I saw her gesture toward me and heard her say that I had the folder they wanted. This is how I met Jim Beall and his father, Robert Beall.

Such serendipitous encounters made it seem as though an invisible hand were repeatedly guiding my research to new and more startling discoveries. When I went to the National Archives to review the deeds on property Yarrow owned in Georgetown, I found a copy of his signature, which, to my amazement, was in Arabic. Then there was the time I was looking at a map of rural Washington County, Maryland, when my eyes fell on the name Yarrowsburg Road.

The most remarkable break in my research came from a visit to the community of Yarrowsburg. Mt. Moriah Baptist Church, which is nearby, has a small, predominantly black congregation, and the pastor had invited me to a church reunion. He thought I might obtain oral histories about Yarrow's daughter-in-law, Polly Yarrow, for whom Yarrowsburg was named. Surprisingly, no one had heard of her. However, one person, Gloria Dennis, spoke up, saying, "I don't know anything about Polly Yarrow, but my family was named Turner. We came from here and are related to Nat Turner. Are you interested?"

My research up to that point had focused on Yarrow alone. However, that two major figures in black history—Yarrow Mamout and Nat Turner, who led a slave revolt in Virginia—were somehow connected to this obscure little community in Western Maryland added a new dimension and changed the direction of my research. I ultimately concluded, as you will read, that Mrs. Dennis and other Turner descendants could not be related to Nat Turner, but they are related to Polly Yarrow. Her maiden name was Turner, and it was her nephew's grandson who went to Harvard.

This book covers a period of 275 years, from Yarrow's birth in Africa in 1736 to the present time, and spans six generations. Since records on individual slaves are almost nonexistent and records on free blacks such as the Yarrows and Turners are often sketchy, there are gaps in the history that have been filled with less than perfect information.

Two of the generations discussed are Yarrows, and four are their in-laws, the Turners. To help readers keep family members straight, a family tree begins the photo section and shows the relationships. For those who were slaves, the tree lists the names of the owners as well.

The book is organized into fifteen narrative chapters that tell the family's story in a historical context. The first five focus on Yarrow and the Bealls and provide background about the region of what is now the District of Columbia in colonial times, when Yarrow lived there, and the origins of slavery in Maryland and Virginia. The paintings, particularly Yarrow's sitting for Peale, need a chapter of their own.[1] Next are three chapters on Yarrow's sister, niece, and son, respectively. The narrative then moves to the family of his daughter-in-law, Mary "Polly" Turner Yarrow, and follows the Turners through the Civil War to Harvard and today. At the end of the book is an epilogue with a guide for seeing the buildings, places, documents, and art that are still around. I have also included maps from the period to show where the events took place.

The cast of characters is large, and so is their story. It begins in the highlands of Guinea and Senegal in West Africa in a place known as Futa Jallon, where Fulani people had settled. The Fulani were Muslims who in Yarrow's day were warring with their non-Muslim neighbors. During this period of warfare, Muslims were on rare occasions captured and sold into slavery. This seems to be how Yarrow, an educated Muslim, and his sister found themselves on a slave ship bound for America.

At roughly the same time as the Fulani were moving into Futa Jallon, settlers from England were sailing to the American colonies of Virginia and Maryland. The settlers, in desperate need of something to export in exchange for finished goods from England, turned to the surest moneymaker they could find, the addictive tobacco leaf. Agricultural factories called plantations sprang up, and the planters began buying indentured servants and convicts from Great Britain and, later, slaves from Africa to do the work.

Ironically, the Beall family, which owned Yarrow, traces itself back to a man who came to America through battle and enslavement similar to Yarrow. The English were fighting their neighbors in Scotland when the English captured the Scotsman Ninian Beall and shipped him off to America as a prisoner of war for a term of years. Ninian found life in Maryland so agreeable that when he ultimately was freed, he urged his relatives in Scotland to join him, and they did.

Yarrow's first owner, Samuel Beall, was descended from these relatives and was a prominent figure in early Maryland. He bought Yarrow right off the slave ship on June 4, 1752, and made him his body servant. Yarrow was a savvy, hardworking man. When he was freed forty-four years later, he quickly earned enough money to buy a house in Georgetown, invest in bank stock, and make interest-bearing loans to merchants. It was as a small-time financier that he came to the attention of Peale. The artist was hobnobbing with presidents, politicians, scientists, philosophers, and the rich and famous when he heard of the African. That such a great man wanted to paint a former slave made a big impression on Yarrow, and Yarrow made a lasting impression on Peale as well.

The record is thinner on Yarrow's immediate family: his sister, wife, and son. His sister seems to have been a slave named Hannah who worked at a tavern in Rockville, Maryland, about thirteen miles north of Georgetown. When she finally got her freedom, she moved to Georgetown and called herself Free Hannah and later Hannah Peale.

Yarrow's wife, or partner, was a slave when she gave birth to Yarrow's son. Her name appears to have been Jane. Freed on the death of her owner, Ann Chambers, she called herself Jane Chambers.

Yarrow Mamout was fifty-two years old when his son Aquilla was born. By law, Aquilla was the slave of his mother's owner. Therefore, Yarrow had to buy the boy's freedom. Yarrow taught Aquilla everything that he knew, and he even arranged for his son to be taught to read and write.

Yarrow's niece was named Nancy Hillman. She was Hannah's daughter and was every bit as clever as her uncle. Twenty years after Yarrow died, Hillman discovered that an old loan of his was in default. She hired a lawyer, filed suit in court, and recovered the unpaid principal plus interest.

In the meantime, Aquilla left Georgetown to purchase a small house in the farming region of Washington County, Maryland, known as Pleasant Valley, forty-five miles northwest of Georgetown. He moved apparently because his wife, Mary "Polly" Turner, wanted to live near her brother, who was a slave there. Aquilla died seven years after buying a small parcel in the valley, leaving the widowed Polly to carry on alone. She became a midwife. As demand for her services grew, the place where she lived ended up being called Yarrowsburg, even though the community itself was white.

This part of Maryland is steeped in black history. John Brown rented a farm nearby. He used it as staging ground for his raid on Harpers Ferry. It was a mile and a half from Polly Yarrow's house. The Battle of Antietam, or Sharpsburg, was fought five miles away. Union and Confederate troops chased each other through the valley on their way there.

Polly may have delivered her brother's son, Simon Turner.[2] The family history after his birth is more certain. Born a slave, Simon asked for his freedom when he grew up and enlisted in the Union Army during the Civil War. He fought in the famous, and controversial, engagement of black troops known as the Battle of the Crater and returned home after the war.

With the postwar constitutional amendments guaranteeing freedom, the family turned its attention to education. Simon had married Lucinda Sands, the daughter of an ambitious and respected ex-slave named Arthur Sands. Although Sands and his children were illiterate, he did not want his grandchildren to be, so he helped start the first black school in Pleasant Valley.

Simon and Lucinda Turner's daughter, Emma, was gifted academically, and the family sent her to Storer College in Harpers Ferry to get a teaching degree. She met Robert Ford, a young theology student from Howard College in Washington, and the two were married.

It was their son, Robert Turner Ford, who entered Harvard University in the fall of 1923. He was the grandson of slaves. Polly Yarrow was his great-great-aunt, and Yarrow Mamout was her father-in-law. Ford graduated from Harvard in 1927, almost exactly 175 years after Yarrow had arrived on a slave ship.

The sixth generation of the family consists of Ford's daughter Alice Truiett and her four cousins, Gloria Dennis (the woman I met at Mt.

Moriah Church in Yarrowsburg), Emily Willis, Cynthia Richardson, and Denise Dungee. Among them, the five women hold eight college degrees. All are married and live in Baltimore.

What follows is the history of this family—and a case study of race in America.

1 Yarrow Mamout, a West African Muslim Slave

Yarrow Mamout was born in West Africa in 1736 and brought to America as a slave in 1752. He was Fulani, also called Fulbe and Peul, a nomadic people that had converted to Islam. Although the Fulani were associated with West Africa in Yarrow's time, today they may be found as far east in Africa as Sudan. They are a minority in all countries in which they live except Guinea, where they are the largest ethnic group.[1]

The Fulani were originally from what is now the country of Mali, but by the time Yarrow was born, they had migrated southward into the region known as Futa Jallon. That highland has been called the Switzerland of West Africa even though the highest spot is only 4,790 feet above sea level. Futa Jallon receives a great deal of rainfall and is the headwater for three major rivers, the Gambia, Senegal, and Niger. It was also called Senegambia historically, and sometimes simply Guinea. It lies within the eastern sections of today's Guinea and Senegal.

There is more to Yarrow's name than meets the eye. The spelling Yarrow Mamout in America would have been Yero Mamadou in Africa. The Fulani usually consulted an Islamic holy man when a child was born for guidance in choosing a name, and Yero was one of several male names for a woman's fourth child. Mamadou, a variation of Mohammed, could be selected for a boy born on a Monday. In other words, the name Yarrow Mamout tells us that he was his mother's fourth child and was born on a Monday. However, consulting a holy man was not mandatory, and Yarrow's parents may have had other reasons for choosing these names.[2] In any event, since he went by Yarrow Mamout most of his life and used Yarrow as his last name—even though both Yarrow and Mamout were given names—this is how he will be referred to in this book.

Yarrow would have had a Fulani surname and possibly a nickname, but neither of these is known. There were four basic surnames in Futa Jallon: Diallo, Bah, Sow, and Barry.[3] Conceivably, the name Yarrow was not derived from Yero but rather was a misheard rendering of Diallo. This seems unlikely, though.[4] Even today, surnames are infrequently used in this part of West Africa and, when they are, it is only for formalities such as financial and government records.[5]

Yarrow had a sister who was enslaved at the same time he was. Her African name is not known, but it is believed that she was known variously as Hannah, Free Hannah, and Hannah Peale in America. What is known for sure about her is that after Yarrow died, a woman named Nancy Hillman brought suit in court claiming she was entitled to inherit from Yarrow as the daughter of this sister. A judge found this to be true. For this reason, her mother is said to be Yarrow's sister and is called Hannah in this book, although in West Africa the concept of a sister might include a cousin or a close female friend.[6]

Fulani Muslims as Slaves

Yarrow, who was sixteen at the time he was enslaved, was neither the first Fulani nor the first Muslim to be brought to America as a slave. Still, Muslim slaves were uncommon. In early America, literate men knew Shakespeare's *Othello* and tended to think of black Muslims in Shakespearean terms, distinguishing them from other Africans. Shakespeare's Othello was not Fulani, but white Americans in colonial times did not make such fine distinctions. They were intrigued by these educated, black Muslims and referred to them as Mahometans or, perhaps through Shakespeare's influence, Moors, and they tended to treat them better than uneducated slaves. In Africa, Muslims were typically the ones who owned slaves and sold them to traders for transport to America.

The circumstances surrounding Yarrow's capture and enslavement are unknown, but they were probably similar to those of two other Muslims from Futa Jallon, whose stories are known. In early June 1731, twenty-one years before Yarrow arrived, a Maryland attorney named Thomas Bluett was attending court in Kent County, Delaware, when he heard of one such unusual slave. Bluett was told that the slave had escaped from his owner and was being held at the jail.[7] The local tavern doubled as the jail, so, curious, Bluett went there to interview the man. He later wrote his story.

The jailed slave was Ayuba Suleiman Diallo.[8] He was a Fulani from Futa Jallon, and Bluett took care to learn his full name. Diallo's father was an imam and an important man in Futa Jallon. Diallo was educated in the Quran and learned to read and write in Arabic. In February 1730, his father gave him two slaves and told him to sell them to Captain Stephen Pike aboard the slave ship *Arabella*, anchored in the Gambia River. Servants went along as guards. Captain Pike did not offer enough money, though, so Diallo broke off negotiations and found a better deal by exchanging the slaves for cattle in a nearby village.

Diallo made the mistake of sending the servants home while he stopped to visit a friend. His father had warned him to avoid the Mandingo people, but they found him while he was at his friend's and took him prisoner. They then sold him as a slave to the same Captain Pike with whom he had been negotiating. Pike seemed unfazed by this turnabout, and he enslaved the man with whom he had recently been haggling. Pike made one concession and allowed Diallo to write his father for help, yet Pike sailed before receiving an answer. Hence, Diallo found himself on board a slave ship bound for Annapolis, Maryland. He heard later that upon receiving his letter, his father dispatched a party with slaves to exchange for him, but the *Arabella* was gone by the time the delegation reached the river. Diallo also heard that the king of Futa Jallon retaliated against the Mandingo and "cut off great numbers of them."[9]

Pike's slave voyage was financed by men in England whose representative in Annapolis was Vachel Denton. He was a lawyer and seemed to be the man to call when there were slaves to be dealt with.

For example, according to *The Maryland Gazette* of January 21, 1729, a slave named William Robinson was brought before Denton, the city magistrate, and charged with striking a white man in an argument over a fight between their dogs. Denton ordered that one of Robinson's ears be cropped.[10] Several years later, the *Gazette* contained a notice from Denton that Mrs. Elizabeth Beale had two Negroes for sale.[11] He was presumably acting as her attorney. Even later, the paper announced that he was attorney for William Hunt, a merchant in London, and had slaves for sale at Hunt's plantation in Maryland.[12] Thus, when Captain Pike arrived in Annapolis with his cargo of slaves in the *Arabella* in 1730, the London sponsors of the voyage chose Denton as the man to sell the cargo.

Denton sold Diallo to a planter on Kent Island across the Chesapeake Bay from Annapolis. Initially, Diallo was put to work in the tobacco fields. However, the young, aristocratic Fulani proved unsuited to hard field labor and so was assigned the easier job of tending cattle. The Muslim later told Bluett he "would often leave the Cattle, and withdraw into the Woods to pray; but a white Boy frequently watched him, and whilst he was at his Devotion would mock him, and throw Dirt in his Face."[13]

Diallo's loneliness and unhappiness were made worse by the fact he could not yet speak English, and finally he ran away from the plantation. He only made it as far as the next county, in Delaware, before being arrested. This is where Bluett went to the tavern to meet and talk with him.

Bluett offered Diallo a glass of wine. Diallo refused. Instead, as Bluett described, "he wrote a Line or two before us [in Arabic], and when he read it, pronounced the Words *Allah* and *Mahommed*."[14] From these actions of refusing alcohol and writing and speaking a strange language, Bluett concluded Diallo was a "Mahometan."

After release from jail, Diallo was sent back to his owner. Once again he sought his father's help and wrote a letter to him in Africa. The letter was delivered first to Denton, since he represented the slave traders in England. He forwarded it to his principals in London. Eventually the letter worked its way into the hands of James Oglethorpe, who was in the process of setting up the colony of Georgia. Oglethorpe was intrigued by what he heard of this educated Muslim slave. Therefore, he arranged, probably through Denton, for Diallo to sail to London, accompanied by Bluett.

When the two arrived, Bluett set about finding a publisher for his book about the Muslim, *Some Memoirs of the Life of Job Son of Solomon.* Diallo, meanwhile, became a celebrity, or at least a novelty. He was persuaded to sit for a formal portrait by the English artist William Hoare.

Diallo then returned to Africa, and the English public soon lost interest in him. He supposedly helped the British, who were competing for colonies with the French, before being captured by the French and dying in a French prison somewhere in West Africa.

Another Muslim slave to have his history recorded was Abdul Rahman Ibrahima Ibn Sori, a name shortened to Abdul-Rahman. He too was Fulani, born in 1762 in Timbo, the largest town in Futa Jallon. As a young man, he was sent to Macina and Timbuktu in Mali to study.[15] Upon returning to Timbo, he served in his father's army. Abdul-Rahman was captured in a battle in 1788, sold to slave traders in Africa, and transported to America, where he ended up as a slave on a cotton plantation near Natchez, Mississippi.

Through luck, Abdul-Rahman was eventually freed and went back to Africa. The process began when he was in town on his owner's business. There he ran into an Irish doctor who remembered meeting him in Africa years earlier. The doctor had fallen ill there, and Abdul-Rahman's family had nursed him back to health. Now, to return the favor, the doctor tried to buy the slave's freedom, but to no avail. After the doctor died, Abdul-Rahman set about the task himself but was also unsuccessful.

Finally, a local newspaperman took up his cause and got the attention of a United States senator from New York. The newspaperman mistakenly concluded that because Abdul-Rahman could speak Arabic, he was a Moor from Morocco, and he conveyed this mistake to the senator.

The upshot of this comedy of errors was that senator turned to the sultan of Morocco for help. The sultan petitioned President John Quincy Adams to let Abdul-Rahman return to Africa, and Adams agreed. Abdul-Rahman became a celebrity in America, much as Diallo had been in England. He and his wife toured several states and were feted in Washington. After that, he sailed to Monrovia, Liberia. However, within six months of his arrival in Africa, Abdul-Rahman died of fever at the age of sixty-seven. He never made it back to Futa Jallon—or to Morocco, for that matter.

Thus, although no one recorded how Yarrow Mamout became a slave, it was probably in a fashion similar to Diallo's or Abdul-Rahman's. Yarrow's sister must have been brought to America on the same ship. That both Yarrow and she were captured at the same time suggests that the capture came after a battle or by stealth, or, conceivably, that Yarrow's family was the loser in a power struggle.

Stinking Slave Ships

Going from freedom and a position of wealth and education in Futa Jallon to slave and confinement on a filthy slave ship was a tremendous emotional and physical shock. Yarrow left no record of what his voyage was like, but the renowned John Newton did. He captained a "snow" or "snau" in the slave trade at this time.[16] The ship was of the same design as the one that brought Yarrow. The shallow-draft, two-masted vessel displaced one hundred tons and held about two hundred slaves, packed tightly below deck. The ship's shallow draft allowed it to sail up the rivers of Africa to collect slaves but caused it to roll on the high seas.

So awful were the slave ships that Newton soon lost his stomach for the job. He left the sea to take up the ministry, penned the hymn "Amazing Grace" to celebrate this remarkable conversion, and became an outspoken opponent of slavery. In fact, Rev. John Newton was the driving religious force behind the movement in England that eventually abolished the slave trade.[17] He wrote this firsthand account of conditions on a slave ship for the human beings who were the cargo:

> [T]he great object is, to be full. . . . The cargo of a vessel of a hundred tons, or little more, is calculated to purchase from two hundred and

> twenty to two hundred and fifty slaves. Their lodging-rooms below the deck . . . are sometimes more than five feet high, and sometimes less; and this height is divided towards the middle, for the slaves lie in two rows, one above the other, on each side of the ship, close to each other, like books upon a shelf. I have known them so close that the shelf would not, easily, contain one more. . . .
>
> [T]he poor creatures, thus cramped for want of room, are likewise in irons, for the most part both hands and feet, and two together, which makes it difficult for them to turn or move, to attempt either to rise or to lie down, without hurting themselves, or each other. Nor is the motion of the ship, especially her heeling, or stoop on one side, when under sail, to be omitted; for this, as they lie athwart, or cross the ship, adds to the uncomfortableness of their lodging, especially to those who lie on the leeward or leaning side of the vessel.[18]

In his book *The Slave Ship,* Marcus Rediker calls the ships floating prisons, with the slaves being the inmates and the crew being the guards. A snow, like Newton's *Duke of Argyle* and Yarrow's *Elijah,* with 200 to 250 slaves would have a crew of about thirty sailors. Outnumbered seven-to-one by its captives, the crew took a number of precautions. When below deck, each male slave was shackled to another man, thus limiting his ability to move. Even if he remained motionless, the rocking of the ship caused the shackles to dig into his flesh.[19]

Buckets and tubs served as toilets on the rolling ships if the men and women were able to get to them, which was often not the case. The stench was overpowering. Because of the smell, other vessels, spotting a slave ship, gave them a wide berth even on the open ocean. A slave ship, it was said, could be smelled a mile away.

Disease and death stalked the ships. The crew and the slaves themselves brought illnesses aboard. What is more, bacteria and viruses left behind from the previous voyage stayed aboard and looked for new hosts. Once disease did break out, it spread rapidly in the cramped, unsanitary conditions.

Slave ships also had to contend with the perils of the sea, which were often greater for cargo than for crew. In 1762, ten years after Yarrow's voyage, the slave ship *Phoenix* was bound for Annapolis when she sailed into a storm that knocked her on her side. The crew righted the prophetically named ship, but the food and fresh water were lost. While the crew supposedly survived on vinegar, the slaves were left with nothing to drink. After five days, they tried to take over the ship. Fifty or sixty slaves were killed in the uprising. Vaughn Brown recounted what happened next in his book *Shipping in the Port of Annapolis 1748–1775*: "The next day, the derelict was sighted by the *King George*, Captain Mackie, from Londonderry to the Delaware Bay. Although the *King George* was quite low on provisions and had 198 passengers aboard, Captain Mackie took off [of the *Phoenix*] Captain McGachen, his crew of 33, and two passengers. The slaves were left to go down with the *Phoenix*."[20]

The loss of another slave ship struck closer to home for Yarrow. The schooner *Good Intent*, sailing out of Liverpool and carrying three hundred slaves, went down off Cape Hatteras in 1767. Francis Lowndes of Georgetown helped finance the voyage. He was the son of Christopher Lowndes, one of the men responsible for bringing Yarrow to America fifteen years earlier.[21] Yarrow was living in or near Georgetown by this time, and the tragedy—or at least the financial loss it represented—would have been of great concern to Lowndes and his neighbors in the small Potomac River port.

Of course, not every ship went down, and not every slave aboard died. The aim of the slave trade, and the slave ships, was to make money for the financiers, ship owners, captains, and crew. Having the cargo perish before it could be sold was not good business in this sordid trade. Slavers made money only if slaves arrived at the destination alive and in marketable condition.

For this reason, the ships' inmates were fed regularly and periodically unshackled and brought on deck for exercise. Having large numbers of adult, male slaves on deck was dangerous for the crew. To protect themselves, the crew would build a "barricado" or barricade across the deck in the stern of the ship. In the event of an uprising by the slaves, the crew retreated to the protection of the barricado. From there, they could fire muskets and canon into the rebellious group. The *Elijah* was a "pink" snow with a raised rear deck, which enhanced the protection of its barricado.

Getting crews for slave ships was not easy. Typically, it was a job of last resort for sailors out of money and down on their luck. John Newton referred to slave ship sailors as "the refuse and dregs of the nation."[22] Worse yet for the slaves, the job attracted sadists who found the cruel conditions on a slave ship an accepted outlet for their passions.

Still, the cargo sometimes needed to be impressed as crew for the ship and hence might learn the rudiments of sailing. This was clearly needed when the regular crew took sick or died. In *The Slave Ship*, Rediker writes, "When nineteen of the twenty-two crew members of the *Thetis* fell ill in 1760, they 'set sail with the assistance of our own slaves, there being no possibility of working the ship without them,' wrote the ship's carpenter."[23] On some ships, slaves routinely worked on deck. Rediker found that boys and teenagers, whom the crew did not consider a threat, might work topside even on a fully crewed ship.

The ship that brought Yarrow was called the *Elijah*. He was only sixteen and looked even younger.[24] He may have worked topside. Records of his life later in Georgetown show that he knew his way about a ship and water. His owner at that time rented him out to work on the oceangoing sailing ship, *The Maryland,* while it was in port. The *Maryland*'s owner said Yarrow was the best swimmer ever seen on the Potomac River. So perhaps Yarrow had more freedom to move about the *Elijah* than slaves normally did, and he might have learned the rudiments of the sailing trade on the voyage that brought him to America.

In sum, although no one knows for certain about how Yarrow was sold into slavery in Africa or about his voyage on the *Elijah,* informed guesses can be made. He was sixteen years old when he arrived in Maryland. He was able to read and write Arabic and schooled in the Quran and Islam. He and his sister were taken prisoner at the same time and sold to Captain James Lowe, who may have anchored the small *Elijah* in an African river while buying slaves. Lowe surely had Yarrow shackled and chained below deck, and the ship may have remained anchored in the heat for days or weeks, while the buying continued, before it had enough slaves to set sail for America.

Since the crew had less to fear from female slaves, Yarrow's sister would not have been put in shackles. She was younger than Yarrow.[25] Fewer female slaves were imported from Africa because women were less valuable for work in the tobacco fields. During the voyage, they were kept in a separate section of the slave ship.[26] The *Elijah* was so small, though, that Yarrow and his sister would have been able to see each other from a distance and perhaps speak, particularly when Yarrow was on deck for exercise. Yarrow was educated and relatively young, so he may have been given more freedom than usual, perhaps helping cook, serve meals, or crew the ship. If so, he would have had additional chances to talk to his sister.

The time required for a slave ship from West Africa to cross the Atlantic varied between one and three months. Since the *Elijah* was in the Chesapeake Bay in May, it must have sailed from Africa between January and April 1752.

The Money in the Transatlantic Slave Trade

James Lowe, the captain of the *Elijah*, may have been a Marylander. There was a James Lowe in Talbot County, Maryland, in this period. His descendants identify him as the *Elijah*'s captain, although this cannot be said with certainty.[27] Yet even if the captain was a Marylander, the *Elijah* sailed out of Liverpool.

The ship arrived off Annapolis in time for this advertisement to be placed in the May 28, 1752 issue of *The Maryland Gazette*:

> JUST IMPORTED
> *In the* Elijah, Capt. James Lowe, *directly from the Coast of* Africa
> A Parcel of healthy slaves,
> consisting of Men, Women, and Children,
> and will be disposed of on board the said Vessel in
> *Severn* River, on Thursday the 4th Day of *June*
> ~~news~~ for Sterling Money, Bills of Exchange,
> Gold, or Paper Currency.
>
> *Benjamin Tasker*, junior,
> *Christopher Lowndes.*

The arrival of the *Elijah* would have generated a great deal of interest in the Maryland colony. Ships with slaves from the Caribbean islands on average stopped annually at Annapolis, but this was first slave ship from West Africa in nine years. The *Maryland Gazette* had carried an advertisement two years earlier, on May 16, 1750, by the same slave traders, Tasker and Lowndes: "A Ship with Negroes consigned to Messieurs Tasker and Lowndes; which had Orders to leave the African Coast by the First of April, is every Day expected here; and will dispose of her Cargo in Severn." But there was no later advertisement announcing the ship's arrival as was the case with the *Elijah*. Nor does this ship show up in the Trans-Atlantic Slave Trade Database as reaching Annapolis. It may have sold its entire cargo en route at St. Kitts and not continued on to Annapolis.[28]

Vachel Denton, the slave handler retained twenty-two years earlier to sell the *Arabella*'s cargo, which included Ayuba Suleiman Diallo, was still living in Annapolis when the *Elijah* arrived. He undoubtedly had long been regaling listeners with tales about educated black Muslims from West Africa, whetting Marylanders' appetites for the possibility that some day another slave like Diallo would come.

As the ad said, the sale took place on board the ship.[29] This may have been because the good citizens of Annapolis objected to having a putrid-smelling slave ship anchored too close to town. Even the governor's house was only a few blocks up the hill from the dock, within smelling distance. Or it may have been because the water at the wharf was not deep enough for the ship, even with its comparatively shallow draft. In a letter describing the arrival of a passenger ship from England at about this time, an Annapolis resident reported that the ship "anchored a bit below the mouth of the [Severn] river" and the passengers transferred to a pilot boat. Because of high winds that day, not even the smaller pilot boat could get to the dock, so the greeter rowed out in a "canoe" to meet it.[30] Perhaps such ferrying was necessary for all oceangoing ships into Annapolis. Another possibility was that Captain Lowe did not want to take the risk that slaves would see how close they were to shore and try to jump over the side in hopes of gaining their freedom. There might also have been security concerns. Annapolis was a small town with about 150 homes. The two hundred or so slaves on the *Elijah* outnumbered the adult male inhabitants. But the most likely reason the slaves were not disembarked at Annapolis prior to sale was because it was common practice to sell all sorts of cargo, whether human or other, whether slave or indentured servant, from on board the ships, so that at the end of the day the anchor could be raised and the ship could sail with its remaining cargo to the next port.[31]

The two slave traders named in the advertisement, Tasker and Lowndes, were brothers-in-law. They were prominent, well-respected men in the colony. Tasker's father was the acting governor, while Lowndes had married his partner's sister, making him the governor's son-in-law. He was also a merchant, rope maker, and ship builder.

With such important men involved, talk of this slaving voyage would have been in the air for months. The powerful tobacco planters, who were the principal buyers of slaves, would have discussed it when they ran into each other at the tavern, store, tobacco warehouse, church, or court. This was Lowndes's business, so he would have personally told everyone he met. His message was simple: For planters and slave traders in the market for West African slaves, this was a rare opportunity.

Lowndes was known locally as a merchant. He dabbled in slaves, to be sure, buying from this man and selling to that, and he handled Yarrow's voyage and the one in 1750. However, since these were the only times that Lowndes himself publicly advertised the importation of slaves from Africa, Marylanders might not have been aware of his deeper involvement in the business of importing men, women, and children from Africa in the transatlantic slave trade.

The slave trade was complicated and risky and required experienced men with deep pockets who could withstand the financial loss from a slave ship's sinking or the loss of its cargo to disease or who could afford insurance for such risks. The Trans-Atlantic Slave Trade Database, an important scholarly collection available online, holds the names of the owners of the slave ships. These records suggest the men of Liverpool formed syndicates to own the ships. While the individuals in a syndicate varied from ship to ship, many owned multiple ships and were, therefore, in multiple syndicates. For example, in 1754,

Christopher Lowndes's brother Edward owned the *Ann Gally* in conjunction with three other men, and he owned the *Cato* with five entirely different men.

North America was a relatively minor destination in the slave trade, though. Indeed the slave trade had begun in the year 1501, more than one hundred years before the first permanent European settlement there. Only 369,252 slaves, or 4 percent of an estimated 9.4 million transported during the 365 years of the transatlantic slave trade ended up in North America. Some 1,763 ships sailed there out of a total of 30,279 to all destinations in the Americas. The principal destinations were the Caribbean islands, Central America, and South America.

Christopher Lowndes was senior partner of Christopher Lowndes and Company in Maryland, but the company had an office in Liverpool as well. The other partners in the company were John Hardman, William Whalley, and Edward Lowndes. The company did not own the *Elijah* but was just the local agent or factor, selling the slaves upon arrival in Annapolis. The company itself financed only one ship, *Tryton,* which carried 352 slaves to Florida in 1756. Still, the four partners in the company, investing on their own behalf, regularly participated in slave ship syndicates. Ships with at least one of the company members as an owner made a total of ninety-nine different voyages carrying 14,834 slaves.[32] The Lowndes family alone—Christopher and Edward Lowndes, their brother Charles, and Christopher's son Francis—invested in ships that made thirty-seven voyages between 1746 and 1770 and carried 9,637 slaves.

Unlike Christopher Lowndes, who at least had to be around when his slave ship docked, most of those financing ships in the slave trade were sedentary investors, working from offices or clubs in Liverpool, investing in ships, and dispatching them on slaving voyages to destinations throughout the Americas: Jamaica, Virginia, Antigua, Barbados, St. Kitts, Florida, South Carolina, Guadeloupe, Tortola, and, of course, Annapolis. John Newton never worked for any of these men on his three slave voyages, but he fought against their kind when, as a clergyman, he pushed for the abolition of the slave trade in England.

Thus, although Benjamin Tasker Jr. and Christopher Lowndes were named in the newspaper ad as being responsible for the sale of slaves from the *Elijah,* they did not finance the voyage. They were merely on the marketing end of the venture and would be on hand to sell the cargo when the ship arrived.

The *Elijah*'s owners were Charles and Edward Lowndes and John Salthouse. Salthouse was the biggest fish in this group. He participated in the ownership of ships that made seventy-one voyages and carried 19,200 slaves.

The Trans-Atlantic Slave Trade Database contains grimmer statistics on these voyages—estimates, really. On average, 13.5 percent of the slaves on a Lowndes ship died in transit, while 20.2 percent of those on Salthouse's ships did. Most of these ships sailed to the Caribbean rather than to North America.

The Major Artists Who Painted African Slaves

Seen as a statistic, Yarrow Mamout was simply one of nine million. But Yarrow was not just a statistic. He was a living human being who went through the unimaginable experience of being an inmate on one of these ships. And, as his portraits prove, he survived.

So exceptional was the man and his luck that his is one of the few portraits by a major artist of someone who knew what it was like to be the cargo on a slave ship. One was of Ayuba Suleiman Diallo, who sat for the British painter William Hoare. The other was of Ignatius Sancho, painted by the famous British artist Thomas Gainsborough. Of course, since Sancho was on a slave ship only because he was born to a woman making the journey, he, unlike Yarrow and Diallo, would not have remembered the experience.

There are other paintings, engravings, and drawings of slaves, but not by artists of Hoare's, Gainsborough's, and Peale's caliber. For example, the former slave Equiano, who was active in the movement to end the slave trade in England along with John Newton, claimed to have been on a slave ship from Africa to America. There is an oil portrait of him as the frontispiece of his book, but the artist is unknown. A handsome black and white engraving of Abdul-Rahman exists, but again it was by an unknown artist. Likewise, a crude engraving by an unknown artist was done of the slave poet Phillis Wheatley. Much later, in 1837, during the trial of the slaves who took over the *Amistad* and sailed it to America, commercial illustrators supplied drawings to the newspapers covering the trial. And of course, there are a multitude of drawings, paintings, and sketches of slaves and the slave trade in operation.

The Hoare and Peale portraits are different, though. They are of men who came on a slave ship as adults, and they are works of art. The fact that only a handful of those on slave ships succeeded to the point of having a formal portrait done by a major artist demonstrates how destructive the experience was to its victims.

But why did slavery get started in America? Who were the men that owned slaves? And what kind of person traded in them? In short, why was Yarrow brought to America?

2 Tobacco and the Importation of a Labor Force

When the first English settlers made landfall in Maryland on March 25, 1634, a full 118 years before Yarrow came, slavery was the last thing on their minds. One hundred and fifty of them arrived on two sailing ships. One was the 350-ton, full-rigged *Ark*, the other the smaller *Dove*. They had barely survived a winter crossing of the Atlantic. Their ships had become separated in a storm, and, for a time, each group thought the other had gone down. They found each other at the port in Barbados then sailed on together to Point Comfort in Virginia. The Marylanders had been admonished to create a different kind of colony from the Virginia one, however, and the ships left the Old Dominion to sail up the Chesapeake Bay.[1]

In a few days, the *Ark*'s captain, Richard Lowe, ordered his two ships to turn into the mouth of the Potomac River. The ships carried not only the settlers but also, in the cargo holds, all the provisions and equipment they would need to start life from scratch in the New World. It was the first day of spring, a propitious sign for beginning the work of God and king. Captain Lowe dropped anchor at St. Clements Island, not far from present-day St. Mary's City, Maryland. Once ashore, the colonists cut down two trees and fashioned them into a cross. Then Anglicans joined Catholics to celebrate mass and thank God for their safe passage.

The voyages of the *Ark* and *Dove* are the stuff of legend in Maryland, and their arrival is commemorated annually in the state. The idyllic scene is how Americans prefer to think their ancestors arrived. But it was in stark contrast to how Yarrow and other slaves arrived. That moment came on a warm June day in 1752, when the small, two-masted *Elijah* with Yarrow aboard ended its transatlantic voyage by sailing up the Chesapeake Bay. Commanded by a Captain James Lowe, the *Elijah* continued past the mouth of the Potomac River, where the *Ark* and *Dove* had turned off, and dropped anchor at Annapolis, the capital of a Maryland colony that was thriving by this time.

The one-hundred-ton snow *Elijah* was less than one-third the size of the *Ark*, yet it carried more people than the *Ark* and *Dove* combined. There were an estimated two hundred souls and a crew of perhaps thirty aboard the *Elijah*. It carried no equipment or provisions for life in the New World, though. The passengers would not need them, and in any event, the *Elijah* did not have a cargo hold. The passengers were the cargo. They filled the entire ship. They were the men, women, and children of Africa, to be sold into slavery.

The 118 years that separated these two arrivals was less than two lifetimes. Children of passengers from the *Ark* and *Dove* could still have been alive when Yarrow Mamout arrived. The time between them was roughly the same as that between Henry Ford's first automobile and today, and the changes in America were about as radical. The colonists in Maryland in 1634 started from scratch in a virgin wilderness. The nearest human settlements were Indian villages. The only manufactured goods were those the settlers brought with them. Over time, tens of thousands more followed from England and continental Europe. Towns sprang up. Roads were built. The wilderness gave way to farms and plantations. Sailing ships arrived regularly with manufactured goods from Europe and left with American products bound for foreign ports.

Servants, Convicts, and Slaves

Slavery, and all that it brought, was not preordained in America. It was a choice the colonists made. Immigrants came from Great Britain fleeing oppression and poverty and seeking a better life. They knew that slavery existed in other parts of the New World, but they did not come to America with the idea of developing a slave-based economy, at least not at first. Yet once given root, slavery grew to be not only a part of the economy but also a part of the culture.

The insidious vice of American slavery sprang from another vice, tobacco. It started with the founding of Jamestown, the first permanent English settlement in America in 1607, twenty-seven years before the *Ark* and *Dove* arrived. The Virginia Company, which sponsored the colony, hoped it would profit from its colonists exporting the riches of the New World to England. Tobacco was not part of the plan. Although the company's directors knew that the plant grew wild in Virginia and was harvested in the fall by the Indians to be smoked on special occasions, they saw no commercial use in the weed. But within seven years, colonist John Rolfe, himself a smoker, mastered the art of growing tobacco as a crop and profited handsomely by shipping it to England for sale.

A mania for tobacco swept England and the rest of Europe. Virginians were ready and willing to service the demand. The plant was grown on the farms and even in the streets of Jamestown. King James of England denounced the commodity as that "deceavable weed," but in vain. His subjects liked to smoke; they were hooked. The Virginia Company worried about Jamestown's reliance on a single crop and nagged the colonists to diversify. If a whole year's tobacco crop were lost to disease, it argued, the colonists would have no way of supporting themselves. It suggested fisheries and facilities for the production of iron, lumber, glass, and ships. The Virginians ignored the advice. By 1619, five years after Rolfe's first crop, the colony exported only tobacco and some sassafras, whereas three years earlier it had exported eleven commodities.[2]

This is why the Maryland colony was supposed to do things differently. George Calvert, known more commonly as Lord Baltimore, planned the colony. He imagined that his colonists would apply themselves to fur trading, farming, and making crafts for export, just as the Virginia Company had advised the Jamestown settlers to do. But the idea did not take hold in Maryland any more than it had in Virginia.

The failure stemmed from fundamental differences between how men sitting in their clubs in London visualized the functioning of an American colony and how men sweating on a hot summer day in the fields of Virginia and Maryland experienced the reality of an American colony. The colonists did not lack for raw materials. Land, wild animals, and natural resources were in abundance; it was the hallmarks of civilization that were missing. There were no fabrics except wool, no manufactured goods, such as needles, pins, utensils and plates, and no luxuries like wine, sugar, and books. The colonists had to import all these things. They were, in short, in sore need of a commodity that they could export to Europe and elsewhere in exchange for finished goods and delicacies. Tobacco quickly proved it could do this more surely than anything else in Maryland and Virginia. The colonies developed barter economies with tobacco functioning as cash. By 1650, a mere sixteen years after the founding of Maryland, exports of tobacco from Maryland and Virginia to England totaled over four million pounds. By 1700, this grew to thirty million pounds.[3]

In the beginning, English settlers worked the tobacco fields themselves. That is, they owned small farms, just as they had in England. Jamestown founder Captain John Smith estimated that whereas a man's work in growing grain for sale earned him £10 per year, he could earn £50 or £60 annually from tobacco.[4]

The potential for such profits naturally attracted more settlers from England. But tobacco was a labor-intensive crop. One technique for planting was for a farmer to rake soil into a mound around his own foot. He then pulled his foot out and replaced it with a seedling and moved on. At the end of the growing season, the heavy tobacco plants had to be harvested, moved to barns for curing, and then packed into barrels for shipment. It was backbreaking work. One present-day resident of Prince George's County, Maryland, who worked a tobacco farm for one season and had the benefit of machinery, called it "terrible" labor and never did it again.[5]

It did not take many seasons of this kind of labor before tobacco farmers realized that although one man could profit nicely by working a field alone, he could make even more, and do it more easily, if he employed others to work beside him, particularly if he did not pay them. For this reason, early tobacco farmers began buying indentured servants from England.

This transformation from farmers who worked their fields alone to businessmen who employed others to do the work was a distinguishing characteristic of the southern colonies. It marked the rise of a class of men known as "planters" and of their large farms, "plantations," that were agricultural factories.

The bulk of the labor for these factories historically was from one of three sources: indentured servants, convicts, and slaves. This labor force had to be imported, but which type of labor was imported varied widely over time. In the early years of the Maryland colony, it was primarily indentured servants. Later, convicts became perhaps the largest group. Still later, slavery held sway. At the end of the colonial period, Maryland again turned to importing mainly indentured servants and convicts. A recent, unpublished study of Annapolis port of entry records by Jean Russo showed that between 1756 and 1775, 43 percent of the new arrivals who had not paid for their own passage were indentured servants, 38 percent were convicts, and only 11 percent were slaves.[6]

Indentured servants were men and women from the British Isles who signed a contract agreeing to work for a fixed number of years, commonly seven, in exchange for transport to America and room and board. Once they signed the indenture, or contract for their labor, they became by law a commodity like a bolt of fabric or a barrel of gunpowder. The business was thus depersonalized, with the commodities represented by pieces of paper that could be sold to someone else while the reality was that human beings boarded ships bound for the colonies for final disposition by profiteers there. This bit of commercialization made the tawdry process palatable to gentlemen and hence financially viable. Financiers, who put up the money to send someone to America, did not have to know, see, or touch the poor wretch who was selling his or her soul for a chance at a better life.

By 1660, one thousand indentured servants were arriving in America each year.[7] An obvious drawback of indentured servants was that when their indenture expired, they were free to work for themselves, and they invariably did.

English convicts were another source of cheap labor. These were men and women who had their sentences of death commuted to sentences for fixed periods of servitude in America. Being a convict did not mean that a man was a murderer, although he might well be. Fully three hundred crimes in England were punishable by death.[8]

The transportation of convicts to America was big business. In the eighteenth century, the English company of Forward, Reid, and Stewart transported a total of 17,740 convicts for sale over a period of years. The tobacco-growing colonies of Maryland and Virginia were the principal destinations.[9]

Coming to America as a convict was not considered particularly shameful. Many famous Americans have counted themselves as descendants of convicts. The father of Charles Willson Peale, the artist who painted Yarrow Mamout, came as a convict. So did John Jackson, the great-grandfather of the Confederate military genius Thomas Jonathan "Stonewall" Jackson. The elder Jackson had been found guilty of larceny and sentenced to death before having the sentence commuted to seven years' servitude in America. He met Stonewall's great-grandmother on the prison ship. She, too, was escaping a death sentence for larceny. They landed in Annapolis in 1749, just three years before Yarrow did. They were purchased by different owners but stayed in touch and eventually married.

Since they were white, the Jacksons' prospects were brighter than Yarrow's, but even indentured servants and convicts would have had difficulty finding each other in the New World if they arrived on different ships. Of course, one downside of convict labor was that convicts, like indentured servants, became free after they served their term.

Another problem with convicts was that some had a propensity for crime and for escaping their masters once they got to America. The planters were hard men, who treated fleeing servants and convicts, as well as slaves, like errant livestock. Newspapers in those days were filled with promises of rewards for the return of runaways along with crude descriptions, such as this one from the *Maryland Gazette* that gives a sense of how planters viewed their human property, even if it was white:

> Ran away the 26th of June last, the three following Servants viz.
>
> *William Beall*, by Trade's Gardener, about 30 Years of Age, is a short thick well set Fellow, with a full broad Face, and a pale swarthy

> Complexion, with brown Hair, and light Hazle Eyes; He has a Scar or Dent on his right Jaw, and a Sore on his right Leg; He was born at *Whitehaven* in the North of *England*, speaks very slow, and is a very palavering Fellow.
>
> *Thomas Starkle*, an *Englishman*, about 30 or 35 Years of Age, is a tall well made likely Fellow, has a thin Face, and is of swarthy Complexion, with pretty long black curl'd Hair, and smokes a great deal of Tobacco.
>
> *Nathaniel Sweeting*, born in *London*, about 25 or 30 Years of Age, by Trade a Shoemaker, of a middle Stature, is of a very pale yellow Complexion, has black Eyes, is somewhat bloated in the Face, and has swelled Legs. Had on when he went away, a brown Cloth Jacket, and a stripped Linsey Woolsey Jacket under it, a Check Shirt, a Pair of Osanbrigs Breeches, a Pair of new turn'd Pumps, and a new Felt Hat.
>
> Whoever takes up the said Runaways, and brings them to the Subscriber, at Bladensburg, shall have TWO PISTOLES Reward for each; and if taken fifty Miles from home, THREE PISTOLES for each, paid by *David Ross*
>
> This is the fifth Time of *Beall's* running away; he was taken up three Times in *Kent County* [on the Eastern Shore of the Bay], and the last Time near *Frederick Town* in *Virginia* [Fredericksburg]. *Starkle* has likewise made several Trips back, and it is thought they have now taken the same Road.[10]

The third source of labor was slaves from Africa, like Yarrow. Initially, slavery was driven more by economic considerations rather than by any inherent racism. That is, the first Europeans did not arrive in the New World with preconceived, prejudiced views of Africans. At least two passengers on the *Ark* and *Dove* were mulattos. Legally, they were not treated any differently from the white settlers. One, Francisco, was a Portuguese servant of a passenger. The other, Mathias Sousa, was an indentured servant. He served out the term of his indenture, became a free man, and voted in the Maryland colonial assembly.[11]

However, with the importation of large numbers of African slaves to work the tobacco fields, this tolerant attitude changed. Colonial legislatures began enacting laws intended to control the slave population.

The collection of colonial laws aimed at not only slaves but also at free blacks became known as slave codes. Among other things, the slave codes decreed that African slaves were slaves for life and that their children would also be slaves.

The profit potential of the slave trade was stupendous. At the end of the seventeenth century, the purchase price of a slave on the African coast was about £5. Once transported across the ocean and delivered in Maryland or Virginia, the same human being sold for about £20.[12] This price was still a bargain as far as the slave owner was concerned. If Captain John Smith's calculations, which were done about seventy years earlier, were still valid, a slave who was purchased for £20 could be expected to produce tobacco worth £50 or £60 every year. Based on these numbers, a slave on a tobacco farm could return his purchase price three times over by the end of the first year of ownership.

The price of slaves rose over time. By the middle of the eighteenth century, when Yarrow was brought to Maryland, the price was about £40. This was still cheap. In the same period, the going price for a convict was between £8 and £20 pounds.[13] While slaves were more than twice as expensive as convicts, they never had to be freed and thus had a much longer working life. In addition, they would produce children, who would in turn be slaves for the rest of their lives and who could be sold to others. In a sense, slaves were seen as an investment that paid for itself many times over.

Whether for indentured servant, convict, or slave, trafficking in human cargo was a sordid business. Disease and death stalked the transport ships as the cargo was packed as tightly as possible in order to maximize profits. On a ship carrying convicts from London to Annapolis in 1729, ten of ninety-five passengers died. A year later, thirty-two out of 109 convicts died on the voyage.[14]

Slave ships were much worse, of course. Servants and convicts were not shackled and laid side-by-side in the holds of ships the way slaves were. The system for selling servants, convicts, and slaves in the colonies was generally the same, though. Typically, the trader placed advertisements in newspapers announcing the arrival of the ship, the date and place of sale, and details about the cargo to lure buyers. Arthur Middleton describes the scene in his book on the early economy of the Chesapeake Bay region, *Tobacco Coast*: "The disposal of servants and convicts in the colonies was a sight that would have distressed modern observers. Like slaves—and indeed like cattle—these human beings were displayed to the prospective purchasers who felt their muscles, examined their teeth and mouths, and otherwise formulated opinions of their health and morals."[15]

Tobacco determined not only who immigrated to the southern colonies but also where the population in those colonies lived. Since tobacco was grown for sale in Europe, plantations and farms needed to get their output to a seaport. To do this, after harvest and curing, the tobacco leaves were stuffed tightly into large barrels. These hogsheads as they were called were four feet in height and two and a half feet in diameter and weighed 1,000 pounds when filled. Water was the preferred mode of transporting them from plantation to port. The heavy barrels were loaded onto shallow-draft boats and floated down streams and rivers. Otherwise, the barrels had to be put onto wagons or simply turned on their sides and rolled to the nearest body of water. The practice of rolling the barrels was not uncommon, but rolling tobacco barrels more than ten miles risked damage to the contents.[16] In Maryland, this meant that the early settlements were on the Eastern Shore, the land east of the Chesapeake Bay, and on the long strip of land between the Bay and the Potomac River, all areas readily accessible by ship.[17]

Tobacco even shaped how and where towns sprang up in the tobacco-growing colonies. There were two systems for colonists to sell their tobacco to Europe. The first was through consignment merchants in London.[18] The large Virginia plantations shipped on consignment. The other system for selling tobacco was for the planters to go through American agents or "factors" of the British merchants.[19] These factors were the men who would bring Yarrow to America and influence his life. They were particularly attractive for the tobacco farms of Maryland, which were generally smaller than those in Virginia. Factors maintained warehouses where planters would send their tobacco for collection before being loaded onto oceangoing ships. This allowed tobacco to be planted along smaller rivers that were inaccessible to the bigger ships. The result was that tobacco warehouses sprang up at natural ports in the rivers where larger ships could anchor, and the factors settled in these ports to buy tobacco and to sell goods from Europe in exchange.[20]

The main ports in the middle Atlantic region were Norfolk, Virginia, and Baltimore, Maryland, but there were several smaller ports, including—significantly for Yarrow—Annapolis and Bladensburg in Maryland.

Yet, the planters, restless for more land, kept moving west, and so within a few years the last and most northern port on the Potomac River was established where a rivulet called Rock Creek flowed into the river. The port was the brainchild of the Scotsman named Ninian Beall, who owned the adjacent land in Maryland. In later years, a warehouse was built and tobacco loaded on ships bound from there to England.

This port became known as Georgetown, and there Yarrow Mamout would spend much of his life. Other parts of Ninian's land also are of significance. They became the District of Columbia; the White House supposedly sits on land he once owned.[21]

An Insidious Dependency on Slaves

By 1700, tobacco had become the mainstay of the Maryland economy in the counties nestled against the Chesapeake Bay and Potomac River. Lord Baltimore's vision of a colony with diversified industry had been dashed. The planters were in charge.

Slavery had not yet taken hold and would not do so for another decade. The importation of slaves was a trickle of what it would become. Maryland's colonial governor, Francis Nicholson, reported in a letter of August 20, 1698: "There hath been imported this summer about four hundred and seventy odd negroes viz. 396 in one ship directly from Guiny, 50 from Virginy, 20 from Pennsylvania, which came thither from Barbadoes: a few others from other places."[22]

The rate at which slaves were imported actually decreased slightly over the next decade to average about three hundred per year, with an estimated total of 2,938 slaves arriving. These all came from Africa, except for 126 from Barbados, which, like other Caribbean islands, was another source of slaves. One ship, the *Henry Monday*, brought 320 slaves to Maryland, but the other ships carried considerably fewer.[23]

The fact that so few slaves were being brought in meant that for the first seventy years the labor force on Maryland tobacco plantations was composed primarily of English, Irish, and Scottish farmers, indentured servants, and convicts. The African slave trade did not bring in large numbers until 1710 and ended shortly before the outbreak of the American Revolution, when Britain prohibited all forms of trade with the colonies, including the slave trade, and did not allow it to resume until American independence. In other words, the bulk of the transatlantic slave trade took place in a sixty-six-year period, from 1710 to 1776. That is roughly how long the modern civil rights movement has been going on. Yarrow Mamout arrived in about the middle of that period.

In its time, slavery was morally unremarkable. In Maryland, at least, it came about through an insidious process, instituted without any conscious, collective decision among the colonists and without public debate. The transatlantic slave trade was an accepted and regular practice, and it tainted the highest levels of the colony's society and government and later the early government of the United States.

The Ignominious Arrival and Later Ascent of the Bealls

Samuel Beall, Yarrow's first owner, was enlightened for the times with respect to slaves. Indeed, although the Maryland colony's government followed the common form of a governor appointed by the king and an indigenous assembly—and thus displayed some characteristics of a modern democracy—its social structure, as well as its treatment of servants, convicts, and slaves, was a throwback to feudal times. For example, it was common to use marriage to cement political and business alliances. Benjamin Tasker Sr., the governor at the time the *Elijah* docked, was related by marriage to his two immediate predecessors.[24] He had married the sister of one and then married off a daughter to another. He married off two other daughters for business reasons, one to Christopher Lowndes and the other to Robert Carter of the powerful Carter family of Virginia. Colonial Maryland was, in short, controlled by a relatively small number of families who intermarried and who were quite comfortable not only with owning slaves but also with participation in the transatlantic slave trade.

Samuel Beall was different. For one thing, the Bealls were Scottish, not English. For another thing, and more important, although he was a wealthy planter, his ancestors had started in America at the very bottom of the social ladder. The first Beall in America, Ninian Beall, had not even come willingly. Instead, he had come as a prisoner of war, sentenced to seven years of involuntary servitude, a slave for all practical purposes. Captured in battle and transported to America, he had followed a path that was little different from those followed by the slaves Diallo, Abdul-Rahman, and Yarrow Mamout.

Ninian, who was probably Samuel's great-great-uncle, got into trouble because in Scotland he was one of those who had pledged allegiance to the exiled King Charles II. In 1650, English forces under Oliver Cromwell had invaded Scotland to rid it of such men. Just outside Edinburgh, Cromwell attacked the larger Scottish army. In the two-hour Battle of Dunbar, Cromwell defeated the Scots and took five thousand prisoners. Conditions for the prisoners were appalling, and most died. Eventually, about 1,400 survivors were put on ships and sent to Barbados or America as slave laborers for a period of years.

Thus, Ninian Beall arrived in Maryland as a military prisoner in service to Richard Hall of what was later called Prince George's County. He probably was not treated any better than a slave initially. In fact, as an enemy of Cromwell, he may have been treated worse.

Over time though, Ninian became a legend, mainly as a fighter. The colony was in dire need of someone that could deal with the Indians, who were increasingly resorting to violence to counter the swelling numbers of settlers. Purportedly six feet seven inches tall and with bright red hair, Ninian was a fearsome giant for those times. His physical strength and military prowess allowed him to rise above his ignominious arrival in the New World. He formed a company of rangers whose duty it was to move, or "range," along the border between the plantations and the Indians. In Ninian's day, that border was only a few miles north of what is now Washington.[25]

As soon as he was freed from servitude, Ninian began buying land. He was later rewarded for his military accomplishments with grants of additional land. He used his profits from these to purchase even more. By the time he died, the former prisoner of war owned 18,755 acres.[26]

Ninian also owned slaves. In 1699, the colonial assembly passed an Act of Gratitude that included a gift of three slaves. For this reason, Ninian had both land and slaves to pass on to his heirs. His will stated: "I doe give and bequeath unto my son George, my plantation and Tract of Land called the Rock of Dunbarton, lying and being at Rock Creek and containing four hundred and eighty acres" and "I doe give and bequeath unto my son in law Andrew Hambleton my negro woman Alie." Today, the Rock of Dunbarton is known as Georgetown. Ninian's residence at the time of his death is believed to have been in present day Georgetown near M Street on the west side of Rock Creek, a location now occupied by elegant restaurants, shops, and a luxury hotel.[27]

Ninian's remarkable success in the New World led relatives in Scotland to follow him. Four Bealls came to Maryland a short time after Ninian. Their relationship to Ninian has never been established with precision. They have been described variously as brothers or cousins, but most likely were his nephews. Among this group was Alexander whose grandson, Samuel, purchased Yarrow right off the slave ship from Africa.

The Bealls were prolific. Ninian sired eleven children and Alexander five. The sheer number of Bealls and the marriages among them make it difficult for genealogists to keep lineage and relationships straight. Prospective brides and grooms in the family may have had an equally difficult time determining how closely related they were to their betrotheds because first cousins sometimes married each other.[28] Perhaps they did not care—or perhaps they did not have a say in the matter.

The early generations of Bealls were planters. The first tobacco port in the Washington area was named Bealltown, on the Anacostia River, also called the Eastern Branch of the Potomac. The port, opened in

1720, could accommodate oceangoing ships that picked up the hogsheads of tobacco and carried them to England. But the planters did not know about soil conservation. When it rained, the soil was washed off the land into the rivers. Within twenty years, the river at Bealltown silted up from the runoff and was closed to larger ships.

In 1742, a new port opened a mile farther down river, named Bladensburg after Governor Thomas Bladen, to whose sister Benjamin Tasker Sr. was married. The town plat had sixty lots of one acre each.[29] In the same year, fifteen miles to the south by water, the father of ten-year-old George Washington began construction of the Mount Vernon plantation.

Life was good for the planters. Tobacco was making them rich. Some of those with plantations along the Anacostia also bought town lots in the new Bladensburg, but all the planters formed friendships and alliances with the warehousemen, merchants, and tobacco factors there. For more than a decade, the port was the principal commercial center for the planters in the Washington area.

The connections among these men of equal social and financial status would be called networking today and certainly would have felt comfortable to the Scotsmen who came from a clan structure in their native land. These family-based networks lasted for generations and served not only the planters and businessmen and their descendants but also their slaves and their slaves' descendants. Yarrow Mamout and his kin seemed to network within his owners' networks.

Samuel Beall, Yarrow's first owner, was born into this complex web of democracy, feudalism, and family in 1713. He was the son of John and grandson of the immigrant Alexander Beall.[30] He added "Jr." to his name, supposedly, in order to distinguish himself from a descendant of Ninian who was also named Samuel Beall.[31]

Samuel Beall acquired large land holdings around Washington. By the time he died, sixty properties had passed through his hands. His residence at the time Yarrow arrived was on a tract called the Charles and William. When surveyed in 1734, the property contained 1,100 acres.[32] It lay between Sligo Creek and the Northwest Branch near Takoma Park, Maryland, a Washington suburb. A tax assessment done after Beall's death recorded a large dwelling house forty-feet by twenty feet, three tobacco barns, and old log houses.[33] The log houses were where slaves would live and probably where Yarrow lived when Beall owned the property. There is no trace of these buildings today.

Samuel owned other large parcels of land scattered for sixteen miles along Rock Creek from its mouth at the Potomac River in Georgetown northward to Olney, Maryland. The Watergate complex may sit on land he once owned. The National Zoo certainly does. Beall also acquired the land surrounding Ninian's Rock of Dunbarton. On the west side of Georgetown, Samuel owned Noise Enough. To the north of Georgetown, he had Azadia and Gizer, which stretched almost two miles east to west from what is now the Tenleytown neighborhood to Rock Creek in Washington.[34]

When he was twenty-nine years old, Samuel Beall married Eleanor Brooke. She was a member of the fourth generation in the distinguished Brooke family of Maryland. Like other planters, Samuel served in the local militia. Since Indians and bands of armed men still roamed the colony, the planters needed a military force at the ready. Samuel was in the Captain George Beall Troop of Horse. He was also an inspector at the Bladensburg tobacco inspection warehouse, a position that was appointed by the vestry of the Episcopal Parish of Prince George's County.[35]

Beall was a man on his way up in life. He later was a sheriff, justice of the peace, revolutionary, and a one-quarter owner of the Frederick Forge, a major ironmaking facility in Washington County, Maryland, at the mouth of Antietam Creek on the Potomac River. His partners, Dr. David Ross, Joseph Chapline, and Richard Henderson, were part of the network of friends he acquired during his life.

Beall's network centered on Bladensburg and radiated outward from it. He was among the original purchasers of lots in the town, although he never lived there. His good friend and fellow planter, James Edmonston, had a place in the town. In fact, he conducted the sale of the lots.[36] Other original lot buyers included Dr. David Ross as well as the slave traders and merchants Christopher Lowndes, Edward Lowndes & Company, and Francis Lowndes. Beall's network included men from surrounding areas as well, men whose lives or whose descendants' lives would cross with Yarrow's later: Turner, Clagett, Chapline, Lowe, Tasker, Henderson, and Boteler.[37] They all knew, or knew of, one another. They might swap land or meet at the store, tavern, or inn when they brought their tobacco to the warehouse in Bladensburg. They might serve together in the militia or government or arrange a marriage between their families. It was a network of well-to-do men who for the most part trusted one another, or at least trusted each other more than they trusted other men.

Lucre and Taint in the Trade in Human Beings

At the time Yarrow arrived, Bladensburg was still the commercial center for the Washington area. As the lives of two of the town's merchants, David Ross and Christopher Lowndes, show, this commerce involved not only the export of tobacco and the import of finished goods and delicacies but the importation of human cargo as well. These were prominent men with connections at the highest level in early America.

David Ross carried the title "Dr." and was a physician. However, he was really in the business of making money in whatever way he could.[38] He was sometimes a merchant. In this capacity, he had done business with George Washington during the French and Indian War and corresponded with him about provisions Ross had supplied Washington's troops at Fort Cumberland, Maryland.[39]

He must have had other contacts with Washington though. Washington's Mount Vernon plantation was relatively close to Ross's house in Bladensburg, only fifteen miles down the Potomac River. Ross felt comfortable enough with his relationship to Washington to write him in 1769 with the almost treasonous suggestion that Virginia join other colonies to protest Parliament's taxes. Washington seemed to know Ross, for he not only agreed with what he said but also forwarded the letter to his friend George Mason. Ross's letter moved Washington into thinking for the first time about taking up arms against England. In forwarding it to Mason, Washington wrote: "At a time when our lordly Masters in Great Britain will be satisfied with nothing less than the deprivation of America freedom, it seems highly necessary that something shou'd be done." He continued by saying that armed resistance should be considered, but hastily added only as a last resort.[40] The pot of revolution was beginning to boil, and Ross was one of the men adding fuel to the fire.

Ross's various enterprises made him a wealthy man. His Bladensburg house was so large that it was used as a field hospital in fighting during the War of 1812. In recent times, the house was still considered valuable enough that when it was torn down, the rubble was taken to a site outside Baltimore and rebuilt using the original nails, wood paneling, floors, windows, and bricks.[41] Even by today's standards, its dimensions are impressive.

Ross did not shy away from the unsavory ways of making money though. He bought contracts on indentured servants and convicts from England and imported them. An issue of the *Maryland Gazette* reported: "We are inform'd that Capt. Johnson is arrived in Potowmack River, with a Number of Convicts, consigned to Dr. Ross of Bladensburg." In another issue of the *Gazette,* Ross offered a reward of "Five Pistoles" for the capture and return of John Maxfield, a shoemaker originally from Yorkshire. Ross described Maxfield, an indentured servant or convict, as "lusty" and as a "sly palavering fellow." And of course, the *Gazette* carried the previously quoted advertisement by Ross for the return of three runaways.

Ross's life crossed with Yarrow Mamout's in strange and subtle ways. His wife's aunt was married to Vachel Denton, the Annapolis lawyer who had handled the sale of Ayuba Suleiman Diallo. His son married Elizabeth Bordley, daughter of John Beale Bordley of Annapolis.[42] Bordley became benefactor of and protector to Charles Willson Peale. Ross himself became a business partner of Yarrow's owner, Samuel Beall, in the Frederick Forge complex on Antietam Creek in Washington County, Maryland.

Ross died wealthy. The inventory of his estate showed that in addition to land, his share of Frederick Forge, and the house in Bladensburg, he owned ten horses, twenty-nine cattle, twenty-nine pigs, one hundred and eight sheep, seventy-nine hoes, fifty-two axes, and forty-four slaves. According to the appraisal, his personal property alone was worth £4,115.[43]

Slave merchant Christopher Lowndes was wealthier still. One source of that wealth was of course the transatlantic slave trade, but his mercantile business was what he was known for.[44] In 1748, he built a mansion in Bladensburg called Bostwick. It is still there, as is a smaller stone house he had built nearby known as the Market Master's House. Today, the City of Bladensburg owns both. Its website describes Lowndes's business activities broadly: "His trading company imported spices, building materials, dry goods, and slaves. He also owned a shipyard where ocean-going vessels were constructed as well as a ropewalk that manufactured the cordage necessary for shipping lines."[45]

Lowndes's obituary in the *Maryland Journal and Commercial Advertiser* referred to him simply as "an eminent merchant" in Bladensburg.[46] The inventory of his personal estate spoke to his wealth and opulent lifestyle. At death, his personal estate included: a "chariot" or carriage, thirty-one slaves, ten horses, twenty-three sheep, thirty-six cattle, thirty-six pigs, 2,700 pounds of bacon, 150 pounds of pickled pork, 1,600 pounds of pickled beef, forty-two gallons of Madeira wine, twenty gallons of port, and eighty gallons of other spirits. The inventory of the goods at his store and other businesses in Bladensburg counted, among other things, 1,800 pounds of hemp for rope, thirty-seven pounds of chocolate, nine yards of black lace, and 2,394 pounds of sugar. All told, Lowndes was worth £8,321, not counting his real estate holdings.[47] He was twice as rich as Ross. A tiny fraction of that wealth came from the £40 he earned (using the going rate then) from selling Yarrow Mamout.

To the extent that Lowndes's contemporaries knew of his deep involvement in the transatlantic slave trade, they saw nothing wrong with it. His son-in-law, Benjamin Stoddert, served as an aide to General George Washington during the Revolutionary War. When John Adams, who always claimed to be opposed to slavery, later became president, he made Stoddert the first secretary of the navy.

One other merchant of note in Bladensburg was Glassford and Company. Portions of its accounting ledgers survive. They show 214 customers in 1753. Twenty-three were named Beall. Yarrow's owner, Samuel Beall Jr., bought a hammer, powder, and a pair of shoes called double channel pumps. Samuel Turner, one of whose slaves would marry Yarrow's son and have a relative go on to Harvard, purchased "sundry goods." Other customers included Richard Henderson, Dr. David Ross, and Christopher Lowndes.[48] Glassford's store, like the churches and taverns, was a meeting place for the planters.

From Bladensburg, the tobacco planters soon moved west and began sending their hogsheads to the port at Georgetown since it was closer. But in 1752, when Yarrow arrived, Bladensburg was still a tobacco port, and tobacco drove the slave trade.

In England, Liverpool had emerged as the center of the slave trade. Its financiers put fifty-three ships into the trade in 1752. The factors in America were key players in the slave trade because planters bought slaves on credit, and the American factors knew which planters could, and which could not, be trusted to pay.[49] The Lowndes firm with offices in Liverpool and Bladensburg was uniquely positioned to make big money from slaving, and it did.

By the time Yarrow arrived, it was clear that Lord Baltimore's expectations for Maryland had not worked out as intended. Instead of exporting their abundant natural resources to England, the colonists had devoted their attention to growing the addictive, labor-intensive tobacco plant. While they modeled their government after that in England, the upper crust planters adopted a near-feudal social structure. And the Maryland economy depended greatly on African slaves. To an extent, Scotsmen like the Bealls may have come with different ideas, but over the generations they too joined in owning slaves. Indeed, servitude and slavery were so ingrained in the culture that such major figures in that business as David Ross and Christopher Lowndes were respected citizens who had the ears of the most distinguished men on the continent. This was the slave-owning, feudal society that Yarrow Mamout was about to enter—as a slave.

3 Welcome to America

Annapolis was teeming with visitors on June 4, 1752, a Thursday. A new session of the colonial assembly had convened the previous day, and the town was full of legislators and favor-seekers. In addition, planters and slave traders from around the colony were there to look over the newly arrived slaves from Africa, including Yarrow, that were to be sold that day on board the *Elijah.* Then there were the curious. They had come to town simply to watch these strange-looking, frightened black men, women, and children as they came ashore in small boats with their new owners. Everyone in town could see the small snow riding at anchor there in the Severn River. Everyone knew, or knew of, the men conducting the sale, Benjamin Tasker Jr. and Christopher Lowndes.

For those interested in slaves, the excitement was palpable. Ships with slaves from Africa rarely came into Annapolis. Only twelve ships, with 2,241 slaves, came into Annapolis and the upper Chesapeake Bay from Africa during the sixteen years from 1743 until 1759.[1] Slave ships from the Gold Coast and Senegambia, the regions from which Diallo's *Arabella* and Yarrow's *Elijah* sailed, were even rarer. The last ship to come from either of these places was the *Gambia Merchant* in 1743, nine years earlier. The next ship, *Venus,* would not show up for seven more years, in 1759. In the sixteen-year period, the *Elijah* may have been the only source of Muslim slaves arriving directly into Annapolis from these two places. Rarest of all were these Muslim slaves. Merely because a ship came from Senegambia did not mean that it carried Muslims.[2]

The African slaves saw things differently. They surely had a mix of feelings. They would have been relieved that the terrible voyage was over. They would soon be rid of the confines, shackles, and dangers of the stinking ship and away from the oppressive crew. Land beckoned. But they did not know what lay ahead. Whatever it was, they knew it would not be good. It certainly would not mean freedom. The crew may have communicated this to them. They could guess they would be split up, and in this there was fear. They might not speak exactly the same language, but they could understand one another. What is more, they had been through the terrors together and had bonded. They could not know if they would ever see each other again.

Sold!

The previous day, Benjamin Tasker Sr. had spoken to a joint session of the assembly. Although he had served in the upper chamber for years, Tasker had recently become the acting governor, and this was his inaugural address. His predecessor, Samuel Ogle, had died earlier in the year.[3] The succession provided a bizarre example of what the feudal society of the Maryland colony meant: Ogle had been Tasker's son-in-law. Although the two men were about the same age, Tasker had married his daughter to the much older Ogle. The strategic marriage undoubtedly helped Tasker rise to the post he now held. One member of the upper chamber listened to the new governor's short speech with special attention—his son, Benjamin Tasker Jr.

Both chambers of the assembly convened again on the morning of June 4. Since the upper chamber had little to do, Benjamin Jr. was free to attend to selling the slaves on the *Elijah.* The walk from capitol to wharf was a short one. Besides, the slave trade was really the business of Tasker's brother-in-law, Christopher Lowndes, and he would have played the more active role.

The lower chamber of the assembly was busier. The morning that Yarrow was sold into slavery in America, a bill was introduced, the first of the new session, to amend the Maryland slave code. The bill prohibited old and useless slaves from being freed by their owners lest they become a burden on the public. It also prohibited manumission—

the grant of freedom to a slave—by last will and testament.[4] The assembly was not putting out the welcome mat for Africans.

The mere presence of the *Elijah* in Annapolis riveted the attention of residents of the city. If you were there that day, you looked across an expanse of water and saw the ship bobbing gently at anchor in the river. If the wind were blowing from the north, you smelled it too. You heard wafting over the water the din of the crew readying the ship and sprucing up the slaves for the sale, along with a blend of African languages welling up from below deck. The children in the town, particularly the boys, would be down at the dock, taking it all in and perhaps jeering at the slaves as they stepped ashore.

Since the sale took place on board, Tasker and Lowndes would have arranged for boats to row prospective buyers out to the ship. Planters such as Samuel Beall had come from around the colony to look at the slaves, possibly to buy some, and then to return home. Others with nothing better to do stood at the dock and gawked. Slave traders were there too; they would buy slaves for resale. The Africans on this ship would soon be scattered across the colony.

Before the sale, a committee of appraisers came aboard the *Elijah* to examine the slaves and determine their ages. The slaves' ages would establish the price they could command. Whether this procedure was standard for slave sales in Annapolis or whether it was just something Christopher Lowndes dreamed up to assuage buyers is unknown. In either event, the appraisers set Yarrow's age at fourteen or a little older, and Samuel Beall paid accordingly. Indeed, when Charles Willson Peale talked to Yarrow's last owner, Margaret Beall, she told him that there was a committee that determined the slaves' ages and that the slaves' ages determined their prices.

Beall was the kind of person Lord Baltimore had in mind when he founded the Maryland colony. While Beall had tobacco on some of his land, he was becoming more interested in industry than agriculture, and his industry was waterpower. He even called his water mill at Burnt Mills, Maryland, a Washington suburb, Beall's Industry.[5]

Beall owned or operated at least two other mills in the Washington area: one at Kensington, Maryland, and the second in Rock Creek in the District of Columbia where the restored Pierce Mill is today.[6] He may have owned more. Many of his properties were in creek beds surrounded by steep hills. The relatively small, narrow, twisty, sinews of land that show up in the surveys he commissioned seem ill-suited for farming. It is hard to imagine they were used for anything other than water mills.

At the time, water was the only source of power, other than human and animal muscle, available to the colonists. They used it to grind grain, to saw wood, and to "full," or wash the lanolin from wool. They also used it to power hammers that forged or pounded iron.[7]

Beall may have been in Annapolis to do more than just buy slaves. On Friday, June 5, a bill was introduced in the lower chamber of the assembly to repeal "An Act for the Encouragement of such Persons as will undertake to build Water-Mills."[8] Whether Beall was the beneficiary or the target of the bill is unknown. That is, maybe he benefited from the old law and was there to fight its repeal, or maybe his competitors benefited and he was there to promote the new bill. In either event, he could accomplish two tasks while in Annapolis: He could buy a new African slave from Christopher Lowndes, and he could lobby the assembly about the bill.

To planters like Beall, slave buying was serious business because their livelihoods depended on their workforce. Beall was a man who paid attention to detail, and he was there in person to buy Yarrow—for Margaret Beall told Charles Willson Peale that her father-in-law had purchased Yarrow right off the boat. Beall knew the Taskers, both father and son, and the Lowndes family. He may also have known James Lowe, the captain of the *Elijah*. These were men of substance that he could trust. So Beall probably chose Yarrow not merely because he liked what he saw in the African, but also because of what Tasker, Lowndes, or Lowe may have said about the "merchandise."

Once the sale was complete, Beall should have taken personal possession of his new slave. However, he had other business to attend to and probably wanted to hear the reading of the bill on water mills the next day. Therefore, he may have left Yarrow on the *Elijah* until this other business was done. But within a day or two, he would have gone back to the ship and gotten Yarrow. The two of them were then rowed ashore.

The two had different agendas on their first meeting. Of greatest importance to Yarrow was the fate of his sister. If Beall did not buy her, then who would, and how was Yarrow going to stay in touch with her? Only Beall could supply answers, and Yarrow would have been frantic to get his help.

Beall, for his part, was probably thinking about what do with his new slave. He could take him back to one of his mills, such as the one in Rock Creek, and put him to work; he could send him to a tobacco plantation to work in the fields; or he could make him a house servant. Beall may have realized immediately that Yarrow was not the kind of man to be put into the fields. He looked to be only fourteen years old. Ayuba Suleiman Diallo's owner had learned the hard way not to put an educated Muslim in the fields. He tried this, only to discover that Diallo could not do the work. Perhaps Captain Lowe noticed Yarrow's talents during the voyage from Africa and, on arrival, told Tasker and Lowndes how to market him. Maybe Lowndes made more than the going rate of £40 from selling Yarrow.

Beall had plenty of time to think. On horseback by himself, he could have ridden from Annapolis to his home at the Charles and William tract in a day, but he needed longer with a wagon carrying a slave or slaves over the rough, meandering roads. In a wagon with Yarrow and perhaps other slaves, the trip would have taken a day and a half or two days. Unsure if he could trust Yarrow, Beall probably kept him shackled. A slave newly arrived from Africa would not have understood that he was bound to his owner by law and that the law would be enforced by every sheriff and able-bodied man in the colony. If this were not enough to get a runaway returned, Beall could place an ad in the *Maryland Gazette* and post notices offering a reward. But why should he go to that trouble? It would be much easier to keep Yarrow in chains until he learned the ways of American slavery.

That Yarrow's sister was on the *Elijah* was established by deduction from an 1850 court decision in the District of Columbia. The judge had declared Nancy Hillman of Frederick, Maryland, to be the daughter of Yarrow's sister and, as his only surviving heir, entitled to enforce a loan Yarrow had made on a warehouse in Georgetown. The court ruling came ninety-eight years after Yarrow arrived. How did he and his sister know where the other was, how did they and their families stay in touch over all those years, and how did Hillman know about the Georgetown property? The only explanation is that, like Stonewall Jackson's great-grandparents, they came on the same ship. Thus, they knew which planter bought the other, and they lived close enough to stay in touch. Given the way arriving slaves were scattered around the colony with no records kept, the siblings almost certainly could not have found each other if they had arrived on different ships at different times.

Slaves from the *Elijah*

Among the many ways in which Yarrow Mamout was unusual was that he kept his African name, or at least an Anglicization of that name. For most other slaves, a new name was one of the first things he or she received after arrival. The purpose of this was arguably to strip slaves of their African identity, but the practice was more certainly for the convenience of the owner. He wanted a slave with a name he could pronounce, and it was the owner's preference that mattered. Hence, owners gave slaves European or Christian names such as Sam, Mary, and Benjamin that were more familiar to American ears and tongues. Slaves confined to tobacco plantations did not need last names. If they went off the plantation to travel to town, they could identify themselves by their first name and their owners' last name. For example, the slave named Nathaniel who belonged to Samuel Turner in Southampton, Virginia, was known as Nat Turner.

Thus, when Beall first met Yarrow, he had to decide what he would call him. Conceivably, Yarrow had picked up enough English in Africa or on the slave ship to communicate his name in Beall's language or to have given his name to the slave ship captain. Yarrow called himself Yero Mamadou, but Beall apparently heard and spelled it Yarrow Mamout. The spelling may have come from the yarrow plant, which abounds in Maryland, or from poems about the Yarrow River in Scotland, such as John Logan's "Braes of Yarrow":

Thy braes were bonny, Yarrow stream
When first on them I met my lover
Thy braes how dreary, Yarrow stream,
When now thy waves his body cover!

There are no port of entry or customs records with the names of Yarrow and the other slaves on the *Elijah*, or indeed for any slave ship into Annapolis. Such records simply were not kept, even though customs officers did record the quantities of imported goods on the ships. There may have been records of the sale of the slaves, but those have vanished. Nonetheless, the African names of several slaves in the area are known. The names are in the wills and estate inventories of slave owners in the years after Yarrow arrived. There was slave trader Christopher Lowndes's estate, for example. He owned thirty-six slaves when he died. Two had African-sounding names, Denbigh and Linder.[9] Slaves Tombo and Latchin were listed in the inventory of the estate of Jeremiah Belt of Prince Georges County.[10] The inventory of Richard Brooke's estate listed the slave Joater. When the estate of Richard Chew of Anne Arundel County was inventoried, slaves Benn, Jere, Jema (male), Dida, Minta, Sutha, and Oringe were counted.[11] The inventory of the estate of Joseph Galloway of same county listed a thirty-year-old slave named Whapping and a forty-seven-year-old slave named Cupit.[12] The inventory of the estate of Walter Stoddert of Charles County listed slaves named Bambo, Elowese, and Monemea.[13] Samuel Beall's business partner, Dr. David Ross, died in 1780 owning thirty slaves. Two of these were named Osway and Ossand.[14] The similar-sounding name Ousman was commonly given to boys born on Sunday in Futa Jallon.

Nothing puts any of these Africans on the *Elijah* with Yarrow. Nor are any of the names, except Ossand, as definitely Fulani as Yarrow Mamout.[15] However, several could be poor English renderings of Fulani names or nicknames. For example, the slave named Tombo may have been given that name because he came from Timbo, the largest town in Futa Jallon.

While we cannot know whether these men and women were Fulani, Yarrow obviously did. He would have wanted to stay in touch with people from Futa Jallon, as he did with his sister. A desire among immigrants to stay in touch with others from their native land has characterized American history: Irish with Irish, Italian with Italian, German with German.

Yarrow also would have remembered the names and faces of the slaves with whom he shared that terrible voyage from Africa, even if they were not Fulani. The *Elijah*'s passengers were a significant part of the black community in Annapolis and nearby areas then. Ten percent of those coming from Senegambia and the Gold Coast between 1743 and 1759 had been on the ship.

For these reasons, a slave of James Edmonston of Bladensburg named Nicholas stands out as one of the clearest examples of someone who might have known Yarrow in Futa Jallon or at least from the *Elijah.* The descendant of this slave may have married Yarrow's son; we will hear more about that later. Suffice it to say that if the planters networked, the passengers on the *Elijah* may have, too.

Yarrow's First Days in the New World

Yarrow would eventually become Beall's body servant, accompanying his owner throughout the day, but this would not have happened immediately. Yarrow was straight off the boat with a lot to learn, including English and the rules of slavery, before he could serve in such an intimate capacity.

Within days of getting off the slave ship at Annapolis, Yarrow probably found himself either in the slave quarters at the Charles and William or at Beall's water mill on The Gift property in Rock Creek, near where the National Zoo is in Washington now. The tall oaks that shade the Washington area today were not there in Yarrow's time. The original trees had been harvested for firewood or turned into lumber, perhaps at a sawmill Beall built. There were fruit trees, however. Practically everyone was planting fruit trees on his property.

The hot, steamy, mosquito-infested, bottomland of Beall's mill properties was not at all like the highlands of Futa Jallon. Yarrow would have been miserable. He was cut off from relatives, friends, and people who could speak his language and understand his Muslim faith. He knew that his sister was in America, too, but he might have had no clear idea where she was, when he would see her next, or how she was faring. Beall would have counted on his other slaves to help Yarrow adjust. If they were first-generation Africans, Yarrow would be able to understand at least parts of their language even if they were not Fulani, but he might not have been that lucky. If they had been born in America, they would not have been able to understand Yarrow's African speech. Like Diallo, Yarrow may have been isolated by language until he learned English.

If this were not bad enough, there was the matter of housing. House slaves, typically women, might live in an attic over the kitchen of their owner's house. These quarters were hot in summer and cold in winter, and there was the added irritation of climbing a ladder whenever the slaves wanted to get to their rooms. Given Yarrow's comparatively young age and talents, the privilege of living in Samuel Beall's house conceivably might have been extended to him. This would have been the precursor to his becoming Beall's body servant.

More likely, however, Yarrow lived in slave quarters initially. Cabins made of logs with the gaps between the logs filled or chinked with mud were the cheapest and easiest to build. Log walls longer than twenty-four feet lose stability, so log cabins were small. One such slave cabin that survived into twentieth-century Maryland measured eighteen feet by sixteen feet. It consisted of one room and was one and a half stories high, meaning it had a sleeping loft. Chimneys were made of stone or of sticks and limbs lined with mud. The floor might be mud, although some cabins stood on rock or had raised wooden floors. Single-unit quarters could also be made of stone. These were obviously more comfortable in the heat of summer and cold of winter but took more time and effort to build.

Multiunit slave quarters were not necessarily larger or of different construction. Rather, they were buildings intended for more than a single family. There were barracks, dormitory, and duplex styles. The barracks consisted of a single large room where the slaves ate, slept, and lived. The dormitory style had a common area for eating and living and small, separate bedrooms. The duplex had a wall down the center and was intended to house two families with a degree of separation for privacy.[16]

Since Yarrow was a teenager when he arrived and, especially if he were put to work at a mill, he would have lived in barracks or dormitory-style quarters with other male slaves. This had the added advantage to Samuel Beall of exposing Yarrow to men who could teach him English and the ways of slavery, especially the fact that he was not free and should not try to escape or leave to find his sister.

A survey Beall commissioned to determine the boundaries of The Gift in Rock Creek described the improvements there:

> One old mill house 20 feet by 16, boarded & Lap Shingled, one old barn about 30 feet by 16, boarded & shingled one old house about 16 feet square one old hous [*sic*] about 16 feet by 12, one good new corn house about 30 feet by 12 a Dwelling house 20 by 16 with a brick chimney cover with Lap Shingles an earthen flore [*sic*], one old Logg Quarter about 20 feet by 14, About 699 apple trees, 40 peach Trees, about 12 peach trees, about 5000 finer Rails, an old Garden enclosed by finer rails and Pailes.[17]

Beall did not live on this property. His residence was at the Charles and William tract several miles away. He was owner of at least three water mills and too prosperous to be living in the crude buildings described in the survey, which was done when Yarrow was twenty-four and working as Beall's body servant.

The three small houses at this mill generally fit the descriptions of single-unit slave housing, but these could just have easily been for the miller and his family and for white workmen. However, the "Logg Quarter" was clearly a barracks or dormitory-style slave quarters and could have been where Yarrow might have lived initially.

In addition, there was a mill, a barn, and a corn house. The word "corn" meant grain such as wheat rather than maize, and the corn house was where the grain was stored until it could be ground into flour. The large number of rails on the property suggests the existence of both a grain mill and a sawmill. It was not uncommon to have two or even three different types of mills at one location. The cost of a dam and the waterways was three times the cost of the mill itself, so having two or three different kinds of mills share the same waterway made economic sense.[18]

Based on later descriptions of him, Yarrow was a jack-of-all-trades. He could make bricks, weave baskets, and work on a ship. But he was also an entrepreneur and industrious like his owner. By the time he was free, he had an understanding of real estate, financing, law, and investments in bank stock, so he must have picked up a knowledge of business and finance while still a slave. Samuel Beall and his network of friends seemed to recognize Yarrow's talents and helped him take on as much responsibility and rise as high as colonial racism permitted.

The circumstances surrounding arrival of the *Elijah* stood in sharp contrast to those of European immigrants, such as the ones on the *Ark* and *Dove*. Yarrow was little more than a child. His sister was even younger, and he was about to be separated from her. If he caught the eyes of Marylanders at the wharf in Annapolis that day, he would have seen them looking at him with a mixture of curiosity and hostility. He probably could not speak English, the language they spoke, and few in America, other than slaves from Africa, could understand him. To make matters worse, although Yarrow did not know it, the very day he had arrived, the Maryland assembly was taking up a bill to make it even more difficult for slaves to win their freedom. For him, those first few months in a sweltering climate with no one to talk to and no one to understand his Muslim faith would have been almost as bad as the time he had spent on the *Elijah*. Yarrow surely was amazed at how technologically advanced this place was compared to Futa Jallon, but he probably thought it was morally and spiritually crippled. In its practice of slavery, it was.

4 Slavery and Revolution

Yarrow left few historical traces while he was a slave. Years later, Charles Willson Peale, after investigating Yarrow in connection with painting him, came away with the impression that Georgetown was the only place he had lived in America. Another contemporary writer, David Bailles Warden, heard something different. His source was John Mason of Georgetown, the son of the noted Virginian, George Mason, author of the Virginia Bill of Rights. He reported that Yarrow, "before the American revolutionary war, was brought from Africa to the United States, and there sold as a slave to a family, who lived near Georgetown, on the banks of the Potomac."[1] Neither man had the full story.

After purchasing Yarrow in 1752, Samuel Beall made him his body servant. This was more than a valet. A body servant accompanied his owner throughout the day. Wherever Beall was, Yarrow was there too. This allowed Yarrow to learn far more than a field hand ever would. It meant he could travel, something that slaves could not do on their own, and thus he saw colonial America in a way that few slaves did.[2]

Most important, being Beall's body servant gave Yarrow the opportunity to know and be known by important men. Thus, as Beall climbed professionally from planter to engineer and then moved west and became involved in the revolutionary movement, Yarrow gathered an ever-expanding collection of potential benefactors. When Beall died, Yarrow passed to his son Brooke, giving Yarrow additional contacts. David Warden would observe that by the time Yarrow lived in Georgetown, he was known by the "respectable families" there.[3] He had met many of these people while a slave to the prominent Beall family. After he was freed, they hired him or helped him in other ways.

Samuel Beall: Planter, Engineer, Sheriff

Samuel Beall was living at the Charles and William when he made the trip to Annapolis to buy Yarrow. His house was several miles north of Georgetown and near Rock Creek, not the Potomac, as David Warden's comments suggest. Beall was thirty-nine years old. He had a well-connected wife, tobacco plantations, and water mills. He was a respected and valued member of the network of planters and merchants settled along the Anacostia and Potomac Rivers.

In 1753, a year after acquiring Yarrow, Beall was named sheriff of Frederick County, Maryland, in which he then resided. It was a part-time job, so that Beall could still attend to his tobacco farms and water mills. At the time, Frederick County included Georgetown and extended hundreds of miles west to the untamed mountains of Maryland. Within a year, the French and Indian War, a part of the larger Seven Years' War between France and Britain, broke out. The French urged their Indian allies to attack British settlements up and down the Appalachian Mountains. As a result, Beall probably avoided that part of his jurisdiction and confined himself to the eastern part of the county. However, if he did venture west, then he, and Yarrow, did so at some personal risk.

Beall Buys into Frederick Forge

When the Treaty of Paris brought an end to the war in 1763, Western Maryland became a safer place and attracted the attention of Samuel Beall and his business associates. It was in Western Maryland that John Semple, a Scottish factor from Bladensburg, had purchased from the pioneer Israel Friend a site where Antietam Creek emptied into the Potomac. Friend in turn had acquired it some years earlier from local Indian tribes. According to what was called the "Indian deed," the property began "at the mouth of andietum creek thence up the Potomack River 200 shoots as fur as an arrow can be slung out of a bow."

Semple planned an iron furnace, called Keep Triest, on the Virginia side of the Potomac and an iron forge on the Maryland side.[4] The forge, which was to be used to pound and harden the iron from the furnace, would be powered by a water wheel, and this was something the industrious Samuel Beall knew about.

Semple already owned an iron furnace on the Potomac at Occoquan, Virginia, a few miles south of George Washington's Mount Vernon estate, and he knew Washington. Indeed, Washington himself had been interested in the iron industry ever since his father had dabbled in it as part owner of Accokeek furnace in Stafford County, Virginia. Yet, despite such reputable acquaintances, Semple had the unfortunate habit of running into debt and of trying to keep one step ahead not only of his creditors but also of his brother-in-law, who came to Maryland from Glasgow in a vain attempt to keep Semple out of debt.

To raise capital, Semple sold the forge site at Antietam in Maryland to the Ross Company, but he kept the furnace in Virginia for himself. The Ross Company was a four-man partnership composed of David Ross, Richard Henderson, Joseph Chapline, and Samuel Beall. Ross was the physician and trader in convicts and indentured servants from Bladensburg. Henderson was from there too. He was factor for the merchant, John Glassford and Company.[5] Chapline, who founded Sharpsburg, Maryland, and Shepherdstown, Virginia (now West Virginia), had once lived in Prince George's County, but by this time he lived near the forge in Sharpsburg.

The four partners complemented each other. Samuel Beall brought to the business his expertise with waterpower. Ross's and Henderson's contributions were money. Chapline owned large tracts of land in the area. In addition to waterpower, furnaces and forges needed to burn charcoal to melt the ore at the furnace and to heat the pig iron at the forge, and this charcoal came from the hardwood forests of chestnut, hickory, and oak that covered the surrounding hills. Chapline's land also held the iron ore and limestone that were needed for Semple's furnace.

The contract of sale required the partnership to purchase pig iron from Semple's Keep Triest furnace in Virginia for use in the forge. If the two sides could not agree on the price for this iron, then the question would go to arbiters named in the contract: George Washington, George Mason, Robert Mundell, and Hector Ross.

While there is no reason to believe that Beall or Yarrow met the arbiters, it seems likely that Yarrow would have been present when Beall discussed business with his partners and would have been learning, for future reference, the names of the important men of the times, such as Washington and Mason. This might explain why George Mason's son, John, was knowledgeable about Yarrow's past in telling David Warden about the African years later. The forge is also significant in the narrative of Yarrow's life because much later Yarrow's son settled near it.

The four partners agreed among themselves that "no partner shall have the management or direction of the works but that a stranger shall be employed to superintend."[6] In other words, Samuel Beall was not going to move there, at least not in 1764, but the fact that he had extensive experience with waterpower was surely vital to the partners' hopes that they could make a go of the enterprise. Still, although Beall was not supposed to have management of the works, he placed an advertisement in the *Maryland Gazette* for a forge carpenter and other workmen for the business. The advertisement stated that anyone interested should apply to Beall at Frederick Forge, meaning he was working at the forge soon after buying it.[7]

Witness to Revolution

Such entrepreneurial moves by Beall and his associates took place against a background of continuous political and military turmoil in the colonies that soon turned to revolution. Claiming that the American colonies should at least pay England for what it had spent in their defense during the French and Indian War, Parliament passed the infamous Stamp Act in 1765. The law required the colonists to use stamped paper, upon which a tax was imposed, for such things as legal documents. This put Beall in an awkward position. By this time in his life, he had served not only as sheriff of Frederick County but also as a magistrate. The duties of the latter included signing as witness on legal documents.[8] Thus, on one hand, he knew the adverse financial impact Parliament's mandate of stamped paper for legal documents would have on the colonists. On the other hand, he wanted to stay in the royal favor from which he was deriving these offices.

Yet, revolutionary sentiments were burning hotter and hotter, especially in the western part of the colony, where Beall and his associates were trying to get the forge into operation. Maryland's colonial governor, Horatio Sharpe, heard rumors of seditious actions by Thomas Cresap, a delegate to the lower colonial assembly from Western Maryland. Sharpe told the assembly to investigate Cresap and report back. Not wanting to stir up trouble, the assembly found the rumors to be "without foundation." It forwarded to the governor a deposition given by Beall's business partner, David Ross. Ross recalled being at a meeting in Sharpsburg in November 1765 where his partner, Joseph Chapline, was completing the sale of lots in the town before the Stamp Act took effect. Beall was signing as witness on the deeds in his capacity as a magistrate. Just then a rider arrived with a document from Cresap, saying Cresap wanted the document read to the group and signed. It was a petition in support of an assembly resolution that opposed the Stamp Act. Chapline handed the document to Beall to read aloud. When Beall finished, Chapline turned to him and jokingly asked if he was going to sign the petition as well as the deeds. According to Ross, Beall said no, adding "that he did not like Hanging, or Words to that Effect."[9]

But if Samuel Beall shied away from criticizing Parliament on this occasion, it was the exception. He has gone down in history with the lofty title of one of "the Twelve Immortal Justices of the Frederick County Court who Repudiated the Stamp Act Nov. 23, 1765."[10] The lower house of the Maryland colonial assembly had already done that, but still, Beall had thrown his lot in with the radicals early on. George Washington apparently did not suggest that he might commit a hanging offense until 1769 when he forwarded to George Mason the correspondence from David Ross.

As time went on, Beall became more deeply involved in the day-to-day management of Frederick Forge and was eventually forced by circumstance to move there by the death of partner Joseph Chapline in 1769. In preparation, Beall sold seven properties totaling 1,445 acres for £3,050. On March 27, 1770, he obtained a release of the mortgage on his residence, the Charles and William, and then sold the property to his son Richard. Three days later, he sold the 125 acres of Azadia at Tenleytown to his son Isaac. Then on April 2, he bought a 264-acre tract called Kelly's Purchase a few miles north of Sharpsburg and about five miles from the forge. Once he had Kelly's Purchase, Beall moved there, taking along his wife, Yarrow, and other slaves.[11]

The change of scenery did nothing to reduce Beall's passions for revolution, however. After the battles at Lexington and Concord in the spring of 1775, the colonial Maryland assembly, which owed its allegiance to the king of England, stopped meeting. It was replaced by provincial conventions that were independent of the king. Beall was a delegate to these and served on the Committee of Safety, responsible for military affairs in the colony.[12]

Beall was ready to risk hanging, for he joined in the Declaration of the Association of the Freemen of Maryland in July 1775. The document committed Maryland to helping Massachusetts repel British troops by force of arms if necessary, the same idea that had danced in George Washington's head six years earlier. If Beall were hanged, he would have plenty of company. Other signers included his brother Josiah; Benjamin Mackall, whose descendants would marry two of his granddaughters; and future Supreme Court justices Samuel Chase and Thomas Johnson. The signers were a fraternity of famous colonial Marylanders, whose names are affixed to counties, towns, streets, places, and houses around the state, several of which appear again in this narrative of Yarrow's life: Dent, Chew, Tilghman, Bowie, Carroll, Goldsborough, Brooke, Somerville, and Deakins.[13]

The fledging iron industry in the colonies was crucial to armed rebellion, for it had to produce the weapons of war, the bayonets, rifle barrels, and cannon used by the Continental Army. Of particular importance were the furnaces and forges in the hinterlands of Maryland and Pennsylvania, beyond easy reach of British troops. The Rock Forge Furnace, located near Leitersburg on Little Antietam Creek north of Beall's Frederick Forge, is known to have cast cannon during the Revolution. Its owners, Daniel and Samuel Hughes, secured a contract from the Continental Congress to make a thousand tons of cannon.[14] Beall and the Hughes naturally knew each other and in fact served on the revolutionary Committee of Correspondence for Western Maryland.[15]

The most comprehensive research into the operation of the Frederick Forge, *The Iron Industry in Western Maryland,* could find nothing about its contribution to the Revolution. However, its author, Michael Thompson, concluded the forge must have been vital to the war effort because when majority partner David Ross died in 1778, Maryland passed a law prohibiting his widow Ariana, whose aunt was married to Annapolis lawyer and slave trader Vachel Denton, from selling the operation.

The Death of Samuel Beall

Samuel Beall's involvement with both the Revolution and Frederick Forge ended with his death in 1777, of an unknown cause. His will divided his real estate holdings among his children except for his residence, Kelly's Purchase, which was given to his wife for as long as she should live. The brick house there is still standing. The timbers used in its construction have been dated to 1751, which was before Beall bought it. During the Civil War Battle of Antietam, the house at Kelly's Purchase was used as a field hospital.

Beall had other slaves than Yarrow with him at Kelly's Purchase and the forge. Black slaves commonly worked at iron furnaces and forges alongside free white workers. Tax records for Frederick Forge a few years after Beall's death counted thirty-five slaves, male and female.[16] Thus, just as European settlers of Beall's generation were transitioning from a tobacco economy to an industrial one, so were African Americans. In this new, American industrial economy, blacks and whites worked next to each other and performed same tasks. Their wages were the same. But if the black man was a slave, then his pay went to his owner. A slave had no legal right to be paid directly by the employer—in fact, slaves had no legal rights of any kind—and no right to object to what his owner did with the money.

Beall's last will and testament, drafted in 1774, mentioned the slaves at the forge and Yarrow at Kelly's Purchase. Filed in January

1778, it bequeathed to his heirs nine named slaves. To his wife Eleanor, he left Kelly's Purchase for life, as well as "my Negro Man Dick my Negro Woman Ester my Negro Woman Jenny (now employed at the Forge that is in partnership with David Ross and Richard Henderson)."

Beall bequeathed to his son Isaac "my Negro Boy Jarro who now lives on the Land heretofore given to my wife [Kelly's Purchase]."[17] The slave named Jarro was surely Yarrow Mamout. Yarrow was by no means a "boy"; he was thirty-eight years old when the will was written. Beall was not being patronizing, though. That is, the term "boy" was not used as a synonym for Negro or slave. The will referred to other male slaves as "Negro Man." Rather, Beall used the term "boy" to mean that Yarrow was his body servant, common usage of the term at the time.[18]

While Beall's will mentioned nine slaves—two men, two women, three boys, and two girls—the inventory of his estate, taken in June 1779, counted thirteen slaves: three men, two women, four boys, and four girls. This disparity might have stemmed from a poorly done inventory but more likely was the result of additional slaves being purchased or born since the will was written five years earlier. Two of the men were valued at £100 each. But the third was valued at £200, twice what the other two were. Moreover, this valuable slave was paired, by brackets on the inventory, with a "Negroe boy" valued at £50 and "one Negroe Chato £35" for a total value of £285. The brackets may have been intended to indicate that that the three slaves were connected somehow. Yarrow was forty-two years old by the time the inventory was done. If he was in this inventory, then he was surely the valuable slave.

In any event, upon Beall's death, there was no longer a need for a body servant at the rural Kelly's Purchase. By bequeathing Yarrow to his son Isaac, Samuel Beall was returning Yarrow to the Washington area, where Isaac had the Azadia property. Its location in Tenleytown was north of modern Georgetown, but at that time it was considered part of that city. It was also next to Samuel Beall's properties of Gizer and The Gift, where Pierce Mill is today. Nonetheless, if Isaac inherited Yarrow, he did not keep him long, for Yarrow ended up being owned by Samuel Beall's son Brooke.

Thus, for the first twenty-five years in America, Yarrow was Samuel Beall's body servant, initially at the Charles and William near Georgetown and later at Kelly's Purchase near Sharpsburg. This gave him a chance to see firsthand how the planters conducted business and to meet the influential men of Maryland who were involved in the Revolution. He would make use of all this knowledge and these connections once he returned to Georgetown.

5 Yarrow of Georgetown

Brooke Beall had at least two properties when he succeeded to ownership of Yarrow after Samuel Beall's death. One was a huge country estate called Beallmount near present-day Potomac, Maryland; the other was a business and residence in Georgetown. Yarrow would live at both. It was in Georgetown, though, that Yarrow became famous. He would not have left historical footprints if he had been condemned to work on a tobacco plantation or if he had stayed at the remote, rural Kelly's Purchase or Frederick Forge in Washington County. Georgetown had the wealth and proximity to Washington, the new capital of the United States, to attract the writers and artists who preserved Yarrow's story and image. In addition, a number of men, who had played important roles in the American Revolution and knew the Bealls, lived in Georgetown and spoke well of Yarrow. And of course, Yarrow would not have gotten attention if he had remained a slave. Not even in Georgetown did slaves become famous.

Georgetown owed its existence to the Potomac River. Though the river was relatively shallow there, it had a deep channel, making it navigable all the way to the sea for oceangoing ships of the day. Rock Creek, which today is a trickle of a stream winding through northwest Washington and which separates Washington proper from Georgetown, emptied into the Potomac with enough force in the eighteenth century to gouge a forty-foot-deep-hole in the river bottom. Even when the river was low, large sailing ships could anchor there without their captains worrying the ships might touch bottom and damage their hulls or roll on their sides as the water level dropped. This hole in the river bottom is what made Georgetown a port, indeed the last northern port on the Potomac.

Ninian Beall was the first European to appreciate the advantages of the land at the mouth of Rock Creek. To the northwest, the Potomac extended deep into the unsettled interior all the way to what is now West Virginia. Two sets of falls above Georgetown, Seneca Falls and Great Falls, impeded waterborne commerce from the interior and necessitated portage, but this was manageable, particularly since once the goods got to Georgetown, they could be sent anywhere in the world by water.

Ninian acquired the property on the Maryland side of the river with its natural harbor. He called it The Rock of Dunbarton, purportedly because the rock outcroppings rising from the river reminded him of those at Castle Dunbar in Scotland, where he had been captured by Cromwell's forces. The resemblance is tenuous.

Ninian's grandsons, George and Thomas Beall, inherited the Rock of Dunbarton and literally put Georgetown on the map when they helped incorporate it as a town. Next, they made a fortune by subdividing it into residential lots and selling them. The two large and beautiful homes they built with the proceeds are still there: the Beall-Washington House at 2920 R Street, which was the home of Katharine Graham, publisher of the *Washington Post,* and Beall House at 3033 N Street, which was once owned by Jacqueline Kennedy.

In addition to being a seaport, Georgetown had a vital ferry link across the river to Virginia. During the French and Indian War, British General Edward Braddock led a force of British regulars and Virginia recruits out of Alexandria, Virginia, and across the Potomac via the ferry at Georgetown. Today, on the District of Columbia side, at the bottom of what appears to be a well next to a freeway, lies Braddock Rock, the supposed place where the general stepped ashore. Braddock later met the French and Indians near Fort Duquesne, what is now Pittsburgh, Pennsylvania, where he was killed and his army routed. His aide, George Washington, lived to fight another day and to revisit Georgetown.

The Mason family of Virginia owned the ferry by the latter part of the eighteenth century. The terminus on the Virginia side was on

Analostan Island (now called Theodore Roosevelt Island) with a causeway linking it to Virginia. The best-known member of this family of ferrymen was George Mason, one of the arbiters in the contract for Frederick Forge between John Semple and the Ross Company. He also wrote the Virginia Bill of Rights, which was the model for the Bill of Rights that was added to the Constitution. George Mason's home was Gunston Hall near Mount Vernon, but his son John lived in Georgetown. John knew and employed Yarrow.

Although Seneca Falls and Great Falls blocked river commerce coming from the northwest, goods from there could be floated down to the falls and, for a price, transferred to wagons for delivery to ships at the port of Georgetown. Thus, with a ferry across the Potomac, downriver access to the sea, and upriver access to the interior, Georgetown in the late eighteenth century was a minor but promising transportation hub.

When the Revolutionary War ended, two prominent, entrepreneurial military officers, who had served under General George Washington, settled in Georgetown. Benjamin Stoddert, formerly of Prince Georges County, was one. He had married the daughter of slave trader Christopher Lowndes, so in addition to his own talents for making money, he had married even more. His large home above the river, called Halcyon House, overlooked the Masons' ferry and is still there. He later became the first secretary of the navy under President John Adams, retiring to Bostwick, the house his father-in-law had built in Bladensburg.

Uriah Forrest was the other. He had grown up in St. Mary's County, the place where the *Ark* and *Dove* had landed. His house was a block downhill from that of his friend and business partner, Stoddert. Forrest's house was later purchased by William Marbury, who was related by marriage to Charles Willson Peale and who was one of the men to tell Peale about Yarrow. Today it is known as the Forrest-Marbury house and is the embassy of Ukraine.

George Washington himself was a familiar face in Georgetown. He had returned to Mount Vernon in Virginia after the Revolution, but he ventured into business at Georgetown. He was particularly interested in solving the problem that Seneca Falls and Great Falls presented to water traffic from the northwest and was fascinated with the notion of building a canal to bypass the falls. He became president of The Patowmack Company, organized to improve transportation on the river. He wanted a canal on the Virginia side, but building it took eighteen years, and it was not completed until after his death.[1]

Pending at the time Washington became president in 1789 was the decision of where to locate the new nation's capital. Philadelphia had been chosen to serve on a temporary basis, but it was not to be the permanent capital. After lengthy negotiations between the northern and southern states, Congress decided to locate the capital on the border of Virginia and Maryland. President Washington was to choose the precise place for the government to make its home. With help from his two military and business friends, Forrest and Stoddert, he picked a five-thousand-acre site just east of Georgetown.[2]

The new capital would also include Georgetown, the only existing town in Maryland within what would be called Washington, District of Columbia. Being the seat of government radically changed the character of the area. On lands that had formerly been tobacco plantations and farms were built the Capitol, White House, and government buildings. Hotels, boardinghouses, taverns, offices, shops, and residences sprang up. Thousands of new, urban dwellers moved in, and with them new ways of thinking. They pushed aside the old, feudal, planter networks and cultures, although those still held sway for decades in Georgetown and the periphery of the capital.

The economy, too, was changing. Tobacco and tobacco ports like Bladensburg were in eclipse as wheat farming and livestock raising became far more profitable. A contemporary observer, David Warden, noted this, writing: "Before the American revolution, Bladensburg carried on a considerable commerce in tobacco . . . [but] now presents a miserable aspect."[3]

The changes also meant there were more men like Samuel Beall, interested in industry rather than agriculture. Beall himself had been in the new, iron industry and was interested in floating things, heavy, iron things, down the Potomac River to Georgetown. Frederick Forge was some fifty miles upriver as the crow flies from the ships anchored at Georgetown and even farther by way of the snaking Potomac.[4] Both John Semple's furnace at Keep Triest and the Ross Company's forge at

Antietam needed to get their iron to the ships in Georgetown if they were to sell it to other colonies and England. As early as 1769, Semple calculated how much it cost to ship iron to Georgetown. His analysis indicated that portages in wagons were necessary first around Seneca Falls and then around Great Falls. The combined cost of these two portages plus the cost of hauling the iron over land from the Keep Triest Furnace to the river was almost twice the cost of the waterborne portions of the trip. More than £2 per ton could be saved if the trip were entirely by water as was possible once the Chesapeake and Ohio ("C&O") Canal was built.[5]

Neither Semple nor Samuel Beall lived to see the transportation problem solved, and after Beall's death, his family lost interest. It sold its share of the forge and turned its attention to other endeavors.[6] But these navigation problems would indirectly affect his son, Brooke, whose huge country estate sat between the two obstacles in the river, Seneca Falls and Great Falls. It was surely this property, called Beallmount (and sometimes Beall Mount), that John Mason was referring to when he told David Warden that Yarrow was "a slave to a family, who lived near Georgetown, on the banks of the Potomac."

Yarrow at Beallmount

Born in 1742, Brooke Beall was six years younger than Yarrow. He was thirty-five years old when his father died. Like his father, Brooke speculated in land. He bought his first property, five acres in Maryland near Frederick Forge, when he was only twenty-four.[7] Later, he began acquiring the land for Beallmount in bits and pieces. It was west of today's Potomac, Maryland, and north and west of where Watts Branch emptied into the Potomac near Seneca Falls. Beallmount totaled an estimated 1,900 acres when Brooke owned it and stayed in the family for generations.[8] The old house is gone, but the ruins of Beall's mills on Watts Branch are still there. So, too, are Beall Springs Road and Beall Mountain Road. A subdivision of large homes in a development spelled "Beallmont" marks where the main estate used to be.

Thus, some time after Samuel's death, Yarrow came into Brooke's ownership and moved to Beallmount. If Yarrow had experience with water mills, it would have come in handy. Just like Samuel Beall's mills in Rock Creek and at Antietam, Beallmount boasted both a gristmill and a sawmill using a common dam and waterway.[9] Yarrow's other talents would also have made him a good overseer for the big estate. According to the 1783 tax assessment, Beallmount consisted of nine white persons, twenty-three slaves, thirteen horses, and eighty-four head of cattle.[10]

More than a century later, Brooke's great-granddaughter Sally Somervell Mackall gave an idealized version of a family story about what life was like at Beallmount for Brooke and his family in her book, *Early Days of Washington.* She identified his residence as being on the river and claimed that George Washington was a "frequent visitor."

> Mrs. Brooke Beall [Margaret Johns Beall] was highly gifted in face and form, of a lovable disposition, cultivated and attractive. Their home was the meeting place of the gallant and the brave. General Washington was a frequent visitor, and enjoyed sitting on the broad veranda on moon-light nights, near by the old-time jessamine, listening to Mrs. Beall's charming guitar. In the distance the splash of the boatman's oar and the silver sheen on the moon-lit waters formed a scene of loveliness ever to be remembered.[11]

While not a frequent visitor at Beallmount, Washington stopped there on at least one occasion and recorded the visit in his diary. He was scouting a route for the canal he wanted to build around the falls on the Potomac River. The board of directors of the Patowmack Company had met in Georgetown, then traveled up the river, investigating the two falls that hindered traffic. Washington wrote in his diary for August 2, 1785:

> Left George Town about 10 oclock, in Company with all the Directors except Govr. Lee. . . . And being accompanied by Colo. James Johnson (Brother to Govr. Johnson) and Messrs. Beal, Johns & others who took with them a cold Collation with Spirits wine &ca. We dined at Mr.

> Bealls Mill 14 miles from George Town and proceeded . . . to a Mr. Goldsboroughs, a decent Farmers House at the head of Senneca falls—about 6 Miles and 20 from George Town.

On the second day, Washington and his party started at Seneca Falls and floated down river toward Georgetown. When they got to Great Falls, they turned back and returned to where they started, with Washington writing:

> Having provided Canoes . . . we proceeded to examine the falls [below Seneca Creek]; and beginning at the head of them went through the whole by Water, and continued from the foot of them to the Great falls. After which, returning back to a Spring on the Maryland Side [perhaps Watts Branch] between the Seneca and Great Falls, we partook (about 5 Oclock) of another cold Collation which a Colo. Orme, a Mr. Turner & others of the Neighbourhood, had provided, and returned back by the way of Mr. Beall's Mill to our old Quarters at Mr. Goldsborough's. The distance as estimated 8 Miles.[12]

Washington may not have known all these men personally, but their names were familiar ones from the Revolution. The "Beal" is surely Brooke Beall, since the mill at which they stopped was clearly his. The "Johns" was his wife's family. Governor Johnson was the former radical Thomas Johnson, who later became a Supreme Court justice. Because of Samuel Beall's support for the revolution, Washington probably thought of the Beall family as being radicals like Johnson.

Most important among the names of Beall's friends and neighbors that Washington mentioned was "Mr. Turner." This was Beall's neighbor at Beallmount, Samuel Turner. Twenty-three years earlier, he had been living in Prince George's County, where his name showed up in the accounting records of Glassford and Company of Bladensburg as buying sundry goods. Much later, Yarrow's son, Aquilla, would marry Turner's slave, Mary.

Yarrow Mamout himself was living at Beallmount when Washington visited. Someone had to handle the canoes and prepare the "cold

Collation," and that someone was undoubtedly one of Beall's twenty-three slaves. Ordinarily, a slave with Yarrow's ability and age might not have been assigned to handle canoes and prepare meals. But Yarrow was probably Brooke's body servant, just as he was for Brooke's father, so wherever Brooke went, Yarrow did too. What is more, Brooke would have wanted to impress the general, and there was no better way to do this than by having the amiable Yarrow Mamout along. Besides, since Yarrow was reportedly the best swimmer ever on the Potomac, he would have been a handy man to have aboard when the canoes passed through the treacherous rapids. Billy Lee was still a servant of Washington at this time. However, earlier in the year, he had broken his kneecap and become disabled, so he probably was not on this trip and did not meet Yarrow.

While there is no direct documentary evidence that Yarrow was living at Beallmount at the time of Washington's visit in 1785, there is sufficient indirect evidence to put the matter beyond question: his son, Aquilla, was born to a slave on the farm next to Beallmount in 1787. Yarrow was obviously there nine months earlier and indeed probably had been there since shortly after Samuel Beall died ten years earlier.

The Move to Georgetown

Brooke Beall was in the import/export business in Georgetown. This required a warehouse along the waterfront. He owned lot 73 on what was then called Water Street, less than a block up from the river. On a modern map, the property would be on the west side of Wisconsin Avenue between the C&O Canal and the river. The lot had formerly been owned by Colin Dunlop & Son and Company, merchants in Glasgow, Scotland. However, they were British sympathizers, and during the Revolution, the building had been seized and auctioned.[13]

Eventually, the Bealls and Yarrow moved from Beallmount to Georgetown, but exactly when is uncertain. In an unpublished manuscript on the Beall and Johns families that is a seminal work on Yarrow as well, local researcher Eleanor Vaughn Cook concluded the Bealls moved there in 1783. She reached this conclusion in part because

Brooke was clerk of the Montgomery County court and, according to the court's minute book, got permission that year to "remove the Clerk's Office to the house where the Clerk resides in George Town."[14] This conclusion seems to conflict with Sally Mackall's description that suggests the Bealls resided at Beallmount and hosted George Washington at this time. It also conflicts with Washington's diary, which says he visited the Bealls there in 1785. And, most important, it conflicts with Yarrow's fathering a child by a slave woman on a neighboring farm in 1787.

The likelihood is that while Brooke Beall himself obviously spent a great deal of time in Georgetown once he opened his business there, he did not move his family and Yarrow from Beallmount to Georgetown until 1788 or 1789. They were certainly in town by the latter year because Brooke became an alderman then.[15] Lot 73 was too close to the river to be comfortable as a residence in the heat and humidity of summer, and so the Bealls would not have lived there. In her book, Sally Mackall wrote that Brooke still owned his father's tracts in Rock Creek. This included The Gift, which stretched northward along the creek from where the Watergate is today to past the National Zoo. They may have had a house there. Researcher Cook totaled Beall's holdings to three hundred acres on the west side of Rock Creek where Piney Branch enters. This was the same as The Gift.[16]

Beall led a hectic life. He had to divide his time among multiple real estate holdings, attend to his business in Georgetown, and show up at the court in Rockville, where he was clerk. From Beallmount, he could have commuted the five miles to Rockville when court was in session. However, he could not commute the fourteen miles from Beallmount to Georgetown or the thirteen miles from Georgetown to Rockville. Rather, for these longer journeys, Beall would have had to spend the night, and indeed might spend a week or more away from home. At these times, having a body servant, like Yarrow, was useful not only to take care of the details upon arrival but also to be a companion while on the road.

In the 1790 census, Georgetown was still a part of Montgomery County, and Beall's name appears in three different locations in the county. At two of these, including Beallmount, only slaves lived on the land. At the third, Georgetown, were eight slaves and eight white people.[17] The Beall family was there, and so undoubtedly was Yarrow.

Accounting records from Brooke's Georgetown business survive and show the diversity of his moneymaking endeavors. He collected rent from a store at Watts Branch, which was next to Beallmount, and rent from someone working a plantation. He sold salt, herring, flour, rum, snuff, tea, spelling books, bridles, and bedsteads. He was a tobacco shipping agent. And he rented out his slaves.[18] Although the common, modern image of slavery is of a plantation in the Deep South, so-called urban slavery was found in cities. Historian Ira Berlin described the practice this way:

> Urban slaves, unlike their plantation counterparts, lived literally on top of or beside their owners and other white people in attics, backrooms, and closets. The comparative smallness of city houses, shared residence, and disproportionately large numbers of women—at a time when men dominated the plantation population—allowed urban slaves a measure of independence unknown to their rural counterparts. As domestics, laborers, and especially skilled tradesmen and tradeswomen, they moved freely through the towns, often as hirelings rented from one master to another. Sometimes they rented themselves, collecting their own wages and living independently of owner or hirer. Mobile, skilled, and cosmopolitan, urban slaves improved their material condition and expanded their social life.[19]

David Warden provided a contemporary account of the practice of urban slavery in Washington at the time Yarrow lived there.

> Most of the domestic and field labour, at Washington, is performed by black slaves on the subject of which, the same opinion prevails there as in the West Indies, that without them it would be impossible to cultivate the soil. It is difficult to procure white servants whose wages are high. Another inconvenience is, that from interest, caprice, or the love of change, they [white servants] seldom remain long with the same master. They are unwilling to associate with the blacks, and seeing their former companions on the road to independence, their

constant effort is to free themselves from the shackles of servitude. The daily expense of a black slave has been estimated as follows.

His [purchase] price is about five hundred dollars, which, at six per cent, the lawful interest is—30 dollars
For risk or accidents 30
For a peck of Indian meal per week, or thirteen bushels per year, at 50 cents 6 50 c.
Two pounds of salt meat per week 7 50 c.
A barrel of fish per annum 4 dollars
To which must be added, for fowls, vegetables, milk, etc. per annum 5
For clothing 15
In all 98 dollars

According to this calculation, the daily expense is nearly twenty-seven cents.

A white labourer usually earns three-quarters of a dollar, or 75 cents per day; but as he is more industrious, he performs more work. The masters or proprietors of stout black labourers hire them at the rate of sixty dollars a year. Their food and clothing are estimated at thirty-five dollars.[20]

By Warden's calculations, urban slavery was hardly profitable for owners and was, of course, a pitiful arrangement for the slaves, financially and otherwise. A slave owner could expect revenue of sixty dollars per year from the slave's labor less out-of-pocket expenses of thirty-five dollars for a profit of twenty-five dollars per year. This compared to thirty dollars per year in interest that could be earned by instead investing the five hundred dollars that it cost to buy a slave.

Brooke Beall made money from Yarrow Mamout's labor by essentially renting him out. According to the accounting ledger, Yarrow worked "2 days on the Maryland" in September 1790 for Forrest and Stoddert. This was the partnership of George Washington's former associates, Uriah Forrest and Benjamin Stoddert. The *Maryland* was a ship owned by John Mason, the principal source of information about

Yarrow for David Warden.[21] It made at least one Atlantic crossing, but on this occasion, Yarrow just loaded the ship while it was in port for Forrest and Stoddert's trading company.[22] Yarrow worked on two occasions for William Deakins in 1790: six days in May and sixteen in June. The Deakins family had known the Bealls since before the Revolution when Samuel Beall and William Deakins signed the Declaration of the Association of the Freemen of Maryland. Yarrow also worked for Robert Peter. According to a partially illegible entry in the ledger, Yarrow apparently performed the service of "burning coal" for a charge of £3.15. What this means is uncertain. The entry, dated March 16, 1795, might mean Yarrow burned excess coal that Peter wanted to get rid of, or it might mean he made charcoal from wood. All three accounting entries credit Yarrow's earnings to Beall.[23]

Yarrow, too, had an account in Beall's ledger. On May 14, 1790, he bought three yards of osnaburg, a coarse linen fabric used for sailcloth and also for slave clothing. Given the small amount of the material, he must have wanted it for the latter purpose.[24]

The ledger shows how a slave owner like Brooke Beall was doubly advantaged from slavery. With one hand, he took the wages for Yarrow's work. With the other, he took money from Yarrow, who had to pay his owner for the clothes on his back. Of course, the men for whom he worked must have also paid something to Yarrow directly, since he was known to have built up savings even as a slave.

Freedom

Prosperity prompted Brooke to want to move to the higher, more exclusive ground in what is now called Upper Georgetown. This is where Ninian's grandsons—Brooke's cousins several times removed—had built their houses. Brooke asked Yarrow to make the bricks for this new house and the out buildings. Yarrow was nearly sixty years old. Where he learned brick-making is not known, but the most logical place would have been from Samuel Beall at the water mills or at Frederick Forge. A forge was in constant need of bricks and stones for its hearths and buildings. Brooke told Yarrow that once the bricks for the new house were done, he would free Yarrow. Yarrow lived up to his end of the bargain and completed the bricks, but in July 1795 Brooke died before freeing Yarrow.[25] Brooke's widow, Margaret, kept the promise, but not for another year.

According to both Yarrow and Margaret, the offer to free Yarrow was made for the purest of reasons, rewarding a good and faithful servant.[26] This was not always the reason for freeing a slave. The economics were such that an owner was better off if he freed older slaves than if he supported them financially in their old age. A bill to prevent owners from releasing destitute slaves that might be a burden on society had been introduced in the Maryland colonial assembly on the day Yarrow arrived from Africa. That was forty-four years earlier, and before the American Revolution. Later slave codes gave the owners more leeway. They only had to attest that the slave was under a certain age—in Maryland it was forty-five—or that the slave was able to support himself or herself.[27]

Yarrow received his manumission paper on August 22, 1796. It was signed by Brooke's son, Upton Beall, and recorded in the Montgomery County Land Records on the same day.[28] Eleven years later, Upton signed another manumission, which Yarrow recorded in Washington, D.C.[29] Upton never legally owned Yarrow, but since he was so well known and was clearly acting on behalf of the family, no one paid attention to this technicality.

Yarrow was on his way to financial security. He either had, or would soon get, a nest egg of $100 from savings. In addition, but prior to getting his own manumission, he purchased his son's freedom for £20. Thus, Yarrow was sixty years old before he could experience the benefits of life in America that would have been won by a man of his talents many years earlier were he not a slave. On February 8, 1800, he acquired a lot from another Deakins, this one Francis, on what is now Dent Place in Georgetown.[30] Yarrow was not rich, but he had quite a bit of money for someone who had been a slave for so long.

Whether Yarrow's lot had a house on it when he bought it is unknown, but one was eventually built. It was not the log cabin of a slave. It was a wood frame house, not a trivial asset. Tax assessment records from the 1800–1803 period valued the property at $30. By

1807, it had appreciated to a value of $35. The value rose to $200 in 1815 when the assessment noted a "small frame" house there. In 1818, the property was assessed at $500.[31] Its value had increased more than sixteenfold.

This may be compared to the real estate and personal property of Francis Lowndes, the son of the slave trader Christopher Lowndes. Francis too invested in slave ships. He had owned the *Good Intent*, which, as mentioned earlier, sank in a storm off Cape Hatteras with three hundred slaves aboard. Despite this setback, by 1818 he had Georgetown property valued at $24,400. To state the obvious, being a slave trader was substantially more lucrative than being a slave.[32]

In any event, house or not, Yarrow moved onto the lot as soon as he bought it. The 1800 census listed him as a free man in that part of Georgetown with one other person; presumably this was his young son Aquilla.

Then Yarrow did a puzzling thing with the property in 1803. He and Francis Deakins, who had sold the property to him in the first place, signed a deed transferring title to Aquilla. Yarrow still lived in the house, but it was in Aquilla's name. There will be more about what was behind this strange transfer in a later chapter on Aquilla.[33]

The deed has disappeared but the deed book kept by the Recorder of Deeds still exists. The oversized ledger in which the Recorder of Deeds meticulously copied deeds brought into his office is at the National Archives in Washington.[34] The neat handwriting of the Recorder of Deeds remains perfectly legible except at the end, where Yarrow's signature is. Instead of an "X," with which an illiterate person would have signed, there are two sets of symbols. Sulayman Nyang, a professor of African Studies at Howard University, was sent an emailed photograph of the signature and asked if it spelled "Yarrow Mamout." Nyang termed it "distorted Arabic" and speculated that the Recorder of Deeds had attempted to copy a signature that was in Arabic. That is, although the Recorder of Deeds himself did not know how to write in Arabic, it appears that he tried to make a faithful copy of what was on the deed and so drew what he saw. Nyang felt the signature demonstrated that Yarrow was literate in Arabic.[35] Since he retained his Muslim faith throughout his life, Yarrow may have owned and read a copy of the Quran and thus retained literacy in Arabic over all the years.[36]

Kevin Smullin Brown, a scholar of Arabic and Islam at University College London, has also examined an emailed copy of the signature. He concludes that it was a combination of English and Arabic. He believes that the first word, which looks like "Josi," was probably an attempt by Yarrow to write his name in English, spelling it something like "Jaro." The second set of symbols, Brown thinks, is Arabic and may be *Mahmadou* and perhaps *daluh* or *Bismillah,* the latter of which translates to "In the Name of God.[37]

David Warden's book provides a contemporary account of what Yarrow was like. John Mason, George Mason's son, talked to Warden about the ex-slave. Mason knew Yarrow both because he owned the *Maryland,* the ship on which Yarrow had worked for two days, and because Mason had a house in Georgetown and another on Analostan Island, the family's ferry terminus in the middle of the Potomac between Virginia and Georgetown.

While Yarrow may have first met Mason in Georgetown, it seems likely that he also remembered Samuel Beall talking about Mason's father, George, as one of the arbiters on the Frederick Forge contract. In other words, while Yarrow may have gotten to know Mason and other important families in Georgetown on his own, he might have met them and their families earlier and, in any event, it did not hurt to remind them that he had been of long service to the Bealls.

According to Mason, Yarrow "toiled late and early and in the course of a few years he had amassed a hundred dollars." He thought he could retire on the money and gave it to a merchant, but he lost the entire sum when the merchant died insolvent.

Yarrow worried because he was no longer young and strong. Nevertheless, he went back to work for fixed wages during the day. At night, he made "nets, baskets, and other articles for sale." After a few years, Yarrow had again saved $100, which he gave to another merchant in Georgetown. He lost his savings a second time when this merchant went bankrupt. Yarrow then went back to work a third time and acquired an even bigger fortune of $200. This time, wrote Warden:

> By the advice of a friend, who explained to him the nature of a bank, he purchased shares to this amount in that of Columbia [Bank of Georgetown], in his own name, the interest of which now affords him a comfortable support. Though more than eighty years old, he walks erect, is active, cheerful, and good-natured. His history is known to several respectable families, who treat him with attention. . . . When young, he was the best swimmer ever seen on the Potomac; and though his muscles are now somewhat stiffened by age, he still finds pleasure in his exercise.[38]

The respectable families undoubtedly included the Bealls, Stodderts, Deakins, Peters, Marburys, and Brewers. Indeed, they probably included George Washington's heirs. A granddaughter of Washington's wife, Martha Custis, was married to Thomas Peter of Georgetown.[39]

Warden then repeated the story in what he said was Yarrow's dialect:

> Olda massa been tink he got all de work out of a Yaro bone. He tell a Yaro, go free Yaro; you been work nuff for me, go work for you now. Tankee, massa, Yaro say. Sure nuff; Yaro go to work for he now. Yaro work a soon—a late—a hot—a cold. Sometime he sweat—sometime he blow a finger. He get a fippenny bit—eighteen-pennee—gib him to massa to put by—put by a dollar, till come a heap. Oh! Poor massa take sick, die—Yaro money gone. Oh, Yaro, go to work again. Get more dollars—work—hard more dollars. Gib him now to young massa, he young, he no die. Oh, young massa den broke—den go away. Oh, oh, oh! Yaro old for true now. Must work again—worky, worky, get more dollar. Gib him this time to all de massa—all de massa cant die, cant go away. Oh, Yaro—dollar breed now—every spring—every fall, Yaro get dollar—chichen now.[40]

This tale became legend. Yarrow told it to Charles Willson Peale too, and Peale recorded it in his diary. Still, it is hard to square parts of Yarrow's version of the story with other facts. For example, Yarrow said that his owner, Brooke Beall, freed him and, after that, he gave his savings to first one man, who died, and then to another man, who went bankrupt or ran away. It was only after this that Yarrow bought bank stock. But in fact, after Peale heard the story, he went to the bank to ask if Yarrow owned bank stock. Peale was told that Yarrow did indeed. He purchased it soon after the bank was founded in December 1793. This means Yarrow owned the bank stock several years before he was freed in 1796 and before he supposedly lost his savings. Of course, the information that Peale was given could be wrong. Whatever the truth, it makes for a good story, and Yarrow could tell a good story.

Another interpretation of what Yarrow meant in saying that he first gave his money to a "massa" was that he gave the money to his owner, Brooke Beall. This would have happened before Brooke died. Maybe Brooke was treating Yarrow as a financially free man as early as 1790, when he began crediting him with sums in his accounting ledger. He just might not have given Yarrow his manumission paper. In this case, the first time Yarrow lost all his money was in 1795 when Brooke died. As will be discussed in a later chapter, the second time Yarrow lost his money appears to have been in 1803. If so, the bank was wrong in telling Peale that Yarrow had invested shortly after it was founded.

There is also a different, less entrepreneurial version of the legend. This one was in a book, *Old Georgetown,* written by Grace Dunlop Ecker in 1933. Ms. Ecker added details not found in other writings. Whether she based these on oral histories that are now lost—she was a friend of Sally Mackall, the Beall descendant who wrote such a glowing recollection of her ancestors playing host to George Washington—or merely took literary license on what she read in David Warden's book or elsewhere cannot be determined. However, not all of her facts came from Warden. Ecker had to find the location of Yarrow's house herself. She wrote:

> On 6th Street [Dent], between Market (33rd) and Frederick (34th) Streets, was the house which Francis Deakins sold on February 8, 1800 to Old Yarrow as he was called, one of the most mysterious and interesting characters of the early days. It is not know whether he was an East Indian or a Guinea negro, but he was a Mohemmadan. He conducted a trade in hacking with a small cart, and his ambition in life

> was to own a hundred dollars. Twice he saved it and each time ill fortune overtook him. The first time he gave it to an old grocery man he knew, to keep for him. The old man died suddenly and Yarrow had nothing to prove that he had had his money. So the next time he picked a young man to keep it for him. Then he absconded. Some of the gentlemen of the town became so interested that they took up a collection and started an account for him in the Bank of Columbia.[41]

Again, this version does not seem to match what the bank clerks told Peale, that Yarrow got his stock shortly after the bank was set up in 1793 and, therefore, before he was freed. Moreover, Ecker was the only person to say Yarrow was a hacker, by which she apparently meant someone who operated a cart for hire, and to specify that the person to whom Yarrow gave his money was a grocer. In fact, there was a black grocer in Georgetown at this time. His name was Joseph Moor, which suggests that he was Muslim. He was listed in the 1820 census with the spelling Joseph Moore. Since he was still living then, he could not have been the man Yarrow first gave the money to since that man died. Ecker may have heard stories about Joseph Moor, the grocer, and stories about Yarrow and mistakenly assumed Yarrow gave the money to Moor.

However, except for the suggestion that Yarrow got his bank stock as early as 1793, the various versions of Yarrow's financial woes might be reconciled. Brooke Beall may have freed Yarrow around 1788 when Brooke and his family moved to Georgetown with Yarrow. He just did not get around to giving Yarrow his manumission paper then. Thus between 1788 and 1795, when Brooke died, Yarrow may have been in business for himself. The entries in Brooke's accounting ledgers may represent his holding the money for Yarrow rather than his pocketing it for himself. If this were what happened, then the first time Yarrow lost everything was when Brooke died in 1795. Yarrow then went back to work, earned the $100 back again, and gave it to a younger man. But Yarrow lost it a second time through this man's insolvency. Finally, if Ecker is to be believed, several men in Georgetown contributed $200 to buy bank stock for Yarrow.

In sum, legends aside, Yarrow Mamout was Brooke Beall's slave at Beallmount and moved to Georgetown proper in 1788 or 1789. He had once been a body servant, but he became a jack-of-all-trades. He could work on a ship, make bricks for a house, and make nets, baskets, and other articles for sale. He may have been able to make charcoal and possibly been a hacker. Fulfilling her husband's promise, Brooke's widow gave Yarrow his manumission paper in 1796. Yarrow was sixty years old. Earlier that year, he had purchased his son's freedom and four years later acquired a house in Georgetown.

In 1811, when David Warden heard of him, Yarrow was seventy-five—Warden said he was "more than eighty"—and still active, cheerful, and good-natured. Warden wrote that Yarrow walked erect. He was the best swimmer ever seen on the Potomac when he was young and, though stiffened by age, continued to swim in the river in his later years.

Warden added one final tidbit to the legends surrounding Yarrow. "On Christmas, his great delight is to fire a gun under their [the respectable families of Georgetown] windows at break of day, which is intended as a signal for his *dram*."[42] Warden probably intended the word "dram" to refer to a coin, as was a Georgetown tradition. According to writer William A. Gordon, "Christmas was the great time of year for negroes. Ordinarily, they were not allowed in the streets after the town bell rang at nine o'clock at night, but at Christmas this restriction was removed, and as midnight approached, bands of them would go through the streets singing hymns and carols before the houses of their white friends. The next morning the leader of the band called at the house and received a token of appreciation in the way of a small coin."[43] Warden's story would be more amusing if the dram were not a coin but rather a dram of whiskey. Yarrow was a Muslim. He told Charles Willson Peale that drinking whiskey was "very bad." If it were a dram of whiskey, then either telling Peale that he did not drink was another of Yarrow's tall tales, or the adaptable Muslim made an exception for the Christian holiday.

With the elderly Yarrow finally living as a free man in his own house in Georgetown, the stage was set for his encounter with the great artist Charles Willson Peale, who would not only record Yarrow's visage for posterity but also provide, through his diary, the clues needed to reconstruct Yarrow's path to America.

There was surprising chemistry between the artist and former slave in the two days it took to do the portrait. Peale was so affected that, when Yarrow died four years later, he wrote an obituary for him and sent it to newspapers. Yarrow felt honored. His sister must have felt equally so because she apparently adopted "Peale" as a last name. And the Beall family was so impressed—or ashamed—that they later commissioned the Georgetown artist James Alexander Simpson to paint a portrait for them to keep. Peale did not explain explicitly what made him decide to paint Yarrow, but a look into Peale's background and way of thinking sheds light on his motivations.

6 The Portraits: Peale, Yarrow, and Simpson

By the time he met Yarrow Mamout in January 1819, Charles Willson Peale was wealthy, famous, respected, and aging. In addition to being an artist and portrait painter, he had served as an army officer during the Revolutionary War and a state legislator in Pennsylvania. On top of this, he was a scientist, inventor, diarist, museum director, polymath, and entrepreneur. Peale brought all of this not only to his decision to paint Yarrow but also to the artistic choices he made in capturing Yarrow on canvas, an image that mixes Peale's life experiences and views and Yarrow's visage and personality.

Peale's origins were humble. His father, also named Charles, had been born in England. As a young man, the elder Peale had taken financial liberties that resulted in conviction for embezzlement and a sentence of death. He secured the option of emigrating to America instead.[1] Like so many others, such as Ninian Beall and Yarrow Mamout, the father of the great artist came to Maryland more or less involuntarily as a convict.

After completing his sentence of servitude, the senior Peale became a schoolteacher and married Margaret Triggs in 1740. Charles Willson was their first child, the middle name coming from relatives in England. The boy was born in 1741 in Queen Anne's County, Maryland, near the town of Centreville on the Eastern Shore, a peninsula, connected to the mainland at the north, but separated from the rest of the colony by the Chesapeake Bay. After young Charles was born, his family moved to nearby Chestertown.[2]

Peale's father died when Charles was only eight years old, leaving the family without a breadwinner. His mother therefore decided to move to the larger, colonial capital of Annapolis on the west side of the Chesapeake and take up work as a seamstress. There were only 150 or so houses in the town, but it was livelier than Centreville or Chestertown. The family was timely assisted by a young Annapolis lawyer named John Beale Bordley. He had once been a student of Peale's father. The elder Peale had been like a father to Bordley, and so, for the rest of his life, Bordley returned the favor by helping Charles Willson.

As chance would have it, then, Peale was living in Annapolis in June 1752 when Yarrow was brought there as a slave aboard the *Elijah*. There is no record on the matter, but one can imagine the boys of the town going to the harbor as soon as the slave ship dropped anchor. Other memories of life in Annapolis and the wonders that came in from the sea did stick in Peale's head. For example, years later he fondly recalled a boyhood experience of hearing a newly arrived ship's captain read from a foreign newspaper: "The manly expressive sweetness of his voice seems still to vibrate in my ears even at this distant period—and I have enjoyed the remembrance of it a thousand times."[3]

A slave ship coming into Annapolis was a rare and exotic event, and the young boys in Annapolis, particularly ones as curious as Peale, would have gone down to the wharf to witness the spectacle of these frightened black men and women straight from Africa, speaking in strange tongues, brought to shore in shackles. Peale was eleven years old; Yarrow was sixteen, but when they met and talked sixty-seven years later, Peale thought Yarrow was 134 years old. The possibility that he had witnessed Yarrow's arrival never crossed Peale's mind.

Peale fared only moderately better than Yarrow in the near term. With his family still impoverished by his father's death, Peale at age thirteen was apprenticed to saddlemaker Nathan Waters of Annapolis. The apprenticeship lasted eight years. It was not a happy time for Peale, who later characterized it as "abject servitude."

When the apprenticeship ended in 1762, Peale opened his own saddle business. He also took a wife, Rachel Brewer, the sister of a boyhood friend. She was the first of three wives and mother to ten of his seventeen children.[4] And, by one of those curious, circuitous routes that connect events in life, Rachel's relatives introduced Peale to Yarrow many years later in Georgetown.

Peale was constantly in debt. To bring in money, he took up upholstery, metalwork, clock repair, and portrait painting in addition to saddlery. He also was involved with the radical movement, men who supported the causes that would lead to the Revolutionary War. Unfortunately for Peale, his creditors were on the opposite side of these causes, and they began to dog him for payment for this reason. Peale eluded an arrest warrant his creditors swore out against him and fled to Virginia in 1765,[5] the same year that at Sharpsburg, Maryland, Yarrow's owner, Samuel Beall, declined to sign the Cresap petition lest he hang. From Virginia, Peale sailed to Boston where he got his first look at paintings from Italian masters and where he had a chance to spend a brief time with the American painter John Singleton Copley.[6]

In 1767, Peale's artistic talents were apparent enough to those around him that they financed his going to London. Beale Bordley arranged for wealthy Marylanders to pay for the trip. Peale's benefactors included the slave trader Christopher Lowndes and his father-in-law and former colonial governor Benjamin Tasker Sr.[7]

Peale spent two years in England studying art under the American painter Benjamin West. The trip was broadening for Peale, and not just artistically. In London, he met Benjamin Franklin and learned of his work with electricity, evidencing an early interest in science on Peale's part. The encounter was the first of many with Franklin and may have fueled his radicalism. When his teacher, Benjamin West, received a commission from King George III for a painting, Peale worked on it. Yet while he accepted the king's money, he vowed to himself that he would not accept the king's control over America.[8]

In 1769, Peale returned to Annapolis and began building his reputation as a portrait painter. A man with Peale's talents was in demand among the wealthy planters, and in the spring and fall they came to Annapolis and dropped by Peale's studio. The rest of the year, he had to travel to pick up business. It was during this time that he first visited Philadelphia and began to think it would be a better market for him.[9]

Throughout this period, Peale was refining his skills and building a reputation. His personality and approach to his sitters was as responsible for his success as his hand. His biographer Charles Coleman Sellers explains it this way:

> In a portrait artist's faces one often finds the artist also, and this is true of Peale. There are exceptions, but the Peale face is almost always recognizable at once in an expression of gentle, intelligent affability. The eyes are warm, the mouth approves. These are faces of the Enlightenment, the Age of Reason. When you see them in the mass as in the great Independence Hall collection, the impression is that of an audience as a favorite lecturer raises his eyes to address them.
>
> In a Peale portrait of a close friend there is often a warmth and immediacy lacking in other portraits where he did not have a feeling of congenial rapport with the subject. You can see this sensitivity working adversely in the forbidding and awkwardly composed portrait of Samuel Chase, a signer of the Declaration of Independence from Maryland, with whose politics the painter ardently agreed but whose aggressive, ambitious, impatient nature was so different from his own.[10]

In 1772, George Washington invited Peale to come to Mount Vernon, where he painted the first of his portraits of Washington. The artist spent four days there. The two men bonded. On the last night, at the end of dinner, the gracious Washington rose and presented Peale with a cup and saucer to take back to his wife Rachel, saying, "That Mrs. Peale may be associated with our pleasure, will you present this cup to her with my best respects?"[11]

Yet, despite his success and renown, Peale was still in debt. In part to remedy this, he moved to Baltimore in 1775. The city was larger, and the portrait business was better. His decision proved a sound one, for once in Baltimore, he finally broke clear of the debt that had plagued him. Solvency also freed him to indulge his thirst for learning things other than art. He taught himself French and frequented the docks where he found sailors with whom he could speak the language.[12]

In June 1776, Peale took the next step up the ladder of success and moved to Philadelphia. His timing was propitious. The Continental Congress was meeting there. Peale had already finished miniatures of the revolutionary leader John Hancock and his wife, Dorothy Quincy, and he secured a commission from the congress to paint portraits of George and Martha Washington.[13]

Like the subjects he painted, Peale owned slaves. They went with him to Philadelphia. Sellers writes:

> [In Maryland, Peale] even had the distinction, if it can be called that, of owning slaves. I have been inclined to suspect that [slaves] Scarborough and Lucy [Williams] may have been given to him in exchange for portrait work by some planter who counted himself doubly benefited by the arrangement. However this may be, they became a family within the family of the Peales, the births of their children recorded with the others in the Pilkington's book [a dictionary of painters that served as a family Bible for the Peales]. At least one of their offspring was to end his days as a man of considerable property in Philadelphia, over which a white woman presided as his wife. Charles Willson Peale had early deplored the effect of slavery on the manners of the white population (he had had an instance of it in his first meeting with Rachel), and, investigating hypotheses as to differences between the races, was to conclude that given equal advantages of education there were none.[14]

Peale was in Philadelphia when the Declaration of Independence was signed. Given his radical sentiments, he must have been delighted. On July 8, he stood in a great crowd of people in the yard of the state house to hear the document read.

The impending war proved good for his business too. Military officers who came to Philadelphia that summer stopped by Peale's studio to have their portraits painted. In October, Peale himself was elected an officer in the state militia. This is why on December 27, 1776, he found himself in a small boat crossing the Delaware River from Pennsylvania into New Jersey with the rest of Washington's army. However, the famous painting of Washington crossing the Delaware is not Peale's. It was done more than eighty years later by a man who obviously had not participated, as Peale had.

Even in the army, Peale still applied his various crafts. For example, when he discovered that some of his men did not have shoes for the winter, the former saddlemaker bought hides and made moccasins for them. The next winter, 1776–77, he was with Washington's army near Philadelphia at Valley Forge. Peale split his time between the encampment and his family on a farm outside Philadelphia. When in camp, he made money by doing portraits and miniatures of the officers and by selling replicas of his portrait of George Washington.[15]

By 1779, Peale had ended active service with the militia and was back with his family in Philadelphia where he was elected to the Pennsylvania legislature. That November, the legislature took up a bill to abolish slavery gradually. Peale voted for it and freed his own slaves as required, although they continued to live with him.[16]

When the fighting ended in 1781, Peale could have devoted himself full-time to painting if he so chose. But his attentions slowly began to turn to other projects and other disciplines. He realized people were not merely interested in pictures of their own families. They were also interested in the rich and famous and would pay for the privilege of seeing images of them. Since Peale had copies of many of his paintings, he took advantage of the public's curiosity and opened a gallery in Philadelphia to exhibit his portraits of famous Americans. In 1788, he expanded on the idea by creating a museum where, for a price, the public could see not only portraits but also objects of natural history.

In concept, it was a precursor to the Smithsonian museums. Now showman, Peale announced the new museum with this newspaper advertisement:

> Containing the portraits of Illustrious Personages, distinguished in the late Revolution of America and other paintings—also, a Collection of preserved Beast, Birds, Fish, Reptiles, Insects, Fossils, Minerals, and Petrafications, and other curious objects, natural and artificial. Intended to be an easy and pleasant instruction in natural history. As this museum is in its infancy, Mr. Peale will thankfully receive the assistance of the curious. N.B. To pay for attendance, &etc. admittance One Shilling or One Dollar for free Ticket for One Year.[17]

The museum would later make its home on the second floor of Independence Hall in Philadelphia, where the Declaration of Independence was signed, a fitting location for the works of this Renaissance American.

On occasion, Peale's scientific, artistic, curatorial, and entrepreneurial bents came together in a single project. The best example of this followed the discovery of the skeleton of a mammoth elephant, which was mistakenly identified as a mastodon at the time, on the farm of John Masten in upstate New York. Peale traveled to the site, painting landscapes along the way. Once there, he purchased the remains and shipped them back to Philadelphia. The specimen was not entirely satisfactory. Key pieces of the skeleton were missing, so Peale went back to New York and had his men dig in the muck for more. He captured the dig in his famous painting *Exhumation of the Mastodon*. His men dug up two more skeletons on nearby farms. The expedition took five months and cost $1,000, a huge sum for science at the time.[18] Even the scientist-in-chief, President Thomas Jefferson, took an interest in and corresponded with Peale about it.

After it was back at the museum, Peale ordered the skeleton reconstructed in an upright position and put on display there together with a drawing of the complete skeleton and his painting. Peale had the workman fabricate any missing bones in order to make the animal's skeleton complete. Another skeleton was sent to Europe for display under the supervision of his son Rembrandt.[19]

Some of Peale's scientific interests seem odd today, but he usually found support in the American Philosophical Society of Philadelphia, an organization devoted to the pursuit of science.[20] For example, in his declining years, Peale got interested in the subject of longevity for the obvious reason. At the time, most naturalists believed animals should live about ten times longer than the time it took to reach maturity. This meant that humans should live to be two hundred years old. Peale subscribed to a more conservative ratio of one to six. He felt that humans were easily capable of reaching 120 years of age if they avoided alcohol, exercised, and otherwise took care of themselves. In fact, he knew a man in Philadelphia, John Strangeways Hutton, a decent, hardworking man who was 107. Having been married twice, Hutton had twenty-five children and a total of 132 descendants.[21]

As with his painting of the excavation of the mammoth, Peale applied his artistic talent to the cause of science in other instances. Once, when traveling through Somerset County, Maryland, in 1791, he encountered a slave named James whose color had changed from brown to white. The condition, called vitiglio, is a depigmentation of the skin. It is relatively rare and occurs in both white and black races, but this was not known at the time. Peale was interested because if blacks could become white through association with whites or for some other reason, then, he felt, the terrible problem of racism would be solved. Therefore, he painted James's portrait, made appropriate inquiries about his heritage and life, and turned all of his material over to the American Philosophical Society.[22]

Slavery itself was such a part of Peale's life that, despite his opposition to the practice, he generally did not remark on it in his diary. And when he did, he wrote about it in patronizing terms. For example, he acquired for his museum the bow of a slave named Jambo, explaining in the diary:

> An African Prince, subdued in Battle, Capitulated for his bow, and quiver. A Bauble bought his life.—A British Merchant sent him to South Carolina, where he was sold as a slave.
>
> A placid countenance, and submissive manners, marked his resignation, and preserved him, in all situations, the possession of his Arms; the only companions he had left—the sole objects of his affections.
>
> His Stateliness, and strength, recommended him to Colonel Motte, a humane Master in whose service he died, in stedfast faith of a certain resurection in his native state.
>
> The Bow and quiver, were preserved as relicks of a faithful slave in the Colonels family, who gratefully remember the services, the fortitude and the fidelity of the trusty, gentle Jambo.[23]

But the most startling example of Peale's outward indifference to the evils of slavery took place August 16, 1789, when he did a portrait of the wife of slave trader Christopher Lowndes without comment about her husband's profession. Peale was traveling from Annapolis to Georgetown and stopped in Bladensburg to see a woman he referred to in his diary as Mrs. David Ross. She was Henrietta Marie Bordley, daughter-in-law of Samuel Beall's former business partner, Dr. David

Ross, and daughter of Peale's long-time friend and benefactor Beale Bordley. She told him that her neighbor, Mrs. Elizabeth Lowndes, was dying and wanted to preserve her image for her family.[24] Peale paused in his travels and made sketches from which he later made several portraits and miniatures. Elizabeth Lowndes died a short time later. Peale resumed his journey to Georgetown, where he had a commission from Mrs. Lowndes's son-in-law Benjamin Stoddert to paint the three Stoddert children.

Peale had every reason to know that Christopher Lowndes had been in the slave trade. For one thing, Lowndes's name had appeared in the announcement in the *Maryland Gazette* about the arrival of the *Elijah* in 1752 when Peale was living in Annapolis. Even though he was only eleven and might not have seen the newspaper, he surely heard of Christopher Lowndes as someone in the transatlantic slave trade. For another thing, Lowndes was one of the men who paid for Peale's study in London using money that came in part from the slave trade. And finally, Peale was introduced to Mrs. Lowndes by Dr. David Ross's daughter-in-law. The Ross family had known the Lowndeses for decades, they were neighbors, and they certainly were aware of how Christopher Lowndes got his money.

Two Days with Yarrow

Peale visited Georgetown again in 1818, and it was then that he heard about Yarrow Mamout. Much had changed in the town in the twenty-nine years between his 1789 visit to the Stodderts and this one. In 1789, Georgetown was a small, but growing tobacco port at the fall line on the Potomac River. A year later, George Washington made the decision to put the capital nearby, and the government moved there from Philadelphia in 1800. The United States had fought another war against England during which the city of Washington was burned in 1814. Thus, when Peale arrived in 1818, he saw that the little port of Georgetown had become a thriving transportation and financial center adjacent to the capital of a robust United States.

Much had changed in Charles Willson Peale's personal life as well. His first wife, Rachel Brewer, had died, and so had his second, Elizabeth de Peyster. He had remarried a third time to Hannah More. When Peale went to Georgetown in 1789, it was to make money from portrait painting. In 1818, he went to Washington as painter, museum director, and scientist.

Peale planned to spend three months in the city. First and foremost, he wanted to do a portrait of President James Monroe to add to portraits of the four previous presidents in the "Presidential Gallery" at the Philadelphia museum. Second, Peale was willing to paint anyone else for a price. Among those who sat for him were Vice President Daniel Tompkins, Secretary of State John Quincy Adams, Secretary of the Treasury William H. Crawford, Attorney General William Wortley, Speaker of the House Henry Clay, and a bevy of senators, congressmen, and commodores.[25]

One man rejected Peale's invitation for a sitting: William Lowndes, a congressman from South Carolina. He was of the same Lowndes family that had once been in the transatlantic slave trade and a distant relative of Christopher Lowndes. Seemingly hurt by being turned down, Peale wrote about the incident in his diary to which he confided his views on portraiture, giving insights as to how he might have approached his sessions with Yarrow:

> Mr Lounes is a very tall slim man—he has a long nose (and) large mouth, & a thin face, it appears very probable that his aversion to have a picture of himself, that it might (not) be too homely—but in all my exertions to make portraits, I always endeavor to take the most favorable view—being much more pleased to make this agreable, never fearing to give a good semblance, altho' other views might be more remarkable. It is the mind I would wish to represent through the features of the man, and he that does not possess a good mind, I do not desire to Portray his features. The temper of man in a powerful degree fashions as I may say, the turns of the features.[26]

Third, Peale used the trip as an opportunity to catch up with family. Joseph Brewer of Georgetown was the nephew of Peale's first wife

Rachel. Brewer's next-door neighbor, William Marbury, was married to Rachel's niece.[27] Marbury, of *Marbury v. Madison* legal fame, had an elegant house overlooking Analostan Island with the ferry terminus that the Mason family owned.[28]

Peale spent time with both families. Brewer was the one who first mentioned Yarrow Mamout. Peale wrote in his diary: "I heard of a Negro who is living in Georgetown said to be 140 years of age. Mr. Brewer said that he is comfortable in his Situation having Bank stock and lives in his own house. I shall be able to give a more particular account of him as I propose to make a portrait of him should I have the opportunity of doing it."[29]

Free African Americans were not uncommon in Georgetown. The 1800 census counted 277 free blacks, 1,449 slaves, and 3,394 white people. Tax assessments showed other blacks owned property in Georgetown. According to the 1815 assessment not only did "Negro Yarrow" own a house but so did "Negro Hercules, Semus husband." His house was valued at $500 versus $200 for Yarrow's. Brooke Beall's ledger shows that he sold a "plough" and osnaburg cloth to "Negro Tom" and that "Negro Wilks" also had an account with him.[30]

Chronicler David Warden mentions a Scotsman, Mr. Maine, who had a nursery for fruit trees and hedge thorns, such as pyrocantha, on the hill above Georgetown. Maine employed young blacks, whom he taught to read and write and instructed them "in moral duties." Warden added: "Joseph Moor, a manumitted black, who lived with him [Maine] is now a respectable grocer in Georgetown."[31] As mentioned previously, Moor was a contemporary of Yarrow's and, given his name, was probably also a Muslim.

Peale's initial interest in Yarrow seemed to be scientific. Here, to Peale's way of thinking, was someone who might prove men could live to the ripe old age of 140 and who might tell Peale how he did it. Just as he had painted the Negro slave James, who had turned from brown to white, Peale would paint Yarrow and then try to determine the secret of his longevity. There was more than science in Peale's mind, though. Here was a black man of substance, one owning bank stock and a house. Peale might come away with a portrait to prove to the world that black people were the equal of whites if they had equal opportunities. Peale was quite proud of the portrait of the Reverend Absalom Jones, a black minister in Philadelphia, that his son Raphaelle had painted in 1810.

In his diary, Peale described how in late January he and Joseph Brewer went to Yarrow's house to make the arrangements: "[T]hen went to Georgetown to pay a short visit to Mr. Joseph Brewer & Coll. [Colonel] Marburys families—and to know whether I could get an Old Negro named Yarrow to set to me, I went with Joseph Brewer to Yarrows House & engaged him to set the next morning."[32]

Peale worked at Yarrow's house. It was not the best address in Georgetown. Few of the surrounding lots were developed. On one side of the property was the graveyard of the Presbyterian church. On another was a small creek. The portrait took Peale two days. At the end of the first day, he wrote: "I spend [spent] the whole day & not only painted a good likeness of him, but also the drapery and background."[33]

The next morning, before going back to Yarrow's, Peale took time to investigate Yarrow's background. This brief investigation turned up crucial information on Yarrow, which Peale saved in his diary for posterity: "However, to finish it more completely, I engaged him to set the next day—and early in the morning when [went] to see some of the family how [who] had knowledge of Him for many years & whose Ancesters had purchased him from the Ship that brought him from Afreca—a Mr. Bell in a Bank directed me to an ancient Widow who had set him free."[34]

This was in fact Thomas Brooke Beall, president of the Columbia Bank of Georgetown, and the "ancient Widow" was, of course, Margaret Beall, widow of Yarrow's owner Brooke Beall. Naturally, the two Beall men were distant cousins. The name "Beall" was pronounced "Bell." The bank president was a descendant of Ninian Beall, who supposedly was fond of explaining with gusto that his name should be pronounced like a "ringing bell."[35]

Peale's main purpose in going to the bank was to confirm Yarrow's claim. After all, in those days, stock ownership was something for wealthy men, like Brewer and Marbury. Yarrow was not in their league. His small wood frame house at the edge of a creek near the

Presbyterian church's graveyard was a far cry from Marbury's elegant brick house overlooking the river.

Peale wrote in his diary that the bank records on stockholders were not available at the time he visited but that he later received a message from the bank saying Yarrow had acquired the stock twenty-six years earlier and had been one of the first to invest. Today, although many of the bank records have been preserved, Yarrow's name does not appear in them.[36] But if Yarrow was one of the first to invest, then he had purchased the bank stock when he was still a slave. The bank was founded on December 25, 1793, and Yarrow was not freed until 1796. Why did Peale not look into this more deeply? Maybe he did not have time. Maybe it did not occur to him that Yarrow was a slave when he got the stock. Or maybe he realized Yarrow was a slave when he bought the stock but did not think it was unusual. Perhaps in those days, if a black man was willing to give a bank his money, the bank did not ask too many questions. Unless the black man could prove he was legally free, he could not sue to get the money back.

After leaving the bank but before returning to Yarrow's house to finish the painting, Peale stopped by Margaret Beall's house. She was living at Mackall Square with her daughter and her husband. The couple built a large brick house on the property that is still there. At this time, however, they may have lived in the old frame house, which was moved a few blocks away later and is today a private residence across from Tudor Place in Georgetown.[37] Peale wanted to find out if what Yarrow had told him about his age was true.

> [O]n Making inquiry of this Ladey about his age, for he told me that he would be 134 years old in next March I found that he counted 12 Moons to the Year, and that he was 35 years old when he was first brought to America by Capt. Dow—But the Widow Bell told me that it was a practice in former times when Slaves was brought into the Country, they were vallued by a committee who estimated their age and she thought he had been sold as 14 years or thereabout, yet he might be a little older.[38]

Margaret did not know the facts firsthand. She was the daughter-in-law of Yarrow's original owner, Samuel Beall. He had purchased

Yarrow before Margaret married into the family. What she told Peale must have been a family story that was handed down to her. She said Yarrow was fourteen years old or a little older when he arrived on a slave ship. She was sure of the age because a slave's age determined his price, and the practice had been to have a committee judge slaves' ages. Margaret was obviously repeating a story she had heard from her husband or his father, and the fact that such minor details about Yarrow were remembered is evidence of how much the family valued him.

Oddly, although Peale wrote in his diary that the purpose of his visit with Margaret was to inquire about whether Yarrow was 140 years old as he claimed, Peale did not record what she said. She was probably the source for the information in the 1796 inventory of Brooke Beall's estate that Yarrow was sixty years old then. If so, she knew he was not 140 years old or 134 years old. He was eighty-three, just five years older than Peale. In any event, Peale did not understand what Margaret was trying to tell him about Yarrow's age. He left still thinking that Yarrow was at least 134 years old, even if he did not look it. Peale did not even seem to notice the obvious, that according to Margaret, Yarrow was about fourteen when he came to America, not thirty-five as he claimed.

Margaret also told Peale that Yarrow became the property of her husband Brooke upon the "decase" of Brooke's father. She and Brooke had planned to build a larger house in Georgetown and move there when it was done. Brooke asked Yarrow to make the bricks for the house and out houses, promising he would set Yarrow free when the job was done. Peale wrote in his diary:

> Yarrow completed his task, but his master died before he began the House, and the Widow knowing the design of her Husband, told Yarrow that as he had performed his duty, that she had made the necessary papers to set him free & now he was made free. . . . Yarrow made a great many Bows thanking his Mistress and said that ever Mistress wanted work done, Yarrow would work for her—but she said that she never called on Yarrow to work for her.[39]

Peale did not mention what kind of house Margaret was living in, whether it was the older wood frame house or the brick house that her daughter, Christiana, and son-in-law, Benjamin Mackall, built on Mackall Square. Nor did he ask a question that would be useful today: What happened to the bricks? Were they sold? Did her daughter and her husband, the Mackalls, use them in their new house? Or did Yarrow use them for the cellar of his house, because there are old bricks on the property to this day? But then Peale was merely recording things in a diary to jog his memory later, if need be. He was not writing for posterity and publication.

Peale went back to Yarrow's to finish the portrait. The two men talked while Peale painted. Peale later wrote in his diary what Yarrow told him about his financial misfortunes:

> After Yarrow obtained his freedom he worked hard and saved his Money untill he got 100$ which put into an Old Gentlemans hands to keep for him—that person died and Yarrow lost his Money—however it did not disperit him, for he still worked as before and raised another 100$ which he put into the care of a young Merchant in Georgetown, and Yallow [*sic*] said young man no die—but this merchant became a Bankrupt & thus Yarrow mett a 2d heavy loss—yet not disperited he worked & saved a 3d Sum amounting to 200$, some friend to Yarrow advised him to Buy bank stock in the Columbia Bank—this advice Yarrow thought good for he said Bank no die.[40]

This version of the story is remarkably similar to what Yarrow told David Warden several years earlier. Yarrow had not changed it in the retelling. In fact, the words "young man no die" and "Bank no die" appear in both Warden's book and Peale's diary. The two men were directly quoting Yarrow's words.

The quotes from Yarrow also serve as a reminder that English was a second, third, or even fourth language for him and as evidence that he understood investing, business, and law. He was not just blindly following instructions. In law, corporations are said to have a perpetual existence, which Yarrow correctly and poetically simplified to "Bank no die."

Peale could have empathized with Yarrow's fierce determination in the face of financial difficulties. Memories of all the money problems

Peale had as a young man must have come back to him. How much worse, Peale probably thought, to be broke when you were old—and black.

While Peale was working on the painting that second day, he and Yarrow were getting more comfortable with each other. Peale had the opportunity to ask Yarrow about his lifestyle and the secret to his longevity:

> Yarrow owns a House & lotts and is known by most of the Inhabitants of Georgetown & particularly by the Boys who are often teazing him which he takes in good humor. It appears to me that the good temper of the [m]an has contributed considerably to longevity. Yarrow has been noted for sobriety & a chearfull conduct, he professes to be a mahometan, and is often seen & heard in the Streets singing Praises to God—and conversing with him he said man is no good unless his religion comes from the heart. He said he never stole one penny in his life—yet he seems delighted to sport with those in company, pretending that he would steal some thing—The Butchers in the Market can always find a bit of meat to give to yarrow—sometimes he will pretend to steal a piece of meat and put it into the Basket of some Gentleman, and then say me no tell if you give me half.
>
> The acquaintance of him often banter him about eating Bacon and drinking Whiskey—but Yarrow says it is no good to eat Hog—& drink whiskey is very bad.
>
> I retouched his Portrait the morning after his first setting to mark what rinkles & lines to characterise better his Portrait.[41]

Of course, the best evidence of what Yarrow was like is the portrait itself. At age eighty-three, he was still a vigorous, confident, and cheerful man. It is a remarkable image for someone who was imprisoned on a slave ship from Africa through the Middle Passage to America, subjugated as a slave for forty-four years, and then twice penniless in his old age. Perhaps Peale was amazed that after all he had been through the man could still smile.

Since Peale took the painting with him back to Philadelphia, Yarrow obviously did not pay for it. There is no record of whether Peale displayed it in the museum or showed it to the American Philosophical Society. He died in 1829, but the museum continued to operate. When it finally closed in 1852, Peale's grandson Edmund came across the painting and mistakenly labeled it "Billy Lee," thinking his grandfather had painted the body servant of George Washington. That the portrait might be of Lee was not an unreasonable assumption. Peale knew him during the terrible winter at Valley Forge. In 1804, after Washington's death, Peale had stopped by Mount Vernon. While there, he sought out Lee and reminisced about the old days.[42]

This identification of the painting lasted until 1947 when Peale's biographer Charles Coleman Sellers carefully matched the painting to Peale's diary entries and concluded the painting was of Yarrow Mamout. Besides, Sellers wrote, "It is not reasonable to suppose that Peale would have painted Billy Lee in his old age, for, despite faithful service to General Washington, Billy was a drunkard and a cripple in his last years at Mount Vernon."[43] Yet as recently as 1994, a *New York Times* reporter, writing about an exhibit of the painting, could still get justifiably confused. She identified the painting as "Yarrow Mamout, a servant of George Washington."[44]

In concluding that the painting of Yarrow had been incorrectly identified, Sellers did not seem to know that Georgetown artist James Alexander Simpson also did a portrait of Yarrow. This second painting certainly would have cinched it for Sellers. It might also have piqued his curiosity. When Elizabeth Broun, the director of the Smithsonian Museum of American Art, was asked about the two paintings in connection with the research on this book, she focused on the fact that formal portraits of African Americans prior to the Civil War were rare, and yet there are two of Yarrow Mamout.

The Simpson Portrait

Little is known about James Alexander Simpson. The only published research on him concluded he was born in England around 1805, later came to America, and settled in Frederick, Maryland. He subsequently moved to Georgetown. The 1820 census shows a James Simpson living there; of course, it might have been a different man.[45]

Simpson did the portrait of Yarrow in 1822. He became an instructor of drawing and painting at Georgetown College three years later. If the 1805 date of birth is correct, then Simpson was only seventeen years old when he painted Yarrow and twenty when he started teaching at Georgetown. He taught only if there were enough students for a class. Otherwise, he occupied himself by painting the town, the college, and the residents of Georgetown. Many of those paintings still exist. How Simpson himself learned to paint is unknown. His painting of Yarrow is in the possession of the Peabody Room at the Georgetown branch of the District of Columbia library.

Simpson moved to Baltimore in 1860 and died twenty years later. Today, several of his other works are on display at Georgetown University. His painting of Commodore Stephen Decatur, which Simpson copied from a Gilbert Stuart portrait, has hung in the office of the university president.

A comparison of the Peale and Simpson portraits reveals curious similarities. Yarrow is wearing the same style knit cap in both, although the stripes are in different colors. The collar and buttons of his jacket are the same. He has a white shirt and red waistcoat in both paintings, but his jacket is unbuttoned in the Simpson to show more of the waistcoat. Even the pose, forehead wrinkles, and whiskers are the same in the two paintings. Yarrow looks significantly older in the Simpson painting, although he was in fact only three years older. Whether the difference stems from Peale's desire to produce a flattering image or from some illness that caused Yarrow's appearance to age rapidly is not known.

As for the clothes, Yarrow might have worn the same, or similar, clothes to both sittings, even if they were several years apart. While he had $200 in bank stock and a house in Georgetown, he was by no means a rich man. But another curious fact is that in the early 1800s, Georgetown College required students to have a blue jacket, blue pantaloons with yellow buttons, and a red waistcoat to wear on Sundays. One of Brooke Beall's sons went to Georgetown for a semester or two before dropping out. Perhaps Yarrow was wearing a Georgetown uniform for both paintings, one he acquired from Brooke's son or from one of the Georgetown boys, who Peale said were "teazing" him. Yarrow bought coarse osnaburg from Brooke Beall in 1790 and was probably wearing clothes made from that fabric when he was a slave, but he obviously dressed better as a free man, particularly when there was an artist around that wanted to paint his picture.

The only significant difference in clothing in the two paintings is that Yarrow has a leather greatcoat draped over his shoulders in the Peale painting. The expensive coat is something that only a wealthier man than Yarrow could afford. The coat is just the kind of thing that the great Charles Willson Peale might wear when traveling around Georgetown on a cold January day. It contributes to Yarrow's look of wealth and substance. Thus, it seems likely that the painter draped his own coat over Yarrow for artistic reasons or to help make a statement about racial equality. Peale biographer Charles Coleman Sellers wrote this about the portrait of Yarrow Mamout: "When he [Peale] was cool toward the sitter, or uninterested, the portrait is often unrevealing, stiff, and even awkward. But when his heart was warm toward his subject he recorded not only the features but his own friendly feeling with both sympathy and charm."[46]

Yarrow died on January 19, 1823. Even in death, Peale helped distinguish him: He wrote an obituary and sent it to newspapers. Rarely did newspapers then carry obituaries for African Americans. The *Gettysburg Compiler* was one of the papers that carried Yarrow's. Since the obituary contains much the same information and phrasing as Peale's diary, he surely wrote it. But there is an added fact. The obituary said Yarrow's body was interred in the corner of his garden, the spot he usually resorted to pray. Yarrow must have excused himself while sitting for the portrait, gone outside to the southeast corner of his lot, bowed to Mecca, and prayed.

> Died—at Georgetown, on the 19th ultimo, negro Yarrow, aged (according to his account) 136 years. He was interred in the corner of his garden, the spot where he usually resorted to pray—Yarrow has resided in town upwards of 60 years—it is known to all that knew him,

> that he was industrious, honest, and moral—in the early part of his life he met with several losses by loaning money, which he never got, but he persevered in industry and economy, and accumulated some Bank stock and a house and lot, on which he lived comfortably in his old age—Yarrow was never known to eat of swine, nor drink ardent spirits.[47]

That Peale was the author explains why the obituary was in a Pennsylvania newspaper.

Another of Peale's writings, his diary, was the key to unlocking the first part of Yarrow's story. Peale wrote that Yarrow was brought to America by a Captain Dow. No captain by that name is listed in the Trans-Atlantic Slave Trade Database in this period. The only similar-sounding name is that of James Lowe, who captained the *Elijah* into Annapolis in 1752. Yarrow may have been referring to him. Or, he could have been referring to slave trader Christopher Lowndes, who was sometimes called Captain Lowndes. That Yarrow was on the *Elijah* is even more certain given that Margaret Beall said Yarrow was fourteen or a little older when he came to America, meaning that he came in 1750 or later, and that the *Elijah* was the only slave ship from Guinea to Maryland then.[48]

Yarrow's death was not the end of the family or Yarrow's own narrative. He would be talked about in Georgetown for several more decades. Then there was his sister, his son, his son's wife, and her relatives.

7 Free Hannah, Yarrow's Sister

Although there is little direct information about Yarrow's sister, documents and circumstances suggest that she was the slave named Hannah belonging to Joseph Wilson of Rockville, Maryland. Wilson and his extended family were in the tavern business, and Hannah worked at Wilson's tavern. He had purchased her when he bought it. When Wilson died a few years later, Hannah's name appeared in his will. Hannah was a common slave name, of course, but even so, this woman would seem to be Yarrow's sister, especially since Wilson owned other Fulani slaves, including one named Yarrow.[1] The fact that Yarrow had a sister at all, as has been noted, was established in a lawsuit her daughter, Nancy Hillman, filed years after Yarrow died, seeking to inherit his property

Joseph Wilson's Tavern and His Slaves

Rockville, about thirteen miles north of Georgetown, was known as Williamsburg in Hannah's day. The settlement was founded at the intersection of several major roads. To the northwest was the road to Frederick, Maryland, to the south was Georgetown, and to the southeast was Bladensburg.

Early Rockville was nothing more than a rest stop for travelers. One of the first known businesses at the intersection was an inn for travelers operated by Lawrence Owen and called Owen's Ordinary. The tavern was there as early as 1755, and General Braddock's army camped next to it on the way from Georgetown to Fort Duquesne in the French and Indian War.[2]

Joseph Wilson was a relative newcomer to Rockville. He got his start as a planter in Prince George's County, and he had four farms totaling almost six hundred acres. Like all of the old tracts, these had names. Wilson's were the Joseph and James, Two Brothers, Valentines Garden, and Conclusion. Wilson probably lived on the Two Brothers tract. Tax assessments show an old framed house and one new house on the land. The new house would have been where Wilson lived. There were two log houses on the property, too, which were obviously slave cabins. The Joseph and James tract had 270 acres, one house, and one slave cabin. The other two tracts were smaller and had no buildings. In addition to being a tobacco farmer, Wilson dabbled in public service as a justice of the peace and owned lots in the town of Rockville.[3]

He was interested in the tavern business, too. He had married Sarah Owen, the widow of tavern owner Lawrence Owen. Perhaps she was the one to urge Wilson to give the business a try, or perhaps he was already in the business, and this was how he got to know her. In any event, in 1786, Wilson bought the Rockville tavern operated by his son-in-law, Leonard Davis. The establishment was called Hungerford's Tavern after an earlier owner. Hungerford's may have been in the same spot as Owen's Ordinary, but, if not, it was at least in the same intersection. The building is believed to have survived into the twentieth century as a private residence, but a bank building occupies the property today, with only a plaque to mark the spot.[4]

Wilson paid Davis £780 and gave him 16,000 pounds of tobacco. In return, he got farm animals, tavern furniture, and fifteen slaves. The deed of sale named the slaves: Peter, Saundo, Condo, Cato, Page, Dick, Sango, Will, John, Sal, Jeney, Doll, Nell, and Hannah and her child Callaby.[5] This Hannah is the one believed to be Yarrow's sister. She was working at the tavern along with three slaves with African names, Saundo, Condo, and Sango.

Fulani at Hungerford's

Four years after purchasing the tavern, Wilson made out his last will and testament. He named thirty-three slaves, dividing them between his two daughters Ann and Sarah. Seven of the slaves were those he had purchased with the tavern: Cato, Page, Sango, Jene, Doll, Nel, and Hannah. The remaining twenty-six were Yarmouth, Peter, Caesar, Sarah, Luce, Darks, Fiona, Sook, Jude, Anthony, Peg, Jacob, Beck, Bask, Fuller, George, Clem, Joe, Rachel, Fide, Jem, Yarrow, Ellick, Wago, Isaac, and Jim.[6] Some of the names are clearly African, such as Sook, Bask, Fide, Jem, and Wago. Yarrow was obviously Fulani. Isaac and Yarmouth probably were too. The names sound as though they were derived from the Fulani names Issaka and Younous.[7]

That West Africans, probably from the *Elijah*, were slaves in the Rockville area is further evidenced by a newspaper interview almost one hundred years later, in 1879, of a former slave named Shadrack Nugent. Nugent told the reporter he was born near Rockville in 1761. He said his father was brought to this country from Guinea and was called "Bob—Mr. Crampton's Bob."[8] According to Nugent, his mother was an Irish indentured servant named Mary Nugent. He himself was body servant to George Graff in the Revolutionary War and saw combat in Baltimore. After the war, Nugent said, Graff bought a farm three miles from Rockville, settled there, and ultimately gave Nugent his freedom.

Although Nugent was taking liberties with the truth, the essence of his story is plausible and supports the belief that slaves from Guinea were living in Rockville in 1761. The liberties include Nugent's claim that he was 118 years old. Even the reporter was skeptical, and rightfully so. The 1860 census recorded Nugent as seventy years old, and thus he was in fact eighty-nine when he talked to the reporter. In the next census, which was done after he talked to the reporter, Nugent suddenly became 119. He stretched the truth in other ways as well. Since he was born around 1790, he could not have fought in the Revolutionary War.

But Nugent may not have made up his story out of whole cloth. He probably was a body servant to Graff, but in the War of 1812, when the fighting around Baltimore occasioned the writing of the "Star Spangled Banner." Likewise, while Nugent was not born in 1761, he could have been talking about his father. In that case, the man who came from Guinea was his grandfather, and it was Nugent's father who was born in 1761. Since the *Elijah* was one of only two slave ships from Guinea into Annapolis in this period, the grandfather may have come with Yarrow and may even have been a Muslim.[9] If so, then he most likely was on the *Elijah*.

Josiah Henson (Uncle Tom), Yarrow, and Hannah

There was another famous slave in Rockville at this time, Josiah Henson. Born in 1789 in Port Tobacco, Maryland, Henson was still a boy when he was sold to Isaac Riley of Montgomery County. Riley's farm was a few miles south of Hungerford's. Henson's autobiography, written after he fled to freedom in Canada, became inspiration for Harriet Beecher Stowe's *Uncle Tom's Cabin*. He is sometimes called "the real Uncle Tom," and his book gave a slave's perspective on what life was like in the Washington area in Yarrow's and Hannah's day.

Colonial taverns were for more than eating and drinking. They were way stations where travelers might spend the night and gathering places for public meetings and the conduct of civic affairs.[10] They were often the largest building in town. Hungerford's was where the planters of Montgomery County met to pass the locally famous "Hungerford Resolves" that sided with the radicals in Boston after the Tea Party.[11] The resolves were a precursor to the Declaration for the Association of the Freemen of Maryland, which Samuel Beall and the other Maryland revolutionaries signed in 1775.

The most famous tavern in the Washington area was Suter's Tavern in Georgetown. It was frequented by the likes of George Washington and Thomas Jefferson. Washington really did sleep there. It was operated by John Suter, who was related by marriage to Joseph Wilson.[12] Although the location of Suter's Tavern is debated, it was probably on the same block as Brooke Beall's warehouse in Georgetown. Thus, while Hannah worked at Joseph Wilson's tavern in Rockville, Yarrow worked at Beall's warehouse in Georgetown, just a few doors from Suter's tavern, which was run by Wilson's in-law. Suter's Tavern was also the place where stockholder meetings of the Columbia Bank of

Georgetown, in which Yarrow owned stock, were held—as well as occasional slave auctions outside it.[13]

David Warden, who wrote about early Washington, probably had Suter's in mind when he mentioned that slaves were employed in the taverns: "In some of the taverns, they sleep on the floor of the dining-room, which the master for obvious reasons, ought to forbid."[14] He reflected the prejudices of the time by adding that slaves had "an uncommon desire for spirituous liquors." Slaves had a different view. At least Josiah Henson did. To him, the planters were the ones with the uncommon desire for alcohol, which they consumed with their other vices:

> My master's habits were such as were common enough among the dissipated planters of the neighbourhood; and one of their frequent practices was to assemble on Saturday or Sunday, which were their holidays, and gamble, run horses, or fight game-cocks, discuss politics, and drink whisky and brandy-and-water all day long. Perfectly aware that they would not be able to find their own way home at night, each one ordered his body-servant to come after him and help him home. . . . I have held him [his owner] on his horse, when he could not hold himself in the saddle, and walked by his side in darkness and mud from the tavern to his house. Quarrels and brawls of the most violent description were frequent consequences of these meetings; and whenever they became especially dangerous, and glasses were thrown, dirks drawn, and pistols fired, it was the duty of the slaves to rush in, and each one drag his master from the fight, and carry him home.[15]

Hannah would have witnessed this carousing around the tavern where she worked. As early as 1750, the planters were arranging for horse races at Owens's Ordinary. Later, Joseph Wilson surveyed a thirty-acre tract near Hungerford's Tavern and named it "Raceground," a name by which it is still known, and apparently devoted it to that purpose. Just as Henson remembered, the planters had reason to head home at sundown because the sale of liquor at horse races after dark was prohibited by law.[16]

Not only was Hungerford's a meeting place for dissipated planters, radicals, and travelers, it was also a watering hole for lawyers. For a brief period, the court met at Hungerford's. When the permanent courthouse was built, it was only a block from the tavern. Lawyers walked over to the tavern for lunch and dinner, for refreshment between trials, or even perhaps to solicit clients. If Hannah were a waitress at Hungerford's, she would have known all the lawyers and considered them to be her regular customers.

During the time the Davis and Wilson families were running the tavern, Brooke Beall was living at Beallmount, five miles away. He was clerk of the county court, and the courthouse was in Rockville. As his body servant, Yarrow would have gone to Rockville with Beall. If Beall did not need him after they had arrived, Yarrow could go to Hungerford's and visit with Hannah and other slaves from Africa. He could even talk to the three men from Futa Jallon: Yarrow, Isaac, and Yarmouth. Hungerford's Tavern, in short, was a meeting place not only for dissipated planters on weekends but also for slaves from Africa, including Yarrow Mamout and others who had been on the *Elijah*.

Slave Life in Rockville

Life for slaves in Montgomery County was hard. Josiah Henson remembered the meager food: "The principal food of those [slaves] upon my master's plantation consisted of corn-meal, and salt herrings; to which was added in the summer a little buttermilk. . . . In ordinary times we had two regular meals a day."[17] The slaves at a tavern like Hungerford's, where there was ample food around, may have fared slightly better.

Slave housing was cramped. Joseph Wilson's last will and testament named thirty-three slaves, yet the tax assessment on his two big farms counted only four log cabins. This means that unless the slaves were sleeping at the tavern, each cabin housed an average of eight slaves. Josiah Henson wrote about the grim cabins on the Riley farm:

> We lodged in log huts, and on the bare ground. Wooden floors were an unknown luxury. In a single room were huddled, like cattle, ten or

> a dozen persons, men, women, and children. . . . Our beds were collections of straw and old rags, thrown down in the corners and boxed in with boards; a single blanket the only covering. . . . The wind whistled and the rain and snow blew in through the cracks, and the damp earth soaked in the moisture till the floor was miry as a pig-sty.[18]

Hannah gave birth to her daughter, Nancy Hillman, around 1769, seventeen years after the *Elijah* had arrived, when Hannah was probably in her twenties and her brother Yarrow was thirty-three.[19] Joseph Wilson did not own Hannah when her daughter was born; he bought her from his son-in-law seventeen years later. The identity of Nancy's father is not known, but he may have been one of the male slaves named in Wilson's will and given to his daughter Ann Worthington along with Hannah. Those men were Bask, Fuller, George, Clem, Joe, Fide, Jim, Ellick, Wago, Isaac, Jem, and Yarrow.[20] If Hannah was married to Isaac or this other Yarrow, then her husband was from Futa Jallon and had been on the *Elijah*. It is not unreasonable to suppose Hannah would have married a Muslim from Futa Jallon if she had a choice and the chance.

Josiah Henson should have known Yarrow Mamout and Hannah. Henson often took produce from his owner's farm in Rockville to Georgetown for sale during the time that Yarrow lived there. Since everyone in Georgetown apparently knew Yarrow, Henson surely would have. Besides, Henson's owners, the Rileys, owned several lots a few blocks from Yarrow's house.[21]

Henson would have been even closer to Hannah both literally and figuratively. This was because, for one thing, she lived in Rockville and because, for another, they both were owned by the same extended family. Hannah's owners were the Wilsons, who were related by marriage to the Rileys, also tavern owners. Isaac Riley's brother, George, was married to Wilson's daughter Sarah, whose sister owned Hannah.[22] In other words, Isaac's brother was married to the sister of Hannah's owner.

The fact that Henson was closely connected to Yarrow and Hannah takes on historical significance because the people he wrote about in his autobiography became characters in Harriet Beecher Stowe's watershed novel on slavery, *Uncle Tom's Cabin.* Stowe said the enlightened slave owner in the novel, George Shelby, was based on Henson's description of George Riley, whose sister-in-law owned Hannah. The evil overseer in the novel, Simon Legree, was based on George's overseer, Bryce Litton.[23]

While the smiling Yarrow in Peale's portrait might be taken to suggest that life for African Americans in the Washington area at this time was not all that bad, Henson wrote about a violent encounter with overseer Litton that paints a very different portrait of slavery:

> Bryce Litton beat my head with a stick, not heavy enough to knock me down, but it drew blood freely. . . . [H]e suddenly seized a heavy fence-rail and rushed at me with rage. The ponderous blow fell; I lifted my arm to ward it off, the bone cracked like a pipe-stem, and I fell headlong to the ground. Repeated blows then rained on my back till both shoulder-blades were broken, and the blood gushed copiously from my mouth. . . . My sufferings after this cruel treatment were intense. Besides my broken arm and the wounds on my head, I could feel and hear the pieces of my shoulder-blades grate against each other with every breath. No physician or surgeon was called to dress my wounds, and I never knew one to be called on Riley's estate on any occasion whatever. "A nigger will get well anyway," was a fixed principle of faith, and facts seemed to justify it.[24]

Yarrow and his sister surely witnessed the same arbitrary cruelty of slavery that was manifested in men like Bryce Litton.

Hannah Moves to Georgetown

Brooke Beall kept up his connections to Rockville even after he moved from Beallmount to Georgetown. He was still clerk of the court in Rockville. Since it is thirteen miles from Georgetown, he could not have commuted and would have been in Rockville for days at a time. As a result, he got to know and do business with the men there. Joseph

Wilson, for example, had tobacco stored at Beall's warehouse in Georgetown and probably sold through him regularly, as did other men in the county.[25] Moreover, Wilson was a justice on the Montgomery County court while Beall was the clerk. And Beall had known Wilson's predecessor at the tavern, Charles Hungerford; a 1790 entry in Beall's accounting ledger shows that Hungerford had owed him money for fourteen years.[26]

Beall's unexpected death in 1795 changed things for Yarrow in two important ways. First, he no longer went to Rockville regularly with his owner, and therefore he did not have an opportunity to see his sister as frequently. Second, he was freed.

Yet legal freedom did not make Yarrow free in all ways. He was not free to travel alone, for example. He could be stopped on the road and asked to prove his freedom. If he traveled outside of Georgetown, where he was known, he needed to carry his manumission paper to prove he was not a runaway, for vigilantes, slave traders, and even bystanders were always on the lookout for slaves fleeing their masters.[27]

Slave owners were of two minds about stopping African Americans traveling on the road. On one hand, they wanted their own runaway slaves to be captured and returned. On the other hand, many fancied that they themselves might one day manumit a favored slave. As a result, the practice arose of giving freed slaves manumission papers to prove their status. Eventually, laws were passed that required manumissions be reduced to paper if they were to be legally recognized. Freed slaves were well advised to go the extra step and make their manumissions a matter of record by filing them with the recorder of deeds. Still, many did not do this. It cost money to file at the recorder of deeds. Although counties in the state generally copied manumission papers into their most important record books, those for real estate, at least one, Washington County, perversely recorded them inverted from the back of the book used for horse sales.[28] In any event, while a black person might be allowed to live as free without filing a manumission paper, he or she did this at peril. In the event a freed slave's freedom were challenged and he or she could not produce a copy of the manumission paper, a white neighbor would have to come forward to vouch for his or her free status.

Some slaves, like Yarrow Mamout, were freed by their owners as a reward for faithful service.[29] Often this gesture of apparent magnanimity was accomplished through the owner's last will and testament. Other slaves purchased their freedom and the freedom of others, such as a future spouse or an enslaved child or sibling.

Manumission could also be a matter of crass economics when a tight-fisted owner concluded an elderly slave cost more than he produced. Laws theoretically prevented this by prohibiting slaves over a certain age from being freed unless they could support themselves.[30] Just such a bill had been introduced in the colonial assembly in Maryland the day after Yarrow arrived in 1752. But by the time Yarrow was freed, forty-four years later, the practice was for the manumission simply to contain a recitation that the slave was of the right age or that he could fend for himself.

The result of these manumissions was that throughout the tobacco-growing regions of Maryland small enclaves of free blacks began springing up, typically next to tobacco plantations and farms where slaves still worked. Free blacks and slaves often lived side by side in Maryland.

Yarrow may have taken all this into account and decided to move his sister to Georgetown. Since Suter's Tavern in Georgetown was owned by relatives of the Wilsons, she may have found work there. There is no deed of manumission of Hannah by her last known owner, Ann Worthington.[31] She may have simply been told to go free after Wilson's death and moved to Georgetown without bothering to get a manumission paper or, if she did have a paper, she did not bother to file it—and slaves freed at the death of their owners very often had no manumission records in any event. The 1800 census for Georgetown listed "Free Hannah" in one location and Yarrow in a different one. She was living with three other blacks.

After Charles Willson Peale met and painted Yarrow in 1819, Free Hannah began calling herself Hannah Peale. The 1820 census lists "Yarrow Marmoud" in Georgetown and a free black woman named "Hannah Peale" there as well. She was living in the same neighborhood where Free Hannah had lived in 1800, and there was no other free black woman named Hannah in the censuses for Washington or nearby Maryland in this period.[32]

Peale was married to his third wife by this time. Her name was Hannah More Peale, and she was with him during his visit to Washington. While Peale did not mention in his diary that he met Yarrow's sister, he must have. And Yarrow's sister probably decided to adopt the name Peale in honor of the famous artist, especially since she had the same first name as his wife. In doing this, she was displaying the same trait for occasional, eccentric behavior that her brother did.

Thus, while definite proof is lacking, the circumstantial evidence suggests that the slave named Hannah belonging to Joseph Wilson was Yarrow's sister. Indeed, there seemed to be a small community of slaves from the *Elijah* working at Hungerford's Tavern in Rockville then. Hannah got her freedom, and, perhaps with help from Yarrow, moved to Georgetown. After Charles Willson Peale visited Yarrow and painted his portrait, Hannah began calling herself Hannah Peale.

Meanwhile, there was one final connection between Josiah Henson and Yarrow. In their fight, Bryce Litton had broken Henson's arm and in fact had almost killed him. Henson's owner, Isaac Riley, was outraged—perhaps more because it meant Henson could not work than because it was such a vicious and unprovoked attack—and filed a complaint against Litton with the court in Rockville. By this time, Brooke's son, Upton Beall, was clerk of the court. He was also the one who signed Yarrow's manumissions. Upon receiving Riley's complaint, Upton would have reviewed Riley's complaint and referred the matter for trial. Naturally, Litton won the case, for as Henson bitterly wrote: "Of course no negro's testimony was admitted against a white man."[33]

This was not entirely true. Yarrow's niece, Nancy Hillman, would fare quite well when she went to court.

8 Nancy Hillman, Yarrow's Niece

Nancy Hillman was born around 1769, according to a later census. She was nineteen years older than her cousin, Aquilla Yarrow.[1] If Free Hannah was Yarrow's sister, then Nancy grew up in Rockville, and both Hannah and Nancy worked at Hungerford's Tavern.[2] Working at the tavern meant that Nancy had been around lawyers during her childhood and might have learned how useful a good one could be. The tavern was only a block from the courthouse where Yarrow's owners, the Bealls, were fixtures and would have been a gathering place for the lawyers of the town. Nancy later married a man named Hillman and lived in Frederick, Maryland.

Nancy Hillman Frees Herself

The fact that Nancy Hillman may have rubbed shoulders with lawyers from childhood and later moved to Frederick is reason for believing that the savvy black woman named Negro Nancy who filed her own manumission in Frederick in 1811 was Nancy Hillman. The number of manumissions filed in Montgomery and Frederick Counties in this time period was not large, and no other was for a woman named Nancy. In this self-manumission, Negro Nancy asserted she was free because she was born of a free woman. Her purpose in filing was to have her status as a free person on record. However, her only proof was the word of a lawyer named Richard Brooke.[3] He said, for purposes of manumission, that Nancy was twenty-eight years old, 5′3″ tall, of light complexion, and "descended from Negro Hannah a free woman and who has always been *reported* to be free born" (emphasis added).

Lawyer Brooke was a distinguished member of the Maryland bar, having previously practiced in Hagerstown, and was being very careful with his words. He was thirty-seven years old and could not have firsthand knowledge of any of the significant facts to which he was swearing.[4] He could not swear for certain that Negro Nancy was born free. If she were in fact twenty-eight, as the manumission said, then he would have been only nine when she was born. If she were older than that—for example, if she were Nancy Hillman and forty-two years old, which a woman born in 1769 would have been—then she was born before he was.[5] Brooke therefore swore only that the facts were "reported" to be true. A woman who grew up in a tavern next to a courthouse would have learned that good lawyers knew how to talk their way around the facts. Besides, the wife of Yarrow's first owner, Samuel Beall, was Eleanor Brooke. Richard Brooke may have been related to her and connected to the Yarrows through the Beall network.

The Lawyers and the Hillmans of Frederick

For someone comfortable around lawyers, Nancy would have found Frederick the perfect milieu. The small town was home to two Supreme Court justices, Thomas Johnson and Roger Brooke Taney. Its legal community sent eight of its members to be federal courts of appeal judges and another to be attorney general of the United States.[6] Francis Scott Key got his start as a lawyer in Frederick—in fact, he and Roger Taney were law partners as well as brothers-in-law. The small office they shared is still there next to the courthouse.

While Key went on to fame by penning the words to the "Star Spangled Banner," Taney went on to infamy. As chief justice of the Supreme Court, Taney wrote the 1857 decision in the Dred Scott case declaring that African Americans were not citizens and had no constitutional rights. His decision outraged many in the North and was a spark for the Civil War. He nearly destroyed the reputation of the

Court with the offensively racist language that he brought to his opinion:

> They [African Americans] had for more than a century before [the Constitution] been regarded as beings of an inferior order, and altogether unfit to associate with the white race, either in social or political relations; and so far inferior, that they had no rights which the white man was bound to respect; and that the negro might justly and lawfully be reduced to slavery for his benefit.[7]

Yet the Hillmans lived in the same town where Taney got his start, and they were not regarded as inferior. In fact, based on what is known of them, they were quite respected. Their names appear several times in a diary kept by Jacob Engelbrecht, a tailor and minor politician in Frederick. He filled twenty-two volumes with handwritten entries of news, milestones, ruminations, and, most important, marriages and deaths in the town. He wrote about both whites and blacks.

The diary mentions four Hillmans. In an entry of December 5, 1820, Engelbrecht listed "different Negroes in Fredericktown." The first was George Hillman. Engelbrecht wrote that he was "president & secretary." The diary does not explain what organization Hillman belonged to. Engelbrecht may have intended the entry simply as a list of prominent African Americans in town. The same entry mentioned a second Hillman, "Ross's Frederick Hillman."[8] Engelbrecht apparently meant that Frederick Hillman belonged to or worked for the lawyer William Ross.[9] Nancy Hillman, always on the look out for a good lawyer, later hired Ross's sons to write her will. The Ross home is less than a block from Key's and Taney's law office.

The third Hillman mentioned in Engelbrecht's diary was Ignatius. He seemed to be Nancy's husband. The 1820 census showed that Ignatius Hillman was head of a household composed of himself, a free black male over forty-five, and an unnamed free black woman between twenty-six and forty-five. The couple had two teenaged boys. Although this woman is not named, she was surely Nancy Hillman, meaning that by 1820 she was married to Ignatius Hillman and had two sons. In an 1823 diary entry, Jacob Engelbrecht wrote that Ignatius Hillman had been given a plot of land near the paper mill owned by newspaperman Matthias Bartgis. The mill was northwest of town. Engelbrecht called the Hillman property Black Heath.[10]

Ignatius Hillman must have once belonged to or worked for federal court of appeals judge Richard Potts, for in the diary entry about Hillman's death in 1827, Engelbrecht wrote that he was also known as "Pottss Eagy." Ignatius was buried in the cemetery of St. John's Catholic Church in Frederick.[11]

Nancy lived on. She was listed in the 1830 census. So was the fourth Hillman to appear in Engelbrecht's diary, Aaron. He was not living in Nancy's household, but was probably one of her two sons, now grown and living on his own. Her other son may have died or moved away.

Engelbrecht mentioned Aaron Hillman in an 1830 entry about the death of "Negro Bob Smith the fiddler." Engelbrecht wrote: "Bob had been celebrated for bringing in the election return, Presidents messages & distant pressing errands &C. Aaron Hillman author." This entry is in Engelbrecht's handwriting but was signed with an "X." Hillman apparently brought the news of the fiddler's death to Engelbrecht and waited as Engelbrecht entered it in his diary. Hillman then made his mark to show he was the author.[12]

Engelbrecht kept a separate "Death Ledger" in which he recorded Aaron's: "Hillman, Aaron, Septr 21 1832, Colored, Cholera."[13] Aaron's father, Ignatius Hillman, had been buried in the Catholic cemetery a few blocks away from St. John's Church in Frederick five years earlier. But in 1832, the church opened a new cemetery that was closer. Church records indicate that the first person buried in this new cemetery was Negro Henry. He also died of cholera and was buried on September 25, 1832. Thus, it is unclear whether Aaron Hillman was buried in the old cemetery where his father was or whether the church records are wrong and he was buried in the new cemetery where Negro Henry was. The latter seems more likely. During cholera epidemics, the priests were so busy that they tended to miss recording each and every burial.[14] Aaron may have been the first person buried in the new cemetery.

Cholera was a dreaded disease that mysteriously struck down young and old and was not understood at the time. It is in fact contracted from drinking water or eating food that is contaminated with the bacteria. It causes dysentery, with death coming from the resultant dehydration and electrolyte imbalances. Cholera is spread from person to person, and infected humans carry it from place to place and town to town. And so, when cholera came to Frederick in September 1832, Engelbrecht's diary echoed the town's fears.

> The Cholera—The dreadful Epidemic is & has been raging in our City, to an alarming extent. . . . Every countenance looks serious & gloomy. When we rise in the morning we are almost afraid to inquire the news of the cholera, lest we should hear of the attack & death of some of our nearest & dearest friends. Such is this dreadful Malady. The election takes place on Monday next, but we hardly know & seldom hear of it. We pray God he may soon arrest this awful plague.[15]

The deaths of Aaron Hillman and Negro Henry were not isolated events. Cholera stalked Frederick and indeed all of Western Maryland that fall. Engelbrecht filled his diary with the names of residents of all ages, sexes, and races who fell victim: Edward Curran, originally from Ireland, buried in the Roman Catholic graveyard; one-year-old Maria Wenrich; thirty-one-year-old Matilda Lease; Mary Ann Leather; Charles Sin; Elizabeth Lawrence; Mary Ann Walling; Exile Jameson; John Pierce; John Abbott; and Catherine Brown, to name just a few otherwise unremembered souls. There were seven deaths among the German families living at the house of John Dill. And then there was the cholera death of Joseph Worley, an innkeeper, who probably spread the disease to his customers.[16]

On September 25, a newspaper reported that there had been twenty-one cholera deaths that week, six whites, nine "colored," and six "foreigners."[17] As we will see, Aaron Hillman may not have been the only member of Yarrow's family to die in the epidemic. His cousin Aquilla Yarrow, who was living in the adjacent Washington County, died at about the same time.

The Lawsuit over Yarrow's Loan

In 1843, Nancy Hillman again got herself a good lawyer, John Smith, this time to represent her on a loan of $170.86 that Yarrow Mamout made to a man named William Hayman some twenty-two years earlier on March 23, 1821. Smith had his work cut out for him. He had to file first in one court to get himself appointed administrator of Yarrow's estate and then in a different court to proceed on the loan.

Yarrow must have sold his bank stock before making the loan in 1821. It seems unlikely that he had both $200 in bank stock and another $170 to loan Hayman. Besides, the Columbia Bank of Georgetown was in serious financial trouble at the time, and its stock would soon be worthless. Yarrow could not possibly have known enough about the bank's finances to see what was coming and pull his money out before the bank failed. He did, however, know two of the directors, John Mason and William Marbury. Mason was the one who told David Warden about Yarrow. Marbury is the one who told Peale about him. One of them may have advised him to get his money out.

According to Hillman's lawsuit, after borrowing the $170 from Yarrow, Hayman signed a deed of trust—a mortgage—pledging a warehouse on what is now Wisconsin Avenue in Georgetown as collateral for repayment of the loan. William Marbury's son John was the trustee on this deed. This is further evidence that one of the Marburys may have tipped off Yarrow to the dangers of leaving his money in bank stock and then arranged for him to invest his money in the loan to Hayman. But later Hayman needed more money and pledged the same warehouse as security on a second loan from two other men. Even later, without repaying the first two loans, Hayman proceeded to pledge the same warehouse as collateral for a third loan of $1,500.

How Yarrow knew Hayman and why he decided to loan him money in the first place are unknown. Yarrow had been burned by two imprudent loans already and surely would have been careful, so Hayman must have come well recommended. He certainly appeared reputable, and the loan a safe investment. In 1824, three years after he got the loan and a year after Yarrow's death, he was Master of the Grand Lodge of Masons in Georgetown.[18] By 1831, he owned a brewery on the north side of K Street by Rock Creek. There is nothing to suggest Hayman had the brewery when Yarrow made the loan or that the loan related to it. Loaning money to a brewmaster would seem a questionable investment for a man who did not drink spirits. On the other hand, Yarrow's sister had spent her whole life working in taverns, so maybe he did not object to others drinking. Also in 1831, Hayman became a founding director of the Potomac Insurance Company. It was created to meet the demand for insurance after a series of fires had swept the city.[19] John Marbury was on the board of directors of the insurance company with Hayman.[20]

By 1843, Hayman was in deep financial trouble, and the warehouse was put up for public sale. It brought in only $910. Since the three loans were still outstanding, there was not nearly enough money to pay off all of them. Yarrow's loan was the first and, under the law, should have had priority over the later two. Nonetheless, the third and largest creditor, Eliza Moshier, filed a lawsuit seeking to get all $910 for herself. This is when Hillman hired a lawyer and intervened to assert her superior legal right to the money.[21]

Her lawyer told the court that Yarrow's son Aquilla had died seven or eight years earlier and that she was Yarrow's niece and only surviving heir. Thus, she should be entitled to enforce whatever rights Yarrow had.[22] Her lawyer said Hillman was a free woman at the time of filing the suit and free at the time of Yarrow's death. Moreover, he said, her mother had been free. These allegations were all necessary if Hillman were to maintain the lawsuit, since slaves had no legal rights and could not sue. (Negro Nancy asserted the same allegations in her self-manumission.)

Moshier, the largest creditor, knew that in order to prevail she would have to knock Hillman out of the lawsuit, since Yarrow's loan had priority as the earliest. To do this, she first attacked Hillman's right to sue. The court characterized her challenge: "That Yarrow had no relatives in this Country except his son before mentioned; that 'if there were or are now any persons, allied to him by blood or marriage they could and cannot claim any portion of his property because they had not, and cannot have any heritable blood by reason of legal disability.'"

Conceivably, the reference to relatives "by marriage" shows Moshier knew that Aquilla had left a widow. If so, the argument applied to her as well as to Hillman. The "legal disability" was Hillman's race. That is, even though she was free, the creditor was arguing, she did not have a right to sue because she was black. The court rejected this line of attack and found Hillman could maintain the lawsuit. As long as Hillman was free, the court implied, she could sue without regard to her color.

Politics and personalities crept into the case. The judge was James Sewall Morsell, a veteran of the War of 1812 and formerly a lawyer in Georgetown. President James Madison had appointed him a judge. His house, which is still there, was on N Street in Georgetown, a few blocks from Mackall Square, the property Brooke Beall had given his two daughters and the place his widow, Margaret, was living when Peale visited her.[23] As a neighbor of the Bealls, Judge Morsell undoubtedly had known Yarrow.

The trustees on Yarrow's deed of trust were William Redin and John Marbury. Marbury's involvement may have troubled the judge for two reasons. First, he was the son of William Marbury, who had sued Madison in the famous *Marbury v. Madison* case. As a Madison appointee, Morsell may still have harbored ill feelings toward the Marbury family because of the lawsuit despite the passage of time. Second, Marbury had a conflict of interest. On one hand, he and Hayman were in business together as directors of the insurance company. On the other hand, as the one holding Yarrow's deed of trust, he was supposed to protect Yarrow's interest. Yet Hayman had not been making payments on Yarrow's loan for many years, and Marbury had done nothing.

The creditor argued that the Yarrow family's delay in bringing the action so many years after Hayman's default was in itself a reason to prevent Hillman from recovering. Either Yarrow or Aquilla should have foreclosed as soon as Hayman stopped paying, she said. Hillman offered no defense on this matter. But Judge Morsell blamed Marbury. He said that Marbury, as trustee, had the duty to foreclose, because

> [T]he party to whom the *debt was due* [Yarrow] and his descendants *were negroes* a class of people, remarkable for being *almost entirely*

> *ignorant* of their rights, and of the steps necessary & proper to be taken to secure them—they might also well have thought that full confidence might be reposed in the learned and very worthy Trustees [Marbury and Redin], to watch over and protect the interests, entrusted to their care by executing the Trusts, whenever it was proper to do so.

Morsell seemed to rub more salt in Marbury's wounds by citing an opinion of Chief Justice John Marshall, who had decided *Marbury v. Madison,* for the proposition that payment of a loan will not be presumed merely because the creditor did not try to collect.[24]

In truth, neither Yarrow Mamout nor Nancy Hillman was ignorant of the law. They had been around lawyers all their lives. Yarrow was a body servant to lawyers; Nancy grew up in a tavern next to the courthouse. Yarrow, as we will see in the next chapter, understood enough about the law to put his home beyond the reach of his creditors by deeding it to his son. Nancy had essentially freed herself by finding a lawyer to swear her mother was a free woman when Nancy was born even though the lawyer had probably not been born then. And of course, Nancy had the intelligence and vigilance to go to court to foreclose on a loan her uncle had made twenty-two years earlier.

Hillman won. Final judgment in the case was entered in 1850, seven years after it was begun. The court awarded her $451, calculated as principal plus interest on Yarrow's original loan of $170.86. It was a tidy sum for Hillman, who was eighty-one years old.

The Death of Nancy Hillman

To advise her on what to do with her newfound wealth, Hillman hired two of the most respected lawyers in Frederick, William Ross and his brother Worthington.[25] As stated before, one of the Hillmans had worked for the father of these two men. The two lawyers created a trust into which Nancy put $300 of the award and then wrote a will for her.

Nancy Hillman died a year later. Since her husband and son were Catholic, she presumably was too. If so, then she was buried in the newer cemetery at St. John's Catholic Church. The accounting records for her estate show a payment for a gravedigger.[26] There is no tombstone for her in the cemetery, though, but then most of the graves in the African American section of the cemetery are unmarked.[27] There is a tombstone for later Hillmans. Ironically, Chief Justice Taney is buried in the same cemetery, a short distance from where Nancy Hillman, Yarrow Mamout's niece, is probably buried.

The beneficiaries of the trust, which was still intact at her death, are unnamed and unknown. Hillman's will left the trust and the rest of the estate to the two lawyers.[28] Nothing explains why she did this, but these men were reputable. She may have given them oral instructions as to how to distribute the money. Perhaps the money was to go to people who had not filed manumissions or were still in slavery. Hillman was certainly smart enough in the ways of lawyers not to be bamboozled into leaving her estate to enrich them. Conceivably, Aquilla's widow was one of the beneficiaries.[29]

With Nancy Hillman's death in 1851, Yarrow and all his known blood relatives were dead. In legal parlance, Yarrow left no heirs of the body and no blood relatives in America. However, since Aquilla, his son, had married, there was at least a daughter-in-law to carry on the Yarrow name.

9 Aquilla Yarrow

Aquilla Yarrow was Yarrow Mamout's only known offspring. He was born to a slave mother around 1788. He was quite a bit younger than his cousin, Nancy Hillman, and about Josiah Henson's age. Although Yarrow called himself Yarrow Mamout, he treated Yarrow as his last name and so referred to his son as Aquilla Yarrow. Yarrow probably chose the name Aquilla because it was the name of one of Brooke Beall's sons.

Ann Chambers of Montgomery County owned Aquilla and his mother. She and her late father, William, also owned four properties in Montgomery County totaling 433 acres. The properties were called "Montross," "I want thinking about it," "Beggar's Bennison," and "Discovery Boardstones" (also called "Boylstones Discovery").[1] The planters' sense of humor obviously came into play in giving tracts names like "I want thinking about it." The humor in Beggar's Bennison is less apparent. It literally means "beggar's prayer" and has another, bawdy meaning.[2] Montross had a dwelling house. This is where Chambers probably lived. Beggar's Bennison had a log house, two small log houses, and a barn. The small log houses were slave quarters and presumably where Aquilla's mother lived.

Chambers's land was about fourteen miles northwest of Georgetown and close to the Potomac River. The four parcels were not contiguous and were scattered around the edges of Brooke Beall's 1,900-acre Beallmount estate like keys on a key ring. Beggar's Bennison, where the slave quarters were, was next to the mill at Beallmount.[3] A water treatment plant for Washington marks the edge of the property today.

Yarrow surely met Aquilla's mother while he was living at Beallmount and perhaps while working at the mill. The two must have had a solid, continuing relationship, for Yarrow stayed in touch with her and, when Aquilla was seven or eight years old, bought his freedom.

Buying Aquilla's Freedom

Yarrow's own freedom had come as the result of Brooke Beall's promise to him that if he made bricks for Beall's new house in Georgetown, Beall would free him. Aquilla's freedom may have been part of the same deal. Beall's account ledger had an entry under Ann Chambers's name on May 19, 1795, "to cash for Negro boy" in the amount of £37.[4]

Beall might well have been buying Aquilla or advancing money from Yarrow for that purpose. However, Aquilla's freedom did not come at this time, for the plan was disrupted by Beall's death later that summer. While his widow, Margaret, told Yarrow she would still keep her husband's promise, she did not get around to completing the paperwork for another year. The delay spelled trouble for Yarrow because he had already arranged with Chambers for her to free Aquilla. On February 4, 1796, Chambers signed the boy's manumission paper. Since she was illiterate, she marked her signature with an "X."

A month later, on March 16, the paper was taken to the clerk of the court in Montgomery County for filing. The manumission paper recited that Aquilla was seven or eight years old and that his freedom had been purchased for £20. This amount differed from the £37 entry for the "Negro boy" in Brooke Beall's ledger, and so that boy might not have been Aquilla. More likely, however, Chambers had simply forgotten how much she had been paid. Ten months had passed, and since she could not read, she only had her memory to guide her. Whether she received £37 or £20 was of no legal significance.

Chambers took the unusual step of going herself to the courthouse in Rockville to file the manumission. It was five miles from where she lived. Normally, the freed slave would have done this, but of course Aquilla was but a child.

Once there, Chambers had a change of mind. As the clerk copied the manumission into the deed book, she directed him to add the provision: "Above named Boy shall not be taken out of his family till he is able to get his living by any person unless by his Father Yarrow nor even him provided he don't obtain his freedom."[5] A county justice recorded the manumission that day. He duly copied by hand the manumission paper, which Chambers had signed a month earlier, into the big deed book and added the oral statement she made to him. He also wrote that the manumission was filed "at the request of Negro Aquilla." Thus, the boy must have been there too.

Yarrow and Aquilla's mother were probably there as well, for this was more than manumission. It would determine who had custody of the young Aquilla. By freeing him, Chambers was giving up a slave, and his mother was giving up custody of her son. The dictated entry in the deed book suggests that Chambers was under the impression that Yarrow was free when she had signed the manumission a month earlier. She and Aquilla's mother may have thought it was in the boy's best interest to live with a parent who was free. However, once Chambers arrived at the courthouse a month later, she apparently discovered that Yarrow was still a slave. Maybe Yarrow told her, or perhaps Chambers had the clerk check the deed book.

In any event, Chambers seemed to decide on the spur of the moment to condition Aquilla's freedom on Yarrow's getting free and dictated language to that effect to the clerk. Perhaps she felt that Yarrow had lied to her earlier. Chambers was going to stick with her agreement to free Aquilla, but she was not giving Yarrow custody until he was free. The addendum sounds as though it were done in anger or irritation. As a result, Aquilla would have left the courthouse with Chambers, not Yarrow. Yarrow would not get custody unless and until he got his own freedom.

If Chambers intended to goad Yarrow into action, she succeeded. Yarrow surely wanted to get this resolved as soon as possible and would have raised it with Margaret Beall the next time he saw her. Yet, she delayed for some reason, and Yarrow did not file his own manumission, signed by Margaret's son Upton, for six more months.

Once he did, he had satisfied Chambers's condition and should have gotten custody of Aquilla.[6]

Nonetheless, because of the conditional wording of the manumission, there might be doubt about whether Aquilla was free, and so six years later, on October 27, 1802, Ann Chambers signed a second manumission of Aquilla. It removed the condition and said he was entitled to "exercise every right of a freeman."[7]

The Education of Aquilla

Having an eight-year-old boy around would have been a challenge for Yarrow. He was sixty years old and unmarried. The 1800 census for Georgetown showed him living with one other person, presumably Aquilla. Of course, living with an older father in Georgetown was a far better environment for a young boy than a shabby slave cabin on the hardscrabble Beggar's Bennison.

Yarrow had a grander vision, though. He wanted Aquilla to be educated. Getting an education for his son would be a heady accomplishment for an African slave and showed the importance Yarrow attached to it. Yarrow could read and write in Arabic, and while his signature on the deed suggests he may have been able to write in English, too, he could not write well.

However, there were no schools for blacks, and neither Yarrow nor the illiterate Ann Chambers could have taught Aquilla. Frederick Douglass, who grew up a slave in Maryland in a later time, wrote that he had to get the white boys he knew to teach him to read, adding, "It is almost an unpardonable offence to teach slaves to read in this Christian country."[8]

But there was another way to educate Aquilla. In his book about Washington and Georgetown, David Warden told of a Scotsman, Mr. Maine, who operated a nursery on a hillside two miles above Georgetown. He employed "five or six young blacks to cultivate his nursery, whom he nourishes, educates, and rewards with the annual sum of sixty-four dollars. During hours consecrated to repose, he teaches them to read and write, and instructs them in moral duties." The black

Georgetown grocer Joseph Moor had worked there.[9] Yarrow must have arranged for Maine to take in Aquilla, for the inventory of Aquilla's estate, years later, showed that he owned books.

Yarrow Outsmarts His Creditors

In February 1800, four years after being freed, Yarrow purchased a lot in Georgetown. The early Georgetown tax assessment records do not distinguish between lots with houses and those without. Therefore, it is not known whether there was a house on the lot initially. However, Yarrow was counted as the head of a household in that part of Georgetown in the 1800 census, and so he must have been living on the lot whether or not the house was finished.

The house that is on his lot today, while old, does not appear to date from Yarrow's time. The brick cellar that it sits on might, however. The bricks are handmade. This would date them to before 1850, when brickmaking machines came into general use.[10] It is conceivable that Yarrow made these bricks specifically for his house or that they were the ones he made for Brooke Beall five years earlier. Since Beall died before his house could be built, the bricks may have still been lying around there unused. Yarrow might have carted them to his property. He did not need many, and it was not far. In any event, the bricks there today may be ones that Yarrow made with his own hands.

In 1803, Yarrow transferred ownership of the property to Aquilla. This was an odd thing to do. The boy was only fifteen. The wording of the deed is even more suspicious. In it, Yarrow and Francis Deakins, who had sold Yarrow the property in 1800, jointly conveyed the property to Aquilla in his name alone. That is, Yarrow did not transfer it into joint ownership with his son as parents commonly do. Aquilla became the sole legal owner. The new deed said the original was a mistake: the property should have been deeded to Aquilla in the first place.

> Whereas . . . said lot ought to have been conveyed to the said Negro Aquilla or Aquilla Yarrow and doubts are entertained of the legality of

> the said conveyance to cure which and to remove the same and to carry into effect the intentions of the parties it has been advised that the said Francis Deakins and the said Negro Yarrow should unite and join on a conveyance of all their interest estate and title to the said half lot to the said Negro Aquilla.[11]

Although at first glance this appears to be the usual, unintelligible, legalese that is found in deeds, it is not. It makes no sense at all. Aquilla was only twelve years old when Yarrow bought the property. He would never have intended to give a twelve-year-old boy title to his house. He had slaved, literally, all his life for it. Rather, Yarrow's intent in transferring it to Aquilla was to put it beyond the reach of his creditors. Yarrow had lost all his savings, just as he told Peale, and his creditors were dunning him. The house was his principal asset. Someone, presumably a lawyer, advised him that if he put the house in his son's name, his creditors could not get it. It worked. Yarrow was still living there when Peale came to paint him in 1819. Yarrow had access to lawyers just as his niece Nancy Hillman did, and they both knew how to use them. Judge Morsell, who had written the opinion in Hillman's case, was wrong. The Yarrow family was anything but ignorant of its legal rights.

Aquilla's Mother, Jane Chambers

The name of Aquilla's mother is not in any of the documents, but she may have been a black woman who went by the name Jane Chambers. Ann Chambers, Aquilla's former owner, died in 1807. Her will provided that all her slaves should be freed, her property sold, and the proceeds distributed to the slaves. Seven slaves were named in the inventory of her estate, including a woman named Jane.[12] Chambers was not rich. Her personal property, such as livestock, furniture, a loom, and cooking equipment, was valued at $389.48. Her most valuable assets, other than her four farms, were the slaves. They were worth $945. Of course, the slaves could not have both the $945 and their freedom; however, they each stood to get about $55 once Chambers's personal property was sold.

The estate sale was held in the spring following her death, and Aquilla and the woman Jane Chambers showed up, as evidenced by a record of purchasers at the sale. Aquilla was twenty years old. If he were living in Georgetown, he had traveled fourteen miles to get to the sale at Beggar's Bennison. He might have been working next door at Beallmount, though.

The Jane Chambers who came to the sale is the puzzle. No one in Ann Chambers's family was named Jane, so this was surely Chambers's former slave Jane, who had taken her owner's last name when freed. Another slave of Chambers was named Levi, and a Levi Chambers was recorded as buying something at the sale.

While Aquilla purchased only three old pots for ten cents, Jane bought a loom for $3.05.[13] Her purchase suggests that she had been a weaver for her late owner. The loom was an expensive thing for a newly freed slave, but Jane stood to get $55 as her share of the estate, thus giving her money to buy the loom. What is more, the loom was an investment in equipment she could use to support herself in her new life of freedom.

Jane's age is not known. She was valued at $125 in the inventory of Chambers' estate, slightly more than two other female slaves. This would make sense if she were a weaver.

Aquilla's presence at the estate sale and his purchase are puzzling too. He was a twenty-year-old man going to an estate sale for an owner he barely knew—she had freed him twelve years earlier—and coming away with nothing more than three old pots. He may have gone because Jane was going to buy the loom and needed help getting it home.

Jane's relationship to Aquilla is another puzzle. She might have been his girlfriend, but she was not the woman he eventually married. She might have been a half-sister, that is, the daughter of his mother and a man other than Yarrow. Yarrow did not treat her as his child and did not buy her freedom. Or it could have been coincidence that she and Aquilla showed up at the estate sale. But if that were the case, it seems odd that Aquilla would bother to go and then just purchase three old pots.

A possible explanation is that Jane was Aquilla's mother and Yarrow's partner or wife. Yarrow was fifty-one years old and well past the point of sowing wild oats when he had sired Aquilla. He obviously cared deeply for the boy. He could have walked away from the responsibility of fatherhood. Instead, he stayed in touch with Aquilla and his mother. She was still living with Chambers when Yarrow bought Aquilla's freedom. Ann Chambers's addendum to the manumission proved this, for she said that Aquilla should not be taken from his "family."

As long as Jane was Chambers's slave, she was not free to join Yarrow. Given how hostile Chambers was about Yarrow taking a young slave like Aquilla, she would have been even more opposed to his taking Jane, who might be bringing in money from weaving. But Chambers's death opened the way for the newly freed Jane to move in with Yarrow. He was seventy-two years old by this time, and Jane had money and a loom. What more could Yarrow want?

The idea that a man needed a good woman to keep house for him was in vogue in Georgetown. David Warden reported that John Mason's slave urged his widowed owner to remarry, arguing, "That the thing [was] a wife was very useful and comfortable, and that without her his master's house would never be clean."[14] Yarrow may have felt the same way.

Although neither Mason nor Charles Willson Peale mentioned that Yarrow had a wife, the 1820 census showed he was living with a free black woman. Since there were not many free black women in Georgetown, this is another reason to believe that Jane Chambers was Yarrow's wife.

Aquilla Moves to Pleasant Valley

Aquilla had moved out of Yarrow's house by 1820 because the census shows only a woman living with Yarrow. Aquilla was thirty-two years old. He could read and write. If he had worked at Mr. Maine's nursery, then he would have gotten to know wealthy white families in Georgetown that might hire him, and he could tap into the Bealls' network.

In addition to learning nursery and gardening skills from Mr. Maine, Aquilla surely picked up others from his father. He might have known a thing or two about water mills, about iron forges, about ships and swimming, and about how to make charcoal, bricks, and baskets.

As a free man, Aquilla was in the legal position to inherit his father's estate when Yarrow died in 1823, but the estate was not probated then. Tax records showed Yarrow's house was in the hands of his heirs, but the records do not name the heirs. They could have been one or more of the four people who have been mentioned here: Hannah Peale, Nancy Hillman, Jane Chambers, and Aquilla. Yarrow's heirs may have agreed among themselves about who got what, and they may not have bothered with a court filing. If Jane were Yarrow's widow, the others would probably have told her to take whatever she needed. Jane would not have needed much. She was still relatively young, probably in her early fifties, and could make money with her weaving. She must have kept the house, though. Someone paid property taxes on it until 1832. Since that is the year Aquilla died, he might have been paying the taxes to keep Jane in the house.[15]

Aquilla's whereabouts between the estate sale in 1808 and 1825 are unknown. He may have stayed in Georgetown or worked at Beallmount. Most likely, he did both.

In 1825, two years after Yarrow's death, Aquilla finally put down roots in Pleasant Valley in Washington County, Maryland. He bought from Alexander Grim an acre and a quarter of land at the foot of Elk Ridge, for which he paid $56. The land was part of what Grim called "Kusitrion" and included a small house. Kelly's Purchase, where Yarrow had lived when he was the slave of Samuel Beall, was about nine miles north of Aquilla's new place. A justice of the peace named Elie Crampton signed as witness to the deed.[16] Crampton would become a constant in the family's life.

Aquilla's place was too small to be called a farm; an acre and a quarter is barely enough for a vegetable garden. Aquilla needed some other means of support. He may have hoped to make do as a jack-of-all-trades, as his father had done after he was freed, but the farmers in Pleasant Valley had slaves for that kind of general work. Aquilla needed to specialize if he were to make a living. For example, he could have been a collier. Samuel Beall's old Frederick Forge, which was renamed Antietam Iron Works by this time, owned most of Elk Ridge and kept it in hardwood timber. Colliers were men from nearby properties who cut down the trees, stacked them into a teepee-like pile, covered the pile with dirt to reduce the oxygen flow, and set the stack ablaze from the inside to turn wood into charcoal, which they could sell to the iron works. Yarrow seemed to know how to do this, and he may have taught Aquilla.

Pleasant Valley also had its share of water mills that needed attention. Aquilla may have had the skills needed for this although the inventory of his estate upon his death did not list any millwright equipment. Both the iron works and the arsenal at Harpers Ferry needed men who knew how to work with iron. Aquilla could have worked at those. Both places were about five miles from Kusitrion. This was too far to commute without a horse, and according to his estate inventory, Aquilla had none. Closer and just a few miles west of Aquilla's place, over Elk Ridge, the Chesapeake and Ohio Canal was under construction. Aquilla could have gained employment there.

Yet, the potential for such work was surely not the reason Aquilla moved to Pleasant Valley. Employment prospects in Georgetown were brighter. And while the farmers in Pleasant Valley were liberal-minded on racial issues, at least by Maryland standards of the day, they could not be counted on to treat Aquilla as well as the influential men in Georgetown had treated his father. What seemed to bring Aquilla to this place was a woman. Her name was Mary Turner.

10 Mary "Polly" Turner Yarrow

Aquilla Yarrow married Mary Turner, called at various times in her life Mary Yarrow, Polly Yarrow, Polly Yaner, and Polly Jones.[1] She will be referred to as Mary Turner, Polly Yarrow, and sometimes Mary "Polly" Turner Yarrow, depending on the context. The date of her marriage to Aquilla, and indeed whether they were formally married, is not known; Maryland did not issue marriage licenses then. But since Mary Turner began calling herself Mary Yarrow, she obviously considered herself married. They may have had a son that died in childhood.

Mary was born a slave of Samuel Turner on a plantation next to Beallmount in Montgomery County. At least one of Turner's other slaves, Nicholas, may have come from Futa Jallon with Yarrow. He may have been related to Mary, although this is merely conjecture from the circumstances. Aquilla and Mary apparently met while they both lived in Montgomery County. They later married and moved to Pleasant Valley in Washington County. By that time, she was calling herself Polly and was treated as a free woman although she never filed a manumission paper. There was one other person named Turner in Pleasant Valley at this time. He was a slave of Elie Crampton, the man who had signed as witness on the deed to Aquilla's land in the valley. He was surely related to Polly and is treated in this book as her brother, although because Polly was seventeen years older than he, he may have been her nephew.[2] His first name is unknown but may have been Samuel.[3]

The Turners and Nat Turner

Descendants of the Turners of Pleasant Valley tell a story, handed down for generations, that holds that they are related to the Nat Turner who led a slave rebellion in Virginia. If true, this would mean Mary Turner was not only related by marriage to Yarrow Mamout but was also related by blood to Nat Turner. For descendants of two such prominent figures in black history to live in the same rural Maryland community would be an amazing coincidence. But there are problems with this story. First, it conflicts with all the known facts about Nat Turner. And second, rather than being related to Nat Turner of Virginia, Mary Turner and these descendants can, as might be expected, be traced to slaves belonging to a friend and neighbor of the Bealls. His name was Samuel Turner, and he lived in Maryland.

The basic facts of Nat Turner's rebellion are these. In 1831, in Southampton County in southern Virginia, a slave named Nathaniel led more than seventy slaves and free blacks in killing fifty-five men, women, and children before the militia arrived and captured the rebels. Nathaniel had once been owned by a Samuel Turner in Southampton and so was called Nat Turner. He was tried, convicted, and hanged for his deeds. Repercussions from Turner's rebellion were felt clear up in Pleasant Valley and beyond.

The possibility of such slave rebellions had long terrified the white population in the slave states.[4] After Turner's, state legislatures in those states once again tightened the black codes. The legislature in Maryland passed a law requiring county sheriffs to canvass and identify all free blacks.[5] As a result, in the summer of 1832, the sheriff of Washington County did as required and conducted a survey of free blacks in his jurisdiction. He recorded and left for posterity the names of Aquilla Yarrow and Mary Turner in Pleasant Valley.[6] This is the only document that lists them together with first and last names. The sheriff did not list Mary's relatives on the Crampton farm, though, because they were slaves.

The legislature's reasons for distinguishing between free blacks and slaves were muddled. Theoretically it wanted to lessen the chances of a slave revolt in Maryland. It planned to do this by sending free blacks to a colony in Africa, thus reducing their numbers. A private group, the American Colonization Society, was recruiting free blacks to start the colony, and the sheriffs' surveys would help identify potential émigrés. The legislature did not plan to send slaves to the colony because that would have required the state to purchase them from their owners and it did not have that much money to spend on the project. Besides, if the slaves were sent away, there would be no cheap labor to work the fields. All of this was connected to the Nat Turner rebellion, in the legislative mind, because although it would do nothing to eliminate the cause of the unrest, which was slavery, it might marginally reduce the total number of African Americans available to join an uprising.

Elie Crampton, who owned Polly Yarrow's brother, owned a farm about three miles by road from Aquilla's. Its location appears on an 1859 map of the county. A springhouse with living quarters is still there. According to the current owner of the property, the springhouse dates to the early 1800s and was the old slave quarters where the Turner family lived.[7]

Although the Turner descendants do not know why the family once believed it was related to Nat Turner, the fact that the Turners of Pleasant Valley shared last names with Nat Turner probably led to the confusion. Some descendants remember hearing that the relationship to Nat might have been through a half-brother. Yet the story flies in the face of all the known facts about Nat Turner.[8] What seems true is that both the Maryland Turners and Nat Turner were owned by planters named Samuel Turner, but these were different men. The Samuel Turner who owned Nat lived in southern Virginia, whereas the Samuel Turner who owned the Turners of Maryland had a tobacco plantation in Montgomery County right next to Beallmount and Beggar's Bennison, where Yarrow and Aquilla had lived. Perhaps on hearing that Turner's Rebellion was led by Samuel Turner's former slave, someone in the family remembered that the family had once belonged to a Samuel Turner and concluded from this that they were related to Nat Turner.

What is more, the fact the family was once owned by Samuel Turner of Maryland explains not only why there was confusion, it also explains how Aquilla Yarrow met Mary Tuner. They lived on adjacent properties in Montgomery County.

Samuel Turner, James Edmonston, and the Slave Nick

Being a planter in the Bealls's network was like being a member of a small, select men's club. Those in the network knew and did business with one another. Because planters held the economic and political power in Maryland, they were in position to help each other and their slaves, like Yarrow and his kin, and this they surely did.

Samuel Turner entered the Beall network by an unusual yet romantic route: he married the widow of a close friend of the Bealls, James Edmonston.[9] In so doing, Turner acquired Edmonston's slaves, from whom Mary Turner was descended.

The Edmonston and Beall families had been close for generations. Edmonston's mother was the daughter of the legendary Ninian Beall; his wife was Ninian's granddaughter.[10] In other words, Edmonston, like other early planters, married his first cousin.[11]

In addition to intermarrying, the Edmonstons and Bealls were in business together. They once owned much of what are now Washington, D.C., and Olney and Sandy Spring, Maryland.[12] Edmonston and Samuel Beall's uncle jointly held the large Labyrinth tract, which became Silver Spring, Maryland, while Samuel Beall owned adjacent tracts. The Edmonston family founded the town of Edmonston on the Anacostia River a mile upstream from Bealltown near Bladensburg. Edmonston himself owned a lot in Bladensburg across the street from Samuel Beall's business partner, Dr. David Ross.[13] Beall owned a lot there too, but he sold it to Edmonston, who in turn sold it to Ross.[14] In short, the two families followed the planter pattern of being connected by marriage and business, but these families were especially close.[15]

Therefore, when Samuel Beall went to Annapolis to buy a slave off the *Elijah* on June 4, 1752, Edmonston may have gone along. Whether he actually did is speculation, but records show he acquired a new, young slave named Nicholas, or Nick for short, about the time the *Elijah* arrived. Nick was just a teenager like Yarrow and later in life lived on an adjacent farm.[16]

James Edmonston died in the latter half of 1753, and Samuel Turner came into the picture by marrying Edmonston's widow. He thus acquired Edmonston's land and slaves. Some slaves, such as Nick, stayed with Turner for the rest of his life. The 1809 inventory of Turner's estate lists Nick and several others who had been in the inventory of Edmonston's estate more then five decades earlier.

Marriage into the rich and powerful Beall and Edmonston families was a step up the social and economic ladders for Samuel Turner. He had inherited land in Prince George's County from his father, but after marrying Edmonston's widow, he sold it and moved in with her. The two of them lived in Edmonston's house until 1764.[17] Theirs was a May–December marriage; she was forty-three, while Turner was at least seventeen years younger. She had had eight children by Edmonston. However, Turner supposedly fathered eight more children after the marriage, and these children surely came from a second marriage to a different and younger woman.[18]

Turner stepped up the economic ladder again in 1764 by moving to a five-hundred-acre plantation in Montgomery County called The James and The Addition to the James. On a modern map, the properties were at Potomac Ridge at the intersection of Travilah Road and Dufief Mill Road in Montgomery County.[19]

Tax assessment records show that Samuel Turner's various properties had two framed houses, another house, one barn, two tobacco houses, one log house, and four log cabins (slave cabins).[20] Turner moved the slaves his wife had inherited from her first husband in Prince George's County to their new properties in Montgomery County.

This move brought Samuel Turner's slaves to where Yarrow and Aquilla lived. Maps of the old tracts, produced by historical society volunteers in recent times, show that Turner's land was near the large Beallmount estate of Brooke Beall and touched the Montross property owned by Ann Chambers. It was also near the large farms around today's Darnestown that were owned by the prominent Clagett family, which would play an important role in the slaves' lives in the future. Beall's and Turner's names are on the same page of the 1790 census, showing they lived near each other. In the 1800 census, which was taken after Brooke Beall died, the names Turner and Chambers are on the same page. This meant that whenever Yarrow and Aquilla were at Beallmount, they might run into Ann Chambers and her slaves, Samuel Turner and his slaves, and the various Clagetts.

The Slave Girl Mary

Samuel Turner reached the pinnacle of his career when he succeeded Joseph Wilson, who owned Yarrow's sister Hannah, as Register of Wills for Montgomery County in 1779. He served the county in that capacity for thirty years and tended to his farms as well until he died in 1809. This meant that he would have worked for the same court, and out of the same courthouse in Rockville, where Brooke and Upton Beall were the chief clerks.

When Turner died, the inventory of his estate counted twenty-one slaves. Among these was Nick, the slave whom James Edmonston had acquired around the time Yarrow arrived fifty-seven years earlier. Another of the slaves was a woman named Dilly. She, too, had belonged to Edmonston. Both Nick and Dilly were described as "very old" and valued at zero. If Nick were on the *Elijah* with Yarrow, then the two men ended up as slaves on neighboring farms in Montgomery County decades after they had arrived.[21]

The inventory also showed that at the time of his death Turner owned a ten-year-old slave named Mary.[22] She may have been related to Nick and Dilly. Turner owned only twenty-one slaves, so some were sure to be related. Given Nick and Dilly's ages, Mary might have been their granddaughter, but this is only speculation. There are no documents to clarify the matter.[23]

However, it seems reasonably clear that this slave Mary was Aquilla Yarrow's future wife. First is her name. As a slave of Samuel Turner, she would have been known as Mary Turner just as the slave of Samuel Turner of Southampton, Virginia, was called Nat Turner. Aquilla's wife's maiden name was Mary Turner according to the sheriff's survey. Second is her age. Based on the age she gave to census takers later, Aquilla's Mary was born around 1799. The slave Mary in Samuel Turner's estate was also born in 1799. Third is that this Mary lived in the right place. That is, she was Mary Turner living on The James near Beggar's Bennison, where Aquilla lived as a boy, and Beallmount, where Yarrow and, probably Aquilla, worked as adults. Given that

Aquilla later married a woman named Mary Turner, chances are she was Samuel Turner's ten-year-old slave Mary.

There is no proof that Mary was a descendant of Samuel Turner's slave Nick, but it is at least a possibility. Yarrow retained his Muslim religion throughout his life and kept his African heritage. He seemed to be the kind of man who would have wanted his son to marry a woman who was descended from Muslims from the highlands of West African. Someone like Nick's granddaughter might fit the bill.

Getting the Help of the Clagetts

The fact that Aquilla and Mary Turner were neighbors easily explains how they met and married. It does not explain why or how they moved away to Pleasant Valley. This is where the Clagett family may have come in.

In his last will and testament, Samuel Turner directed that all his property should be sold and the proceeds divided among his children. Even the slaves were to be sold. If this were done at auction, families could be broken up, so it was common to arrange private sales to buyers willing to keep slave families together or at least to treat them well, which would include allowing separated families members to see each other. This must have been the case with Samuel Turner's slaves because there is no record of a slave sale. The only property listed as sold from the estate was a lot of grain.[24] Therefore, a plausible explanation for how Mary moved from being a slave on Turner's plantation in Montgomery County to a free woman and Aquilla's wife in Pleasant Valley and how her brother also ended up there as a slave is that a white family made these arrangements to keep the slave family together.

The extended Clagett family most likely facilitated the move, because there were Clagetts in both places.[25] In Montgomery County was Joseph Clagett. He was a wealthy planter whose farm was near the properties of Samuel Turner and the Bealls. He prepared the inventory of Turner's estate on which Mary's name appears. [26]

There were more Clagetts in Washington County. Among them were Zachariah, Samuel, and Horatio. Zachariah was Joseph's brother.[27] Samuel was a cousin. He owned the farm next to Aquilla's in Pleasant Valley. When Aquilla later died, Samuel Clagett probated his estate. Horatio was a medical doctor. He lived north of Aquilla, closer to Elie Crampton's place. Horatio and Crampton knew each other and were both members of the racially progressive American Colonization Society.

Naturally, the Clagetts had connections to the Bealls as well. In fact, the four just mentioned were descendants of Ninian Beall. "Clagett's Purchase" was a tract of 750 acres in Montgomery County that today is the Bethesda Naval Hospital and the National Institutes of Health.[28] It abutted Labyrinth, which was owned by James Beall and James Edmonston, and was near the Charles and William where Samuel Beall lived. Indeed, after Samuel Beall moved to Washington County, one of his daughters, Brooke Beall's sister, met and married Alexander Clagett, who lived there.

Thus, although here are no records, the most likely explanation for how Mary Turner and her brother kept together after Samuel Turner's death and lived near each other in Pleasant Valley was that they had help from the Clagetts.[29]

However it happened, by 1830, Aquilla and Mary were living on the Kusitrion property on the slope of Elk Ridge. Her brother and his family were slaves three miles away on Elie Crampton's farm. But things would soon change.

11 Aquilla and Polly in Pleasant Valley

Aquilla and Polly would have found Pleasant Valley to be all that the name implies. Ten miles long and two miles wide, the fertile valley is largely devoted to agriculture even today. It runs north and south between South Mountain to the east and Elk Ridge to the west. Israel Creek—named for the pioneer Israel Friend, who had purchased the land with the "Indian Deed" mentioned earlier—drains the runoff from the valley into the Potomac River in the south. From Pleasant Valley to the Beallmount estate in Montgomery County is about twenty-seven miles as the crow flies. Georgetown is forty-five miles away.

On the southwest corner of the valley, Elk Ridge rises to a peak called Maryland Heights that overlooks the town of Harpers Ferry across the Potomac River. In the nineteenth century, the entire ridge was covered with hardwood trees, oak, hickory, and chestnut, and it remains forest today.

In 1859, abolitionist John Brown rented a farm on the other side of Elk Ridge from which he staged his raid on the federal armory at Harpers Ferry and called for slaves and free blacks to join him in an uprising. This renewed the old fears of slave rebellions and ultimately led to the Civil War.

Northwest of Pleasant Valley, where Antietam Creek empties into the Potomac, was Samuel Beall's Frederick Forge. The Civil War Battle of Antietam was fought on the north side of the creek. Beall's former home Kelly's Purchase, where Yarrow had lived, was on the edge of the battlefield and served as a field hospital during the clash.

Aquilla died in 1832, only seven years after buying his place and well before those events, but Polly stayed in the house for more than fifty years after that. She became midwife to the community, called Yarrowsburg because of her.

The Question of Race in Pleasant Valley

Today's residents of Pleasant Valley point proudly to a tradition of racial tolerance, a tolerance born of necessity.[1] Early white settlers were a mix of English and Scottish planters, most of them Episcopalian, and German farmers.[2] They did not grow tobacco, because the falls on the Potomac River above Georgetown prevented them from getting a tobacco crop to port, but the planters owned slaves all the same, whereas the Germans were Church of the Brethren, a sect that was related to the Methodist and that was opposed slavery. Given their differences, the two groups needed tolerance if they were to live together peacefully, and they seemed to translate that tolerance to African Americans as well.

George Ross, a slave in nearby Hagerstown, gave grudging support to this assessment. Looking back on his life in Western Maryland, he said:

> I was never down South. I was a little ways in Virginia, but not far. Slavery is harder down there than in Maryland. They have larger plantations & more servants, and they seem to be more severe. Down in Prince George's County, Md., they are a little harder than they are in the upper part of the State. If I had my choice, I would rather live in Maryland than in Virginia.[3]

Another former slave, George Jones, who lived in adjacent Frederick County, Maryland, had different memories. His own experience led him to conclude, "the white people of Frederick County as a whole were kind towards the colored people." However, he continued, "My father used to tell me how he would hide in the hay stacks at night, because he was whipped and treated badly by his master who was rough and hard-boiled on his slaves."[4]

Race relations in Pleasant Valley were not perfect, but they were better than in other parts of Maryland, and much better than in the Deep South.

Aquilla in Pleasant Valley

Alexander Grim had sold Aquilla Yarrow a house and an acre and a quarter of land called Kusitrion in 1825 with Elie Crampton signing the deed as witness. That is where Yarrowsburg is today, just south of the junction of present-day Reed, Kaetzel, and Yarrowsburg Roads. In Aquilla and Polly's day, the road continued past their house and up Elk Ridge to Solomon's Gap. From there, it ran down the other side of mountain to meet Chestnut Grove Road a mile and a half away. The road through Solomon's Gap was later abandoned and has now returned to forest.

Today there would be nothing unusual about a black man from Montgomery County moving to Pleasant Valley and buying land, but that was not the case when Aquilla moved there. People in the valley were tolerant, but they were not that tolerant. A black man with no connections trying to put down roots would not have been welcome. Therefore, Aquilla would have needed help. Some of it may have come from the fact that Pleasant Valley was in the Beall network. Samuel Beall's forge at the top of the valley was still in operation although under different owners and under the name Antietam Iron Works. Beall's daughter had married Alexander Clagett, who had once lived nearby. Zachariah, Horatio, and Samuel Clagett lived there at the same time as Aquilla and Polly, and they were progressive on racial matters. Horatio was listed next to Aquilla in the 1830 census. He would have been a good friend to have, since an old history of Western Maryland deems him "among the most eminent men in the State."[5]

Still, these connections would not have been enough. There had to be more to the story that is now lost to time, probably friendships between Aquilla and Alexander Grim, Elie Crampton, and the Clagetts. Aquilla had forsaken everything his father had accomplished in Georgetown to settle in this pleasant valley, yet it was still a backwater.

The sizable loan his father had made to Mr. Hayman in Georgetown was in default, and yet Aquilla did not bother to foreclose. The only evidence to suggest Aquilla might have kept connections to Georgetown was with respect to Yarrow's old house there. The heirs of Yarrow had kept up the tax payments, and Aquilla may have been one of them.[6]

The house Aquilla had in Pleasant Valley is gone now, but it probably was not much more than a slave cabin. There are abandoned cabins in the woods below Elk Ridge today. Residents say those are slave quarters, but they may instead be the ruins of the homes of poor white farmers. One such building is a story and a half high with a loft. The ceiling of the lower level is only five feet high.[7]

That Grim sold to a black man is surprising. He was descended of English planters and owned slaves himself.[8] He was a founder of St. Luke's Episcopal Church. His grave is in the cemetery behind the church and overlooks his old house, which is still there. He was in financial trouble when he sold to Aquilla and may not have acted for the noblest of reasons. Just a few months before the sale, a public auction of parts of Grim's holdings was announced in the newspaper.[9]

Still, some men in the valley would not have sold to Aquilla under any circumstances. Slavery was a divisive issue even among the congregation of St. Luke's. When the bishop came to consecrate the church in 1843, he was made aware of a dispute among the congregation over slavery and admonished them to resolve things before his next visit.[10] They failed to do so, but the Civil War settled the matter.[11]

Aquilla may have inherited some money from his father. Perhaps that is where he got $56 to buy the small Kusitrion plot. Yet it is difficult to reconstruct Aquilla's life because there are no records of his life except one, the inventory of his estate when he died. Neighbor Samuel Clagett prepared that inventory. His cousin Joseph Clagett had inventoried Samuel Turner's estate in Montgomery County and listed the slave girl Mary. Now another Clagett had come to see Mary and tally the property of her late husband.

Aquilla must have been able to read, because Clagett's inventory listed a "lot of books." There would be nothing unusual about seeing those in the inventory of a white man's estate, but they stand out in the estate of a black man in a state where no one would teach African Americans to read. The inventory gives few other clues as to what Aquilla's life was like. In addition to the books, he owned two cows, five shoats, thirty-three pounds of bacon, a shotgun (perhaps the same gun that Yarrow used to fire off under the windows of the respectable families of Georgetown on Christmas morning as a signal for his dram), a few farm implements, some corn, and household items. None of these things shows how he made a living. He had no plow, no horse, and no mule with which to cultivate fields. His small parcel of land might grow enough for Polly and him to eat but not enough to yield produce to sell to others. In fact, the contents of his garden were valued at only twenty-five cents.

As stated in an earlier chapter, Aquilla would have had a hard time making a living in Pleasant Valley. Conceivably, he worked on water mills there. The Bartholomew family once had a mill on Israel Creek near Aquilla's house, and a mill may have been there in his day as well. Yarrow could have learned about mills from Samuel Beall and passed that knowledge to his son, but the fact that Aquilla did not own mill tools negates the possibility that he was in business for himself as a millwright.

He may have been a collier. Yarrow knew how to make charcoal, and again this is something he might have taught his son. The inventory listed an ax and chains, which Aquilla could have used to chop down trees and drag them into a pile. His house was at the foot of Elk Ridge, where Antietam Iron Works owned ten thousand acres for the precise purpose of keeping it in charcoal. The colliers in the valley hiked up the ridge and turned these trees into charcoal. The job took a week or longer, and the burning required constant vigilance. When they were done, the colliers piled the charcoal into wagons for transport to the iron works. Present-day residents of Yarrowsburg say that circular remnants of these charcoal sites can still be found on the ridge. They also say that charcoal making was an occupation open to free blacks. Since this is where Aquilla lived, these oral histories could refer to him.[12]

Aquilla might have worked at Antietam Iron Works. It was five and a half miles from his house, an easy ride on a horse, but then he did not own a horse, at least not when he died. He could have lived at the iron works and walked the five and a half miles home on his days off. However, an African American minister in the valley at this time, Rev. Thomas W. Henry, wrote an autobiography and talked about life at the iron works. He knew the owner. Henry noted that while free blacks worked there, the owner wanted them to marry free black women and bring their wives to live at the iron works. He described the iron works as being run like what would later be called a company town. The workers and their families lived on the premises, and the iron works ran a store that sold them whatever they needed.[13] Yet since Aquilla and Polly did not live at the iron works, he probably was not employed there.

The arsenal at Harpers Ferry was another local industry that employed free blacks, but Aquilla apparently did not work there either. It was slightly farther away than the iron works. Aquilla could not have commuted there on a daily basis. Moreover, his name does not show up in the existing records of the arsenal.[14]

Most likely, Aquilla applied his hand to several occupations. He probably worked as a collier for part of the time. He was the only free black living in the Yarrowsburg area when the iron works were operating, so to the extent the oral history of free blacks working as collier is correct, it must refer to Aquilla. Aquilla was also slaughtering pigs and probably selling the meat to his neighbors since the inventory showed that he had five hogs, thirty-three pounds of bacon, and a sausage-making machine. Hog butchering is still a tradition in the valley.[15] And a few miles over Elk Ridge, the Chesapeake and Ohio Canal was under construction. Irish immigrants and free blacks were hired to work there.[16]

What Brought Aquilla and Polly to Pleasant Valley

The best explanation for why Aquilla bought a farm too small to support himself and in a location where he could not engage in skilled labor is that Mary Turner wanted to move there, but there is nothing in the documentary record that says this.

Mary was a ten-year-old slave on Samuel Turner's estate in 1809. The next record of her is the 1830 census for Pleasant Valley, which counted Aquilla as living with an unnamed, free black woman, who was surely Mary. She was named in the 1832 survey of free blacks the sheriff took after Nat Turner's rebellion. Still, nothing shows her moving to Pleasant Valley.

She lived as a free woman but did not record her manumission in Montgomery, Frederick, or Washington counties. Of course, this was not unusual. A contemporary observer complained that a number of blacks were living as free persons in Washington County without having been legally manumitted.[17] Likewise, Aquilla's whereabouts between 1808, when he bought three old pots from the estate of Ann Chambers at Beggar's Bennison in Montgomery County, and 1825, when he bought the place in Pleasant Valley, are unknown.

Aquilla and Mary must have first met when she was a girl on Samuel Turner's farm in Montgomery County and he was at Beallmount. Aquilla had a lot to offer. He was a free man, he could read, and his family had money. If Mary's grandfather had in fact come from Futa Jallon, Yarrow or his sister might have arranged or at least encouraged the marriage. In any event, since Aquilla seemed to have no reason to move to Pleasant Valley and Mary did, she might have been the one to instigate the move. Her brother was there as a slave to Crampton, and so she might have asked Aquilla to move to be near him. It would be a natural thing to do.

It was a bold move for both of them. Aquilla was giving up the advantages of Georgetown and his contacts there to settle on an acre and a quarter of farmland in a rural community. Mary went from single to married and from slave to free woman.

The Death of Aquilla Yarrow

Whatever love and happiness Aquilla and Mary found in marriage and Pleasant Valley came to an abrupt end in late summer or early fall 1832 when Aquilla died. It happened shortly after the sheriff had finished counting the couple in his survey of free blacks in the county. Maryland laws generally take effect on July 1 of the year, so the sheriff would have begun his work soon after that. Then, on October 2, 1832, the Register of Wills recorded an order from the orphan's court for an appraisal of Aquilla's estate.[18] The inventory reported its value as $137.70. This did not count the house in Georgetown, which was in the name of heirs of Yarrow. In the margin of the inventory of Aquilla's personal property was the notation "(Polly)." This seemingly was intended to indicate that the next fourteen items in the inventory, including a lot of yarn, eight unfinished quilts, six finished quilts, and seven sheets, belonged to Polly, not Aquilla. Perhaps, the cloth came from Jane Chambers's loom. However, Polly's claim to these items was ignored; they were later sold at the estate sale. Polly even had to buy her own flour sifter from the estate.

The cause of Aquilla's death is unknown. He was forty-four years old. If he were a collier, he might have died in an accident while felling trees. But more likely, he died of cholera. It had killed his second cousin, Aaron Hillman, in Frederick the same month and had spread into Washington County, where Aquilla lived. National and local newspapers were full of stories about the epidemic. The Harpers Ferry and Hagerstown papers reported cholera deaths in and around those two towns and gave advice on how to prevent catching the disease. The newspapers carried poems about "the pestilence," such as this one from the *Virginia Free Press*:

> Are these the widow's weeds I see
> Which deck yon matron's comely form
> Her husband's in eternity
> His body feeds the hungry worm
>
> Oh God! Is this the work of death?
> How long will Plague's destroying breath
> Stalk like a demon through our land,
> Unstay'd by Thy Almighty hand?

The paper's advice on avoiding the disease was of no help, and people continued to die.[19]

The Hagerstown paper mentioned cholera deaths in late September along the Chesapeake and Ohio Canal.[20] It was under construction a few miles from Aquilla's house. The victims were not named. There were Irish and perhaps African American workers on the canal, and a newspaper then would generally not bother to name dead Irishmen or blacks.

The 1832 cholera epidemic brought construction of the Canal to a halt in the vicinity of Harpers Ferry as workmen fled to what they thought were safer places. The canal company put up a hospital in the town for the workmen. At least thirty workers died in a period of a few weeks. Six were found dead in a single shanty. When the bodies of four Irish workers were taken to the Catholic cemetery in Hagerstown for burial, the residents there objected, fearing this would bring the pestilence into town.[21] It came anyway.

Perhaps Aquilla had taken work on the canal, contracted cholera, and died. Or perhaps he had been in Frederick to visit his cousin and contracted cholera that way.

Although Aquilla and Polly had no surviving children, an oral history suggests that they may have had a child that died. A present day resident of Yarrowsburg says when he was growing up, he was shown stone markers in a field by the side of Yarrowsburg Road and told these were the graves of Polly, her husband, and a boy.[22]

Aquilla's death ended Yarrow's line. Nancy Hillman, Yarrow's niece, was still alive though and living seventeen miles away in Frederick. Her son had died at the same time as Aquilla, so both she and Polly Yarrow were in grief together. When Hillman died in 1851 without heirs, Polly Yarrow, though an in-law, was the only surviving member of Yarrow's family. Conceivably, she was the beneficiary of the trust that Hillman had set up with the money from the lawsuit over Yarrow's loan. Perhaps she told her lawyers, the Rosses, that at her death, they should use the money to take care of Polly. In any event, Polly carried Yarrow's name and thus passed it on to the community of Yarrowsburg. The community's name is a rarity as names go, one that adds German to Fulani.

12 Traces of Yarrow

The end of Yarrow's bloodline in America did not end his connections to later events in Maryland, Georgetown, and black history. These are worth noting before turning to the rest of his in-laws, the Turners. Yarrow was long remembered in Georgetown, but other connections to his life emerged after his death.

Aquilla and Peale's Granddaughter

The first and perhaps strangest example of these connections was that Charles Willson Peale's granddaughter ended up in Pleasant Valley. Her name was Priscilla Robinson, and she was the daughter of Angelica Peale Robinson. Priscilla married Dr. Henry Boteler of Pleasant Valley in 1814. He had grown up on the Magnolia Plantation a few miles south of Yarrowsburg. After their marriage, the couple settled across the Potomac River in Shepherdstown, Virginia (West Virginia now), founded by Samuel Beall's business partner Joseph Chapline. Priscilla had four children before dying in 1820 after only five years of marriage. Whether Aquilla had moved to Pleasant Valley before Priscilla died is unknown. Peale painted Yarrow in January 1819, but the brief entries about him in Peale's diary make no mention of his having a son, much less of the son living in the same farming community as Peale's granddaughter.

Francis Dodge, the Pearl, the Edmonsons, and the Turners

Then there is the later owner of Yarrow's house who stopped a major slave escape that involved descendants of the slaves of James Edmonston.

Someone had continued to pay the property taxes on Yarrow's house in Georgetown for years after his death. Tax records show the property belonged to Yarrow's heirs. Since the payments stopped around the time of Aquilla's death, he might have been making them. Five years later, in 1837, the city auctioned the property to pay the tax bill. A speculator bought it, then turned around and sold it to Francis Dodge a short time later.[1] Dodge was a wealthy merchant in Georgetown. His reason for buying Yarrow's lot is not known. Dodge had a large house and family in a different part of the town, so he probably purchased Yarrow's modest property for investment purposes, leasing it out to others.

On Saturday night, April 15, 1848, some seventy slaves in Washington slipped quietly through the streets to board a small schooner called the *Pearl.* Their hope was to sail to freedom in the north. Most were urban slaves, tired of slavery and concerned that they might be sold to slave traders who would ship them off to plantations in the Deep South. Among the escapees were six adult children of Paul Edmonson. Although Edmonson was a free man, some of his children were still slaves. The Edmonsons were surely descendants of slaves of James Edmonston, whose widow had married Samuel Turner almost one hundred years earlier. Now, in 1848, not only was one of the slave descendants, Paul Edmonson, free, but he even owned a forty-acre farm. It was near Olney where the white Edmonston family had once owned so much of the land. Paul's ancestors undoubtedly acquired the name Edmonson from being slaves of the Edmonstons.[2] Mary Turner and the Edmonsons on the *Pearl* were descended from slaves of the same man.[3]

The *Pearl's* departure went undetected for several hours, giving the vessel a head start on pursuers. However, it was a sailing ship. The night was relatively calm, and the ship's progress down the Potomac was slow. Eventually, the slaves' owners in Washington realized what had happened, and a posse assembled on the banks of the Potomac.

Daniel Drayton was the abolitionist behind the escape attempt. His memoirs described what happened next:

> A Mr. Dodge, of Georgetown, a wealthy old gentleman, originally from New England, missed three or four slaves from his family, and a small

> steamboat [the *Salem*], of which he was the proprietor, was readily obtained. Thirty-five men, including a son or two of old Dodge, and several of those whose slaves were missing, volunteered to man her; and they set out about Sunday noon, armed to the teeth with guns, pistols, bowie-knives, &c., and well provided with brandy and other liquors.[4]

The *Salem* chugged down the Potomac after the *Pearl* and found her around 2 a.m. the next morning, lying at anchor at the mouth of the Potomac and the Chesapeake Bay. The posse brought all the slaves back to Washington. Some were returned to their owners; others were sold to slave traders, who in turn packed them off to plantations in the South.

Mary and Emily Edmonson, the two escapees who attracted the most attention, were held for a while in a slave pen in Alexandria, Virginia, before being sent to New Orleans for sale. All the while, abolitionists were trying to find a way to save them. The girls' father, Paul Edmonson, traveled to New York City and asked Rev. Henry Ward Stowe's help in raising money to buy his daughters' freedom. Stowe had not been active in the abolitionist movement up until this time, but he agreed, and, together with others, raised the money.

After the girls' release, Stowe's wife, Harriet Beecher, befriended Mary and Emily and helped them go to college. Four years later, in 1852, Harriet Beecher Stowe published *Uncle Tom's Cabin*, based in part on the life of Josiah Henson of Rockville.

Yarrow Remembered

Yarrow Mamout was remembered after his death in two famous lectures by Rev. Thomas Bloomer Balch on the history of Georgetown given at the Methodist Church there in 1859. Balch was a descendant of the legendary Ninian Beall. As such, he was related not only to the Bealls but also to the Edmonstons and Clagetts. He had grown up in Georgetown and knew Yarrow. Balch's father was pastor of the Presbyterian church a few blocks from where Yarrow lived. The church cemetery backed onto the corner of Yarrow's lot, where he was buried.

Balch began the first of his talks with a discussion of Ninian Beall. Balch did not have the benefit of a raft of Beall genealogists and so was not sure where Ninian came from. But Balch ventured the guess: "We are induced to think that Dumbarton was the part of Scotland from which he came to Maryland."[5] Eventually, he turned to his personal recollections of the town.

> Reminiscences of various kinds are now crowding upon me which evince the strength of the social affections. They consist of parties of innocent amusement; of water excursions; of boat races which came off on the Potomac . . . of distinguished men who resided here for a time, or paid us a transient visit such as Count Volney, Baron Humboldt, Fulton, Talleyrand, Jerome Bonaparte, Pechion, General St. Clair, Washington Irving. . . . Or we might indulge in recollections of such grotesque characters as old Yarrah, who was a Mohammedan from Guinea, and of who an admirable likeness was taken by Simpson, or of Lorenzo Dow, the great itinerant, whose weary limbs found their final repose in one of our graveyards.[6]

Since Balch had seen Yarrow in the flesh, the fact that he termed the Simpson painting an "admirable likeness" is confirmation that the painting captures what Yarrow looked like. Indeed, there was a photographic style to Simpson's approach that is evidenced by his other portraits.

As for the Lorenzo Dow that Balch seemed to compare to Yarrow, he was a traveling, evangelistic preacher. He was more than a bit eccentric, paying little attention to his personal appearance or hygiene. He preached whenever and wherever he was in the mood. Balch's comment that Dow and Yarrow were "grotesque" was probably a reflection on how the two men's flamboyant, public professions of faith on the street contrasted with Balch's own reserved Presbyterianism. To the conservative Balch, Lorenzo Dow's death in Georgetown seemed more Georgetown's misfortune than Dow's.

Yarrow, too, was given to preaching whenever he was in the mood. Peale had written about these street utterances in his diary: "Yarrow has been noted for sobriety & and a cheerfull conduct, he professes to be a mahometan, and is often seen & heard in the Streets singing Praises to God—and conversing with him he said man is no good unless his religion comes from the heart." Balch seemed to agree with Yarrow's religious sentiments, but not the fervent manner of expression. Still, Balch saw a positive side to everything, even death, and so he suggested that living in Georgetown might have contributed to Yarrow's remarkable (but exaggerated) longevity:

> The arrows of death are always and everywhere on their flight. The hearse never stands still. It has discovered the grand secret of perpetual motion, and death on his pale steed never follows it as a mourner, for he has gone elsewhere to wield his darts and brandish his lance. But our town is about as favorable to longevity as any place of my acquaintance. We may safely put down Mrs. Isabella Thompson at eighty-six when she died; my father at the same age . . . and Old Yarrah at one hundred and twenty.[7]

Perhaps the most significance aspect of Balch's lectures was that they were delivered thirty-six years after Yarrow's death. Not only did Balch remember the man, but his audience did too.

The Moon Men

Shadrack Nugent, the man who grew up in Rockville and claimed he was 119 years old and had a father who came from Guinea, seemed connected to Yarrow in other ways as well. Nugent was living on M Street in Washington between Twenty-second and Twenty-third Streets when he was interviewed by a reporter and made his exaggerated claims in 1879. Sticking closer to the truth, Nugent said that after he was freed, he moved to Brookeville, Maryland, north of Washington, and worked in a stone quarry there. He had a brother named Eli. Nugent told the reporter that when the British attacked Washington in 1814, "Eli, who was living with Mr. Dodge, in Georgetown, came to Brookeville with his family, because 'ebberybody in Washington was scare.'" This was the same Francis Dodge who purchased Yarrow's house and who dispatched the *Salem* to chase after the *Pearl*.

The reporter described Nugent as "in pretty good health; walks without a cane; has good teeth; thin, white hair; and talks with considerable animation." The reporter continued: "In addition to the above Shadrack tells some vivid and interesting stories of Braddock's war with the Indians. He is known here by the Bealls, Norris, and other families." The Bealls, of course, were relatives of those who had owned Yarrow.

Nugent said one his sons had been killed in the Civil War; the other was, in 1879, working at the Ebbitt House (the name of which survives as Old Ebbitts Grill in Washington). By the end of the article, the reporter could no longer repress his disbelief with some of the tall tales Nugent had spun and concluded with an observation that might apply to Yarrow as well: "We would remark that we have in this county negroes who are at least four hundred years old—*taking their word for it*."[8]

These same facts and tales are included in Thomas Scharf's *History of Western Maryland*.[9] However, Scharf adds more. He found that Nugent once made a living by the sale of "observations and predictions concerning the moon" and called himself "The Moon Man." He was essentially a human almanac. He based his forecasts on the moon, explaining:

> The first moon in every new year's almanac is March's moon, and the second moon is April's, the third moon is May's, and the fourth moon is June's—the first summer moon which fills for summer.
>
> In every year, you get an almanac; the almanac tells about the weather, and I tell about the moon.
>
> I have been going by the moons for more than a hundred years, and have made it a special study.
>
> And I am one hundred and nineteen years old in this year of 1880.[10]

Nugent's study of the moon was undoubtedly handed down from his father and from his father's father, who probably came from Guinea. His comments seem very much like Yarrow Mamout's remarks to Peale about how he calculated his age. In his diary, Peale wrote that he had gone to see Margaret Beall to ask about Yarrow's age, "for he told me that he would be 134 years old in next March I found that he counted 12 Moons to the Year, and that he was 35 years old when he was first brought to America by Captn. Dow."[11] While Margaret implicitly told Peale that Yarrow was wrong about his age, it appears that Yarrow too was a moon man. That is, both he and Nugent were following lunar calendars. This was a practice that he and Nugent's grandfather brought with them to America. Indeed, Nugent's grandfather was probably Muslim like Yarrow. Islam determines its holidays from lunar cycles, and this could be the reason both men used lunar calendars.

Upton Beall's Daughter Sells Josiah Henson His Slave Brother

Upton Beall is the man who carried out his father's promise to free Yarrow by signing his manumission. Upton's daughter, Jane, gave another famous slave his freedom. She owned John Henson, the brother of Josiah Henson, and then sold John to his brother for the purpose of freeing him.

Upton had followed in his father's footsteps as clerk of the Montgomery County court in Rockville. In 1814, he built a stately brick mansion near the courthouse. It is still there and has become home to the county historical society. Indeed, for many years, the Beall family owned much of what is now downtown Rockville.

Court records show that after Upton and his wife died, their daughter Jane inherited a slave named John Henson from her maternal grandfather. In 1858, she sold this slave to Josiah Henson. Since Josiah wrote in his autobiography that he purchased his brother's freedom, it is believed that John Henson was his brother and that he bought him from Upton Beall's daughter.[12]

Provenance of a Portrait

Yarrow's finest legacy in Georgetown was, of course, the Simpson portrait, and it stayed in the Beall family until the twentieth century.

Brooke and Margaret Beall's two daughters (Upton's sisters) married the Mackall brothers, whose father was a wealthy planter in Prince George's County. The Bealls gave each of their daughters several square blocks of land in Georgetown. Daughter Christina and her husband Benjamin built a large brick house at what was called Mackall Square.

In 1822, Christina and Benjamin must have commissioned Simpson to paint Yarrow's portrait, which they hung in the house. The house and portrait stayed in the family for generations. Finally, in 1911, Herman Hollerith bought the house, furnishings and all.[13] Hollerith was the inventor of the tabulating machine and founder of one of several companies that were later merged into what became known as International Business Machines.

Hollerith seems to have cleared out the memorabilia the Mackalls had accumulated in the house over the years and given Yarrow's portrait to his wife's relatives, the Talcotts, who lived on the Normanstone estate near Georgetown. In 1919, the British government bought Normanstone, tore down the mansion, and built its embassy there. Edmund Myers Talcott acquired the painting when Normanstone was sold because about that time Grace Ecker wrote her *A Portrait of Old Georgetown* and said: "[Yarrow Mamout] must have been quite a figure in his day, for his portrait was painted by James Alexander Simpson, and is now owned by Mr. E. M. Talcott, who inherited it from Normanstone."[14]

In 1932, Talcott's daughter, Mrs. Hugh (Talcott) Barclay, loaned the painting to the Peabody Room of the Georgetown library. It has been there ever since.

Small World

These several stories about how different generations of the same families, white and black, were connected to major events in black history in Washington point to what a relatively small town Washington was in those days, and to a black community that was even smaller.

Francis Dodge owned Shadrack Nugent's brother in 1814. Years later, Dodge bought Yarrow Mamout's house. And, in 1848, Dodge dispatched his sons and his steamboat the *Salem* to bring back the *Pearl.*

The Edmonsons, who had attempted to escape to freedom on the *Pearl* and were befriended by Harriet Beecher Stowe, were descended from slaves of the white Edmonston family. They thus connected with Polly Yarrow, who was descended from slaves of the same family.

Yarrow Mamout and Shadrack Nugent's grandfather came from Guinea, and both were Muslims. This is further evidence of the existence of a black Muslim community in Rockville in the late eighteenth century, probably centered on Hungerford's Tavern.

Meanwhile, Josiah Henson, whose autobiography was inspiration for Harriet Beecher Stowe's *Uncle Tom's Cabin*, bought his brother's freedom from descendants of the Bealls that owned Yarrow.

As for Yarrow himself, he was still being talked about in Georgetown lectures thirty-six years after he died. His portrait hung in the house at Mackall Square in Georgetown for almost ninety years before being passed on to the Talcotts, who gave it to the Georgetown library, where it is today.

13 Unpleasant Valley

Aquilla's death in 1832 left Polly, at age thirty-three, a widow. She lived alone and on good terms with her white neighbors. She was not isolated from the black community, though. Her brother was a slave on Elie Crampton's farm three miles away, and there were slaves on adjacent farms with whom she might socialize. There were a few free blacks in other parts of Pleasant Valley, but they did not live close enough to see regularly.

These were tumultuous times in Washington County. When Yarrow had lived there sixty years earlier, revolution against England was in the air. He may have worried that warfare like that in Africa, which had led to his enslavement, would come to this new land. In Polly's time, slavery was the burning issue. Eventually, abolitionist John Brown rented a farm a mile and a half from Polly's, launched his raid on the government armory at Harpers Ferry, and called for another slave uprising. Brown's action helped spark the Civil War, turning the fields around Antietam Creek, a few miles north of Polly's house, into the bloodiest battleground in history on U.S. soil. Surprisingly, although Brown wanted to abolish slavery and the Union Army would do that, neither paid attention to African Americans in the valley, such as Polly and her relatives. Most blacks there, except for a few young men like Simon Turner, watched from the sidelines as the war played out before their eyes.

Simon Turner and Elie Crampton

Polly's brother was a slave to Elie Crampton. Crampton was the third generation of his family to live in the valley. His grandfather, Thomas

Crampton, had served in the militia in the Revolutionary War with Joseph Chapline, Samuel Beall's partner in the Frederick Forge. After the war, Thomas settled on a farm in the valley on the slope of South Mountain immediately below the notch known as Crampton's Gap.[1] The 1790 census showed him with four slaves. Ten years later, in the 1800 census, he had ten. By 1810, he had sixteen. It is possible that the Turners first came to Pleasant Valley through Thomas Crampton's buying them from Samuel Turner's estate in 1809, but the only thing known for sure is that Simon Turner was born to a slave of Elie Crampton in 1839.[2]

Crampton also had a tract called "Merryland" about six miles southeast in Frederick County, near the town of Petersville. Jacob Engelbrecht, the diarist in Frederick, noted that "The Knights of Maryland and Virginia" had held a tournament at Barracks Ground in Frederick in August 1857 followed by a ball that night. Crampton had won first place.[3] Thus, Elie Crampton must have been known not only in Pleasant Valley but also as far away as in Frederick.

In the early part of the nineteenth century, there were only two ways to get to Pleasant Valley from Frederick. One was to enter the south end of the valley at what would later be called Weverton. The other was to enter in the middle of the valley through Crampton's Gap in South Mountain. That road ran past Elie Crampton's farm.[4]

Life in the Valley for Free Blacks before the Civil War

Freedom for free blacks had its limits. The freedom of their children, for example, depended on the mother's status. Children of a free woman were free no matter who the father was, but the children of a free man and a slave woman were slaves. This meant that if a free man got a slave pregnant, the child was a slave, but if a slave got a free woman pregnant, the child was free. This also meant that the only free black people were those who were children of free women and those who had been freed by their owners.

Free African Americans enjoyed the right to own property and to sue in court for wrongs, but they could not vote. (Of course, neither could women of whatever ethnicity.) They could not participate in government, meaning they could not run for office or be constables, sheriffs, justices of the peace, or judges. They could not be lawyers, either, since lawyers were officers of the court. And they could not serve in the army. In short, although some African Americans were free, they were dependent on the white community to protect their freedom.[5]

Polly's white neighbors were therefore extremely important to her. These included Samuel Clagett. He had inventoried Aquilla's estate and was the nephew of Joseph Clagett, who had inventoried Mary in Samuel Turner's estate.[6] Another neighbor was Dr. Horatio Clagett, also a nephew of Joseph's.

These were men of substance. Many held progressive views on race and would step forward to protect the black community in times of need. Some had undoubtedly helped Aquilla move to Pleasant Valley in the first place. Although most owned slaves, they treated both free blacks and slaves with more decency and respect than others did. But make no mistake; these men were not abolitionists. That is, they did not advocate unconditionally freeing slaves, but they were sensitive on racial issues and occasionally freed some of their own.

Their progressive views led Horatio Clagett and Elie Crampton to become delegates to the American Colonization Society's Maryland convention in 1841.[7] The convention reiterated support for the Society's core principle that free blacks should be helped to emigrate to a colony on the coast of Africa. However, the convention cautioned, this did not mean "modern abolition," a term it defined as "the immediate extirpation of slavery, without any regard to the rights of property under existing laws, and with a blind recklessness of consequences."[8] Nonetheless, the Society believed in basic human dignity and paved the way for the modern abolition it disavowed. Abraham Lincoln, too, favored colonization over abolition right up to the moment in 1862 when he surprised everyone by issuing the Emancipation Proclamation.

Rev. Thomas Henry, the black minister who served in the valley at this time, recalled in his autobiography an instance of how Clagett and Crampton helped Henry and the black community. It was in late spring 1835. Rev. Henry was staying with Dr. Clagett, whose farm was near the African American church that Henry had started in the valley. Rev. Henry was in the middle of Sunday service when a Constable Barnes barged in. Barnes said the service was in violation of a provision in the Maryland slave code that made it illegal for blacks to gather together without the supervision of a white man. He ordered Henry to go with him to see "Squire Crampton." This was justice of the peace Elie Crampton, whose duties, in addition to witnessing legal documents, included resolving minor disputes. Henry explained to Crampton that he had permission to hold the service from a white man named Mr. Grimm.[9] Crampton was satisfied with the explanation and said Henry should return to the church and continue the service.

By the time Henry and Barnes got back to the church, Grimm was waiting for them. Barnes tried to follow the minister into the church but, according to Henry:

> Mr. Grimm caught him by the collar and thrust him back. What happened between these two, outside, I cannot tell as I was seated behind the speaker. The meeting went on glorious all that day; but at night it was an uncommon meeting. The people from far and near were there, and both white and colored seemed to be after the one thing—their soul's salvation.[10]

Rev. Henry was not exaggerating. Many in the valley were tolerant, and both blacks and whites undoubtedly rallied to support him. Polly Yarrow would surely have been among these.

Polly knew Henry's host, Dr. Clagett, both as a neighbor and professionally because she was a midwife. Present-day Yarrowsburg resident Bill Mullenix, who lives across the road from where Polly did, recalled his grandfather telling him Yarrowsburg was named for Polly Yarrow: "She was the midwife in this part of the valley. She was black, you know. Delivered all the babies, black and white."[11]

Midwives did more than deliver babies, though. They provided routine medical care, such as dressing wounds or nursing fevers, freeing doctors for doing surgery and tending the wealthy. Since midwives complemented doctors, they certainly knew the doctors and in a small, close community like Pleasant Valley would have worked with them professionally. Besides, a man as progressive as Clagett, who hosted Rev. Henry when he was in the valley, would surely have sought out a black woman as talented as Polly. Indeed, although Polly was a widow and a former slave, she had risen quite high in life by this time. She was one of the few free blacks in that part of the valley, and as midwife, had as much respect and status as a black woman could hope to achieve before the Civil War. Polly may have been called to the Crampton farm in 1839 to deliver baby Simon to the Turner family there.

Georgia-Men

Although the lot of African Americans in Pleasant Valley would soon change for the better, it was still a violent and dangerous place at this time for both slaves and free blacks. Racial incidents like the one Rev. Henry described hearkened back to the planter mentality, but they were minor compared to what else was going on.

Around Hagerstown, just to the north of the valley, professional slave catchers prowled. Although the slave catchers were mainly on the lookout for runaways from Virginia, even free blacks had to worry about being kidnapped and taken south for sale. The slavers would lay in wait for runaways crossing the Potomac from Virginia at Boteler's Ford on their way north to freedom in Pennsylvania. They were called "Georgia-men" or "soul drivers." Allen Sparrow, a white resident of Middletown, Maryland at this time recalled:

> I have seen from 20 to 40 Negros hand cuft together one on each side to a long chain, the Georgemen as they cald them then with his whip driving them. . . . They paid when the Markets were good high prices, from $600 to $1200 per Men and Five to Eight hundred for women, especially if they were young and good looking. There was men that followed it for a living. They took them to Georgia and sold them to work on Cotton Farms. At that time there was very few people but what thought it was all right and I thought if a negro runaway I was in duty bound to catch him as if a horse or anything else ran away.[12]

George Ross, the former slave from Hagerstown, also remembered the runaways: "I have seen them in droves, 150 or 200 together—men, women and children—linked side by side. There used to be two drivers to a drove, on[e] driver in front and one behind. I have seen them from eight or nine years old and up to 45 and 50; when the mothers were sold, I have seen young babes, from the cradle in these gangs."[13] For free blacks like Polly, such sights must have been terrifying to watch. The only thing separating free blacks from slaves was a legal technicality and a piece of paper.

While African Americans might feel slightly safer a few miles to the south in Pleasant Valley, strange things happened there too. Whispered among valley residents yet today is the rumor that long ago neighbors heard slaves being whipped by the new owners at the house formerly owned by Alexander Grim, the man who had sold Aquilla his land.[14]

Worst of all is the persistent, unsubstantiated rumor of a "slave farm," a place where slaves were raised like livestock to be sold to plantations in the Deep South.[15] The rumors have been around for a century and a half. When asked about such things, former slave George Ross said:

> I don't know as I have known any particular instances where slaves were raised for the purpose of selling them: but I have been on a farm where they had 30 or 40 colored people, & as the younger growed up, they sold off the older; so I rather think by that it was done pretty near for that purpose. . . . I have often heard of slaves being kept for the purpose of breeding, but I have never seen it. That may be done down in Virginia and the other foreign States, perhaps.[16]

Thus, while Polly Yarrow was becoming an accepted and valued member of both the white and black community, she had to be careful. Washington County could be a dangerous place even for free blacks. She could take comfort, too, in the fact that while her relatives were still in slavery, they were slaves to an enlightened man like Elie Crampton, a member of the American Colonization Society who could be relied on to keep mischievous whites like Constable Barnes at bay.[17]

The Sands Family

Even before the Civil War, African Americans in increasing numbers were gaining freedom, and not just by the beneficence of their owners. Like Yarrow Mamout, they were earning money on the side while slaves and using it to purchase their freedom and that of their loved ones.

The Sands family, which married into the Turner family, did this. The Sands may be traced back to Arthur and his older brother Wesley, who were born in the early 1800s.[18] Remarkably, although both were slaves and illiterate, they began the family practice of preserving documents to pass to later generations. The earliest is a handwritten promissory note in the amount of fifteen dollars and dated January 23, 1847, payable to John Gray of Pleasant Valley as administrator of the estate of Thomas Clagett and signed by Wesley Sands with an "X." Justice of the peace Elie Crampton signed as witness.[19] Although Wesley could not read or write, he kept it and passed it along to later generations.[20]

The document is significant for two reasons. First, it shows that a white man in the valley would loan money to a slave—at least to a slave with the drive of Wesley Sands—with the expectation that he was willing and able to repay. In modern vernacular, Sands was creditworthy. He was being treated like a free man. Indeed, he was being treated like Yarrow Mamout might possibly have been treated by Brooke Beall and allowed to work for himself while still a slave. This was certainly cause for Sands to preserve the document for posterity.

Second, the promissory note supports the oral histories that there was a long tradition of good race relations in Pleasant Valley. This seems especially true whenever Elie Crampton or a Clagett was involved.

The John Gray mentioned in the promissory note was connected to the Sands family in a more important way. He owned Henrietta, the wife of Wesley Sands's brother Arthur, and their children.[21] Arthur himself belonged to another farmer in Pleasant Valley named John Mullendore.

Though he owned slaves, Gray reportedly viewed them more as employees. A neighbor remarked that Gray treated Arthur Sands "like one of the family."[22] Still, Gray's views on slavery as an institution were not as progressive as his neighbors'. For example, the split over slavery that divided the congregation at St. Luke's Episcopal Church was purportedly between Gray, who was proslavery, and the Clagetts, who opposed it.[23]

When it came to marriage, the impediments to travel by slaves limited their choice of marriage partners to those living nearby. Yarrow's apparent partner, Jane Chambers, was a slave to one of Brooke Beall's neighbors. His son, Aquilla, married Mary Turner, a slave of another of the Bealls's neighbors. In Pleasant Valley, Arthur Sands married a woman on a neighboring farm.

Thus, when Arthur's daughter, Lucinda, came of age, she married a slave on a neighboring farm, Simon Turner, who belonged to Elie Crampton. They had a formal wedding at the Church of the Brethren in Brownsville in 1855. It was not the church where Rev. Henry had encountered Constable Barnes. This church had a white congregation, and its minister, Rev. Daniel Brown, was white. He presided at the wedding. The newlyweds apparently lived together at the Grays', but they remained slaves to their respective owners, with Lucinda belonging to Gray and Simon to Crampton.[24]

Two years later, on March 7, 1857, Arthur Sands won his freedom by purchasing himself from his owner, John Mullendore. Once again, justice of the peace Elie Crampton signed as witness to the manumission. Nonetheless, although Arthur was free, his wife Henrietta, their married daughter Lucinda, and Lucinda's children by Simon Turner were still slaves of John Gray.

However, Pleasant Valley was slowly becoming home to more and more free blacks. In September 1858, John Gray sold two small pieces of land on the slope of Elk Ridge to "James W. Jones, Col." The abbreviation stood for "colored." The Joneses were free blacks. The lots had come from land that had once belonged to Antietam Iron Works. The enterprise had gone bankrupt about ten years earlier, and its 10,000 acres sold off.[25] Jones's farm was about a mile north of Polly Yarrow's.

For Washington County as a whole, the 1860 census counted 8,216 households, of which 497 were free blacks. This included eight black households in the northern part of Pleasant Valley and twenty-two in the southern part, which was called Sandy Hook. Among the free blacks in Sandy Hook were Arthur and Wesley Sands, James Jones, and Polly Yarrow, with the African part of her name being misspelled as "Yaner."

Abolitionist John Brown Arrives

Pleasant Valley was about to lose its pleasantness. In the fall of 1859, the relatively stable state of race relations was shattered by the events at Harpers Ferry. On October 16, John Brown and his band of men seized the federal armory there. Brown staged the raid from a farm near Polly Yarrow's house. The previous July, he had arrived in the town of Sandy Hook directly across the Potomac from Harpers Ferry, looking for land to rent. He intended to assemble a small band of men and sequester them nearby until the attack. He chose a farm owned by the estate of a man named Robert Kennedy on the west side of Elk Ridge. Although Brown had reached the so-called Kennedy Farm by taking the road north out of Sandy Hook, it was also accessible from Pleasant Valley. At that time, a road ran from the farm over Elk Ridge through Solomon's Gap and on past Polly Yarrow's house. In fact, while the Kennedy Farm was four miles north of Sandy Hook, it was only a mile and a half from Polly's over this rough mountain road.

After renting the farm, Brown had his men join him. For the next three months, the small farmhouse became home to twenty-four people: Brown; twenty-one men; and two women, who served as cooks and housekeepers. Brown thought his efforts would attract free blacks and slaves, but there is no evidence that he approached any of the 497 free black households in Washington County, the twenty-two free blacks in the Sandy Hook district, or any of the many slaves in the area. Polly Yarrow was the nearest black person with medical skills and indeed the nearest free black. Since there is no evidence Brown contacted her, he either did not explore his surroundings enough to meet her or did not have need of her services.

In fact, Brown seemed to ignore both the black community and the progressive white men in Pleasant Valley. He devoted much of his own time to the task of getting weapons, which he had shipped to Chambersburg, Pennsylvania, and of meeting people there. For example, Frederick Douglass met him in Chambersburg. This necessitated travel back and forth between the Kennedy Farm and Chambersburg. Although Brown could have taken the road over Solomon's Gap and into Pleasant Valley to get to Pennsylvania, it is not the shortest or easiest route, and he never mentioned it in his writings. Present-day valley residents speculate that Brown might have preached at the United Brethren Church in Brownsville, where Simon and Lucinda Turner were married, because he did that in other communities, but there is no evidence of this.[26] Nonetheless, the absence of evidence of Brown's contacting people in Pleasant Valley does not mean he did not. Once he was arrested, sensible people were not going to admit they knew the man. Besides, Brown seemed more focused on attracting blacks from Virginia rather than Maryland.[27]

When Brown and his men raided Harpers Ferry that October, they were bottled up in a firehouse and captured. But two groups of men escaped capture and headed north toward Pennsylvania after first stopping by the Kennedy Farm. The best way for them to avoid the militia that captured Brown might have been to go over Elk Ridge at Solomon's Gap. If they did, then they would have passed Polly Yarrow's house and continued over Crampton's Gap in South Mountain. However, both groups apparently hiked along the side of Elk Ridge and then crossed into Pleasant Valley farther to the north.[28] Still, the fact that she was a free black woman living on a possible escape route surely led to Polly Yarrow's questioning by authorities.

John Brown was hanged for his deed, and his actions polarized pro and antislavery forces and soon led to civil war. On one hand, slaveowners and those who believed in slavery feared that Brown's act might lead to more frequent, and more effective, slave rebellions. To them, this was Nat Turner all over again. On the other hand, abolitionists saw the incident at Harpers Ferry as the spark that would ignite broad public support for their long effort to end slavery, which it in fact did.

For the former reason or perhaps just to be vindictive, the Maryland legislature passed a draconian law designed to end the practice of manumission once and for all. It had been pounding this same nail for more than a hundred years, ever since the day Yarrow arrived. Once the law took effect, slaves could no longer gain freedom for any reason whatever:

> No slave shall henceforth be manumitted by deed or by last will and testament, nor shall the fact of a Negro's going at large and acting as free, or not being claimed by an owner, be considered as evidence of the execution heretofore for any deed or will manumitting the party, or as ground for presuming freedom.[29]

The new law was a threat to Polly Yarrow, who had never filed a manumission. She could no longer rely on the fact that she had been acting as free as proof of her right to be free.

In the short term, it had precisely the opposite effect of what was intended. Reports of it appeared on page two of the Hagerstown *Herald and Torchlight* on May 23, 1860: "No More Manumissions, Maryland Law Will Take Effect." Immediately, slaves set about obtaining their freedom either by purchase or by getting their owners to give it gratis. The deed book of the Recorder of Deeds of Washington County is filled with manumissions from late May through June 1860.

Arthur Sands, who had obtained his own freedom three years earlier, rushed to buy freedom for the rest of his family from John Gray. On May 30, 1860, Gray freed Sands's wife Henrietta, their daughter Lucinda, and Lucinda's three children from her marriage to Simon Turner. Sands paid Gray a total of $615. The documents were witnessed by Joseph Grimm, probably the same man who had cuffed Constable Barnes when he tried to follow Rev. Henry into the church years before.[30] Thus, all the Sandses were free, including Lucinda and her children. However, her husband Simon Turner remained Crampton's slave.

Arthur Sands needed room to accommodate this large and extended family, and so a little over a year later, in October 1861, he bought 74.25 acres of land on the slope of Elk Ridge. Like the land that James Jones had purchased from John Gray, this land once belonged to Antietam Iron Works. Sands paid $259.[31] The price was less than half what his wife, daughter, and three grandchildren had cost. The property was a half-mile south of Polly Yarrow's house. Thus, three free black families lived along a two-mile strip on the slope of Elk Ridge: the Sandses, Polly Yarrow, and the Joneses.

War in the Valley

The more significant and deadly result of John Brown's raid was, of course, the Civil War.

In September 1862, both Union and Confederate Armies tramped through Pleasant Valley. They were headed to Antietam Creek where an estimated 130,000 men from the two armies would meet. Preceding the main Battle of Antietam were a series of smaller, separate engagements, including the Battle of Crampton's Gap and the Battle of Harpers Ferry, which were fought where Polly Yarrow, the Sandses, the Joneses, and Simon Turner lived. To residents, these battles meant weeks of danger and occupation by large armies from both sides. Author Kathleen A. Ernst wrote a book about what the fighting meant for civilians and borrowed the reaction of a local white, resident for the title, *Too Afraid to Cry*.[32] That sentiment would be an understatement for black residents.

The Confederate Army came first. One part of it set up camp in the heart of Pleasant Valley on September 11 in preparation for an attack on Union-held Harpers Ferry. St. Luke's Episcopal Church was commandeered first as a headquarters for Confederate General Lafayette McLaws and later as a Confederate field hospital. McLaws described the valley at that time as having one road along the base of South Mountain, which he called the "Blue Ridge." This road ran by Elie Crampton's farm. Indeed, one wing of McLaws's forces had come into Pleasant Valley through Crampton's Gap and had passed by Crampton's farm.

The other road in the valley was along the base of Elk Ridge. This ran by the Sands farm, Polly Yarrow's, and the Joneses. According to McLaws, the road was "very much out of repair and not much used."[33]

This may explain why John Brown had not used the road over Solomon's Gap to venture into the valley.

The Confederates' goal was to capture Harpers Ferry. To do this, McLaws planned to take the Maryland Heights portion of Elk Ridge. From there, his men would be able to shoot "plunging fire, from musketry even," onto Harpers Ferry. But a large Union force occupied Elk Ridge for a mile and a half. The defenses stretched from Maryland Heights above Harpers Ferry northward almost to where Arthur Sandses' farm was.

McLaws intended to drive off these Union troops. On the morning of September 12, after breaking camp, a brigade of his army moved along the old road past the Sandses' and Polly Yarrow's houses and climbed up the ridge at Solomon's Gap. Union forces on Elk Ridge fired down at the Confederates. Errant bullets and shells would have flown past the two houses. Once at Solomon's Gap, the Confederates turned south and drove down the spine of Elk Ridge toward Maryland Heights. The Sandses and Polly, if they stayed around, would have heard the fighting on the mountain above them. By nightfall, the entire southern end of Pleasant Valley, including their houses, was in Confederate hands.

By the time McLaws's men finished taking Maryland Heights the next day, the general was hearing reports of a large Union force moving toward him from the north. He considered the reports "questionable" and continued with the plan to take Harpers Ferry. The reports were true, though. A huge Union army was headed toward Pleasant Valley. On September 14, McLaws was on Maryland Heights, directing the bombardment of Harpers Ferry, when he heard the sounds of fighting to the north. The big Union army was no longer a rumor. It was attacking through Crampton's and Brownsville's Gaps in South Mountain on the opposite side of the valley. Union forces vastly outnumbered McLaws's defenders and soon poured into Pleasant Valley. They fanned out across Elie Crampton's farm in hot pursuit of the fleeing rebels. Union General William Franklin had his men follow what is now Townsend Road past the Crampton farm, and the general settled in at a headquarters just beyond the farm in the town of Rohrersville. That night, the north end of the valley was filled with the campfires and tents of Franklin's troops. McLaws estimated the Union force "engaged and in reserve at Crampton's Gap . . . to be from 15,000 and upward."

By the end of the day, according to McLaws, his losses in killed, wounded, and missing were "very large, and the remnant collected to make front across the valley was very small." He spread this remnant of his army east to west in the valley from South Mountain to Elk Ridge. Polly's house was almost exactly at the western end of the Confederate force. This meant that Polly and the Sandses were behind Confederate lines that night unless they had fled. If they were still there, the two black families looked down on the valley and saw the watch fires of the Union army camped a mile or so away.

By the morning of September 15, although the Union held most Pleasant Valley, Harpers Ferry, just over Elk Ridge, was still under bombardment from McLaws's forces on Maryland Heights. Later in the day, the Union garrison there, about ten thousand men, surrendered. It was the largest surrender in the history of the U.S. Army until World War II.

This led to another shameful incident. An estimated five hundred escaped slaves from plantations in Virginia had taken refuge in Harpers Ferry, believing the large Union garrison would protect them. Once the town was given up, Confederate commanders ordered their men to round up the slaves and march them back to their owners while the rest of the Confederates abandoned the newly captured town and rushed north to join Confederate General Robert E. Lee at Antietam Creek.

The roundup of escaped slaves essentially turned the Confederate Army into Georgia-men. To free blacks such as Polly, the Sandses, and the Joneses, there could not be a clearer signal, if they needed one, that they would not be safe as long as the rebels were around. Of course, given her medical skills, Polly might have been called on to help the wounded from both sides. She might even have been working in the Confederate field hospital at St. Luke's.

The Battle of Antietam took place two days later, on September 17, around the town of Sharpsburg north of the valley. The Union Army was deemed the victor. There were four thousand dead to be buried where they fell, including throughout Pleasant Valley. The bodies were reinterred later in cemeteries. Slaves were undoubtedly pressed into service for this unhappy task. Still, given what happened to the escaped slaves at Harpers Ferry, African Americans in the valley must have breathed a sigh of relief that Lee and his men had fled back across the Potomac River to Virginia and that Union General George McClellan and his army were in the area.

President Abraham Lincoln was far less pleased with McClellan's resting at Antietam. He wanted McClellan to pursue Lee and finish off the Confederate Army. To this end, he visited McClellan at his headquarters on October 3 to put a burr under his saddle. Lincoln did not go through Pleasant Valley on his journey, but people there surely felt his breeze. For the past several months, Lincoln had been mulling over the idea of issuing an emancipation proclamation. Secretary of State William Seward had urged caution, however, telling the President that Union military setbacks argued against immediate release of such a document. He felt Lincoln should wait "until the eagle of victory takes his flight."[34]

The victory at Antietam seemed to be that eagle. Five days after the battle, on September 22, Lincoln announced his plan to issue the Emancipation Proclamation. Thus, as he traveled past on the way to Antietam, the valley was abuzz with the news that Union was now committed to abolition. The proclamation would take effect on January 1, 1863. All slaves in the areas in rebellion, that is, in the Confederate states, would be treated as free under the laws of the United States. The proclamation did not apply to slaves in Pleasant Valley, such as Simon Turner, because it was in Union hands at least for the moment, but the handwriting was on the wall for the end of slavery everywhere.[35]

Simon Turner Goes to War

On October 1, 1863, Elie Crampton died at the age of sixty-three. He was buried in the United Brethren Church cemetery in Rohrersville. His sons-in-law, Benjamin Emmert and Nathan Tobey, were named executors of his estate. The items they listed in the inventory of his estate included six slaves: Simon, April, Jenny, and Barbara Turner, eight-year-old Clara Turner, and three-year-old Lucy Snyder.[36] Simon, of course, had been married for eight years to Lucinda Sands. She and their children were free persons, living with her parents at their farm on Elk Ridge near Polly Yarrow, while Simon had remained a slave.

As one of the executors of the estate, Tobey faced a dilemma. He was a member of the United Brethren Church. In fact, his brother was a minister of the Church and a colleague of church Bishop Milton Wright of Ohio, the father of Orville and Wilbur Wright.[37] The church's national conventions had issued resolutions to the effect that while members who owned slaves could keep them, members could not buy or sell slaves.[38] Thus, as executor of an estate that included slaves, Tobey had to decide whether to follow the law, which required him to prudently dispose of all estate property, or his church.

The Emancipation Proclamation indirectly resolved most of Tobey's moral dilemma. While it did not free slaves in Maryland, it did open the way for African Americans to join the army. As a result, in the spring of 1864, recruiters for the Union Army began working their way through Western Maryland. They talked to Simon Turner. Lucinda later described what happened in an application for a widow's pension: "The colored people were all leaving their masters at that time, and his [Simon's] master said he would be enlisted anyway and he might as well let him go. So my husband went to Frederick MD and enlisted."[39]

Lucinda's recollection was in error; Crampton was dead by this time. Simon consulted the executors, Tobey and Emmert. They told him he was free to do whatever he wanted and on March 29, 1864, signed his manumission. Two days after that, he enlisted in the Union Army at the fort in Frederick, Maryland.[40] Tobey and Emmert freed the other Turners too, except for the child Clara whom they gave to Crampton's widow.[41] Technically, this latter transfer may not have been in violation of church doctrine, since the widow was arguably a joint owner of Clara.

Thomas Jefferson Weedon, who was a slave in the nearby community of Sunnyside, Maryland, also joined the army at this time. His descendants tell about how he got free. Weedon and slaves from other farms agreed to leave together and join the army. They escaped successfully from their respective owners and made it to the post in Frederick. The next day, their owners showed up demanding their return. Weedon and his colleagues decided to confront their former owners. Weedon, according to family legend, stepped forward to announce, "We don't belong to you any more. We belong to Uncle Sam."[42] Simon Turner was lucky to obtain freedom in a less confrontational fashion.

Turner and the other now-free blacks from Western Maryland formed the Thirty-Ninth Regiment, United States Colored Troops. Their officers were white. The commanding officer was Ozora P. Stearns of Minnesota, who, after the war, became a United States senator.[43] The only known photograph of the Thirty-Ninth U.S.C.T. Regiment shows six white officers, sitting in the foreground posing for the camera, and six black troopers standing casually in the background watching.[44] In the center back of the photograph is a tall, young, skinny, black man in a relaxed pose. None of the men in the photograph is identified. However, when descendants of Simon Turner were shown an enlargement of the tall skinny man, one of them instantly said, "He looks like Uncle Mark," and indeed he does. Uncle Mark was one of Simon's grandsons. However, despite the resemblance, it is not likely that the man is Simon Turner, because he was seriously wounded at the end of July 1864, and the photograph was purportedly taken two months later in September.

The confidence evident in the faces of the men in the photograph was not really deserved. The Thirty-Ninth was given little training before marching off to war. Turner enlisted on March 31. General Ulysses Grant had taken command of the Union Army and was about to lead it south. On May 5, barely a month after Turner enlisted, the regiment found itself in a supporting role in the Battle of the Wilderness. It continued moving south with Grant's army but was held back from combat.[45] In the muster rolls, Simon was referred to as Samuel Turner.[46] As stated previously, this may have been the result of confusion with a father named Samuel. Simon himself was referred to both as Simon and Samuel. He was in Company D.

While Turner was marching off to war, the Confederates came back to Pleasant Valley. This time General Jubal Early was in command. His objective was Washington, D.C., but first he wanted to take Harpers

Ferry again. Early adopted the practice of holding Maryland towns on his route for ransom, telling city fathers that he would burn their communities unless they met his ransom demand. He got $21,500 from Hagerstown, $1,500 from tiny Middletown, and a whopping $200,000 from Frederick. The *Middletown Valley Register* of July 8 estimated that in just three days the Confederates had ransomed towns, taken goods from stores, commandeered provisions from farmers, stolen horses and cattle, and damaged fields to the tune of $875,000.[47]

An African American woman in Frederick County passed down to her descendants a chilling story of what the Confederate invasion meant to her. She was sitting outside her house with her infant when a lone Confederate soldier rode by. She noticed him looking back and finally turning around to come for her. She grabbed the baby and fled to her uncle's house. She was too afraid to wait and see what he wanted.[48]

While in Pleasant Valley, Confederate forces once again rode up Elk Ridge past Polly Yarrow's house, and once again they turned at Solomon's Gap as they had done two years earlier. This time, however, Union forces were there in strength and drove them back. Jubal Early's army left the valley without retaking Harpers Ferry and marched on toward Washington, reaching the outskirts of the city on July 11 before deciding it had done enough and returning to Virginia.

What these brief Confederate occupations meant for Polly Yarrow, the Sandses, and the Joneses is not quite lost to history. In recent years, treasure hunters have combed the old John Gray farm with metal detectors looking for Civil War relics. They have dug up dozens of minie balls and smooth musket balls.[49] This was hard evidence of fighting there. The rifled weapons of Union troops fired minie balls. The Confederates had rifled weapons too, if they could find them, but they were also armed with older muskets that fired smooth, round balls. The assortment of both kinds of bullets that the treasure hunters found on Gray farm is evidence that Union and Confederates were shooting at each other there, but it does not tell whether this was in 1862, 1863, or 1864. The treasure hunters also found a belt buckle with "U.S." on it. This suggests a Union soldier was wounded or killed on the farm and stripped of his belt and buckle before being carried away.

Simon Turner and the Thirty-Ninth were not idle while the rebels were looting Pleasant Valley. They had marched south with General Grant and bottled up Robert E. Lee's forces in Richmond. Grant decided that the Confederate's defensive works around the city were too strong to be attacked in a direct assault. Therefore, he approved a plan for coal miners from Pennsylvania to tunnel under a Confederate fortification and detonate ten thousand pounds of explosives. The Thirty-Ninth was one of several African American units that would then charge into the breach in the works made by the explosion. On the morning of July 30, 1864, the powder was lit, and the Confederate fort vanished, leaving nothing but a huge crater in the ground. Simon Turner and the Thirty-Ninth Regiment charged. The ensuing fight was therefore called the Battle of the Crater.

The initial Union attack succeeded. Later in the day, however, the Confederates counterattacked and closed the gap that had been blown in their lines. Sergeant Decatur Dorsey of the Thirty-Ninth Regiment became the first African American to be awarded the Congressional Medal of Honor for his efforts that day. The citation read: "Planted his colors on the Confederate works in advance of his regiment, and when the regiment was driven back to the Union works he carried the colors there and bravely rallied the men."[50]

During the fighting, which was hand-to-hand at times, the enraged southerners tended to single out the black soldiers. The colored troops took heavy casualties. At the end of the day, fifty-eight men of the Thirty-Ninth Regiment were killed, wounded, or missing.[51] Simon Turner was wounded in the arm by a bullet and in the side by a bursting shell. His kidney was damaged. He urinated blood. He never fought again. Turner was discharged on August 10, 1865, five months after the war ended. He had spent much of his army service in hospitals recovering from his wounds. He and Lucinda had not seen each other since he enlisted sixteen months earlier. Neither could write, so they had not been able to communicate except perhaps through friends who were literate or who returned home before Simon.[52] The experience undoubtedly contributed to the burning desire for education that was passed on to later generations in the family. And now, at last, the couple had the chance to do something about that.

14 Freedom

Pleasant Valley had changed radically by the time Simon Turner came home from the war. The Emancipation Proclamation in 1863 did not end slavery in Maryland, but the State of Maryland passed a new constitution in November 1864 that did. All African American families in the valley were free. At the same time, Congress was working on what became known as the Civil War Amendments to the United States Constitution. In 1865, it passed the Thirteenth Amendment to abolish slavery throughout the country. In 1868, it passed the Fourteenth Amendment to guarantee equal protection of the law. And in 1870, it passed the Fifteenth Amendment to protect voting rights. The effects of these changes were noticed at the most basic level. In letter of June 9, 1865, Elie Crampton's daughter Mollie wrote with tongue in cheek and seeming resentment: "We were working so hard yesterday and got so tired that we would stop sometimes to rest—and bless *old Abe* for freeing all the negroes."[1] Naturally, former slaves had a different opinion.

Starting a Colored School

Since Simon did not have money to buy a place of his own, he lived with his in-laws, the Sandses, on their farm on the slope of Elk Ridge. It was just up the road from Polly Yarrow's. Simon's wife Lucinda and their three children had lived there the whole time he was in the army. They had two more children within five years of Simon's return. The farm had a log house and barn.[2] Thus, the 1870 census counted nine people living there: Arthur and Henrietta Sands, Simon and Lucinda Turner, and the five Turner children. The space they lived in was one step up from a slave cabin and terribly cramped.

Although the constitutional amendments ended slavery and removed some of the handicaps that even free blacks had suffered, such as unequal protection of the law and the inability to vote, the amendments did nothing for one of the most fundamental concerns of black parents, particularly Simon and Lucinda Turner, and this was education. To them, freedom without education was like a two-story house without stairs. The Turners' oldest child, Daniel, was twelve by this time, and yet he had never attended school.

Of course, the Turners were not the only ones in this predicament. At the end of the Civil War, there were four million ex-slaves, and no schools for them. Laws in the slave states had prohibited teaching slaves to read. The 1848 slave code in Georgia, as an example, provided:

> Punishment for teaching slaves or free persons of color to read.—If any slave, Negro, or free person of color, or any white person, shall teach any other slave, Negro, or free person of color, to read or write either written or printed characters, the said free person of color or slave shall be punished by fine and whipping, or fine or whipping, at the discretion of the court.[3]

Notably, while this law prohibited anyone, whether white or black, from teaching a slave, it punished only blacks.

The federal government's Freedmen's Bureau was designed in part to remedy this deficiency. It gave $5 million to schools between 1865 and 1870. Of course, that worked out to just over a dollar per ex-slave and was a drop in the bucket. The more valuable contribution of the Freedmen's Bureau was the coordination of efforts by private relief societies in the North. As a result, 3,000 schools serving 150,000 black students were in operation by 1869. So hungry were ex-slaves for education that child and parent sometimes sat next to each other in school.

The Freedmen's Bureau needed local partners if it was to succeed. In Pleasant Valley, it found three: Arthur Sands, Joseph Edemy, and

Robert Anderson. Simon Turner and Edemy's son, James, had fought together at the Battle of the Crater.[4]

Robert Anderson was a mason. A stone house he built still stands along Route 67 at Garretts Mill Road in the valley. He also fashioned the stone basement of Mt. Moriah Church, which would play a significant role in the lives of the Sandses and Turners.[5] In 1867, Anderson purchased a small tract of land on Israel Creek next to the new Washington County Railroad line and near the old Garrett's Mill.[6] A year later, on September 7, 1868, as summer was winding down, he sold the land to himself, Arthur Sands, and Joseph Edemy as trustees "for school purposes for the instruction of colored children forever." The point of their aspirations is evident from the document itself. Anderson and his wife signed with "X's."[7] The trustees might be illiterate but the children would not be. Sands, Edemy, and Anderson were going to pull the black community in Pleasant Valley up by its bootstraps.

According to an August 1868 report filed with the Freedmen's Bureau, classes began that month and would end in November. The local black community, the report said, owned the school building and supported the school financially. It received no support from Washington County. The school had one white and one African American teacher and nine male and five female students. Although ten students were "always present," only eight were "always punctual." Eight students, more than half those attending, were over sixteen years of age. Even though the report was prepared during the first month of school, it found that nine students could spell and read easy lessons. They had somehow learned without the benefit of school and in defiance of custom and the law. Four students had been freed before the Civil War; three of these were probably the Turner children. The report characterized public sentiment toward colored schools in Pleasant Valley as "Rather favorable."[8]

Where these classes were held is unclear. Not until January 1869 did a report indicate the school building was finished. Meanwhile, enrollment had grown to twenty-four, of whom twenty-one were always present. By this time, twenty could spell and read easy lessons, and two were in arithmetic.[9] In February, enrollment reached thirty-five, with twenty-seven attending regularly.[10] Blacks in Pleasant Valley were clearly thirsty for education.

By 1877, "Col'd School No. 6" was marked on a map of the county.[11] It was a one-room schoolhouse. Isabel Johnson, an African American who was born in nearby Yarrowsburg in 1921, said she was told there was once a colored school at that location, but it was gone by the time she lived there. When she was a girl, the schools were still segregated, and the black public school had been moved to Mt. Moriah Church. Johnson observed wryly that there was a school in Yarrowsburg much closer to her house, but since it was for whites only, she could not attend.[12]

The 1880 census showed that although neither of the Sandses could read nor could Simon and Lucinda, all the Turner children could. Surprisingly, the formerly illiterate stonemason Robert Anderson, one of the school's founders, had also learned to read.

Polly Yarrow had not disappeared from the scene. She was still living near the Sandses and Turners at the end of the Civil War. She was sixty-five years old. She was presumably still delivering babies, too. In all likelihood, she had delivered not only Simon Turner but also his children. Indeed, she had probably delivered most of the children that went to original colored school.

The county map that marked the location of the colored school showed the properties of "Mrs. Yarrow" and "A. Sands." However, Polly was living with a man by this time. The 1870 census referred to her as Polly Jones and listed her in the household of Lewis Jones. She may have remarried, or a census-taker may have simply assumed that a man and woman living together were married. Lewis Jones was possibly related to the James Jones to whom the Grays had sold land before the Civil War, but James Jones was not listed in the 1870 census. He and his family must have fled, been driven out, or been killed during the Civil War.

Polly's name appeared again in the 1880 census, still living with Lewis Jones. Her age was given as ninety, although she had been only seventy in the 1870 census. Present-day resident Bill Mullenix recalled his grandfather saying Polly Yarrow's house had burned down at some point, and she moved away.[13] If so, the fire was after the 1880 census was taken.

Polly died on November 21, 1885. She was so well known that the *Hagerstown Herald and TorchLight* felt it should carry a brief death notice, an unusual recognition for a black woman then. Just like her father-in-law, Yarrow Mamout, Polly's obituary was in the newspaper: "An old colored woman, named Polly Yarrow, whose exact age is not known, but was over 100 years, died on last Saturday, at a little village, called Yarrowsburg, near Crampton's Gap, in Pleasant Valley, in this county."[14] She was actually eighty-six-years old. A few months later, Lewis Jones sold her land for $100, although he did not legally own it. It was the same acre and a quarter that Aquilla Yarrow had purchased in 1825.

The newspaper did not make the connection between Polly Yarrow and Yarrow Mamout, but by then Peale's portrait of Yarrow, which was not famous in its time anyway, had gone into storage and was forgotten. Besides, except for their common name, who would have thought these two people were connected—and that name of African origin?

Emma Turner Goes to College

Simon and Lucinda Turner had another child, Emma, in 1875.[15] Polly Yarrow was about seventy-six years old then. She was probably too old to have acted as midwife, but since she lived just down the road, Emma would have known her. Yarrowsburg is so small that even today everyone knows everyone else, black or white. Emma was ten years old when Polly died.

Emma had a passion for learning. She and her siblings were the first people in the Turner family, at least the first in America, who were able to read and write. They went to the school their grandfather helped set up. Colored School No. 6 only had grades one through eight, and there was no black high school in Pleasant Valley. The nearest high school for African Americans was sixteen miles away in Hagerstown. The railroad ran there, but the poor black families in the valley could hardly afford to buy train tickets for their children to ride back and forth each day.

Indeed, no black student from Pleasant Valley is known to have gone to the high school in Hagerstown until almost fifty years later. That was when stonemason Robert Anderson's grandson, Alvin Harris, bought an old school bus for this purpose. Harris's support of education, like his grandfather's, is legend. Local historian John Frye, who grew up in Pleasant Valley, remembered seeing the bus full of black students drive past when he was a boy. Another valley resident, Judy Wolf, remembered the bus as well. Isabel Johnson recalled that when a snowstorm hit the valley one winter's afternoon and prevented Harris from returning his charges to their own houses, he took them to his for the night. Harris's widow, Mary Gross, naturally remembered it.[16]

Despite these difficulties, Emma Turner was bound and determined to get a high school education. She had aunts in Hagerstown and might have boarded with them if she were to go there. She chose instead Storer preparatory school in Harpers Ferry. She was fifteen years old when she started in 1890.[17] Emma boarded at the school, as did most of her classmates. While it was closer to the Turner farm than Hagerstown, Harpers Ferry was still too far to commute on a daily basis. The Turner farm was five miles from Harpers Ferry, a two-hour walk. Former resident Isabel Johnson said that when her mother was a girl, growing up on the side of Elk Ridge in the early 1900s, she would sometimes walk to Harpers Ferry in the mornings to get groceries for her family, return home, and then go to school at nearby Mt. Moriah. Her mother got so tired of this that she dropped out of school in the seventh grade.

The black school at Harpers Ferry got its start immediately after the Civil War, when Rev. N. C. Brackett, a New England Baptist, opened a primary school there. The sixteen teachers Brackett had at the beginning were overwhelmed when 2,500 students showed up, but at least it was a start. Besides, the townspeople of Harpers Ferry welcomed anything that would help them rebuild after a war that had seen the town shelled, burned, occupied, pillaged and change hands seven times.

Yarrow-Turner Selected Family Tree

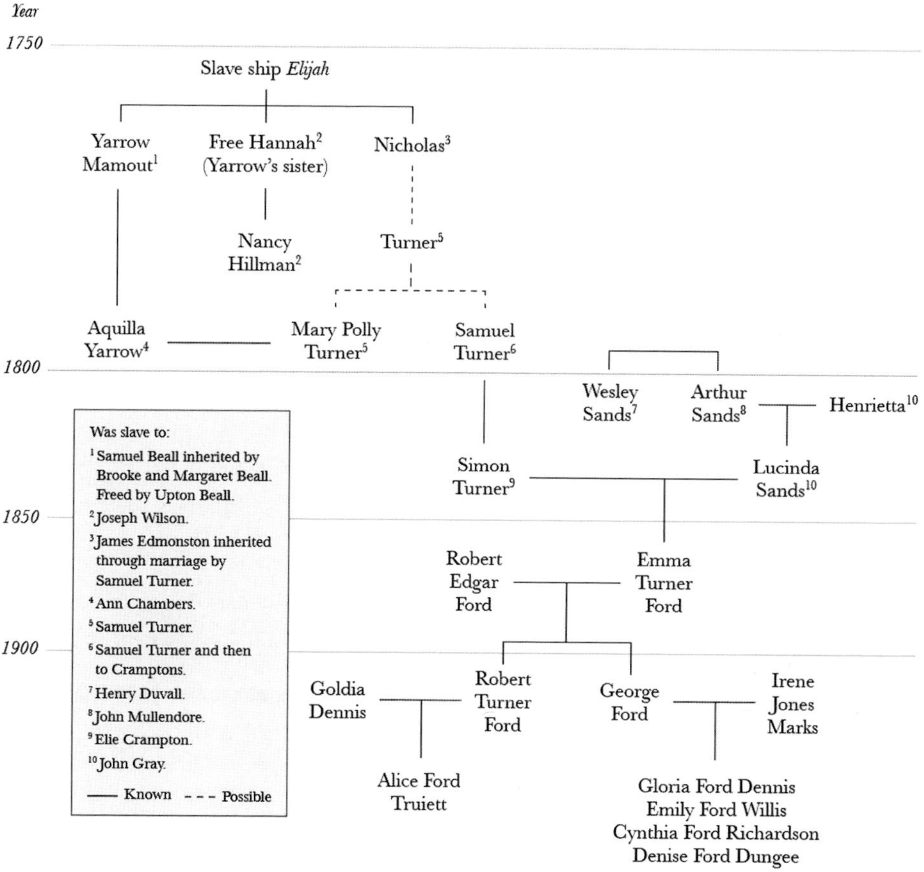

Yarrow and Turner family tree. Graphics by Serrin Ransom.

Ayuba Suleiman Diallo (Job ben Solomon), by William Hoare. 1733. Oil on canvas. On loan to the National Portrait Gallery, London; Property of Qatar Museums Authority (OM.762). Orientalist Museum, Doha.

Yarrow Mamout, by Charles Willson Peale. 1819. Oil on canvas. Philadelphia Museum of Art.

Bostwick, the home of slave trader Christopher Lowndes, in Bladensburg, Maryland, built in 1748. Photograph by the author.

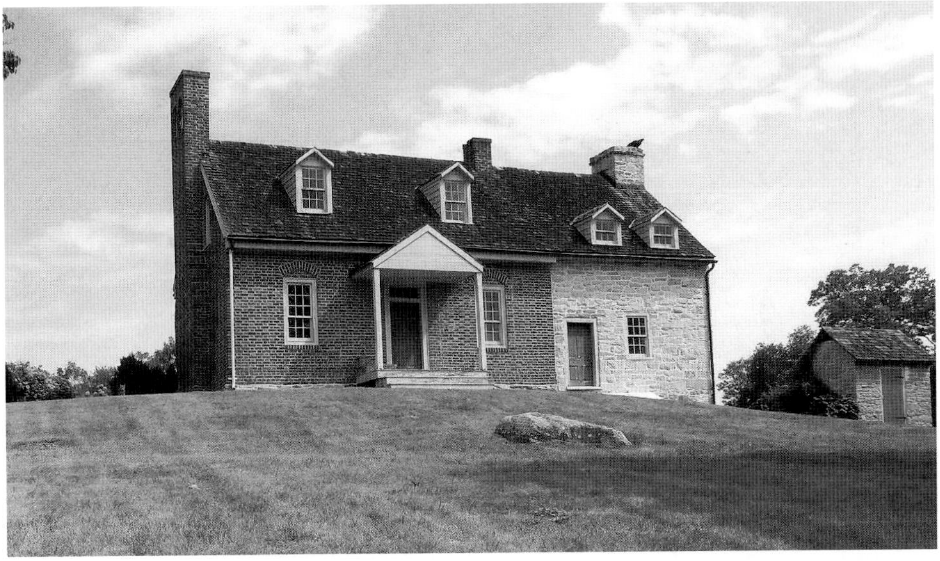

Kelly's Purchase, Samuel Beall's home in Washington County, Maryland. The brick portion is the original house, built in 1770. Beall's will mentioned that "my boy Jarro," his body servant, was living here at Beall's death in 1777. Photograph by the author.

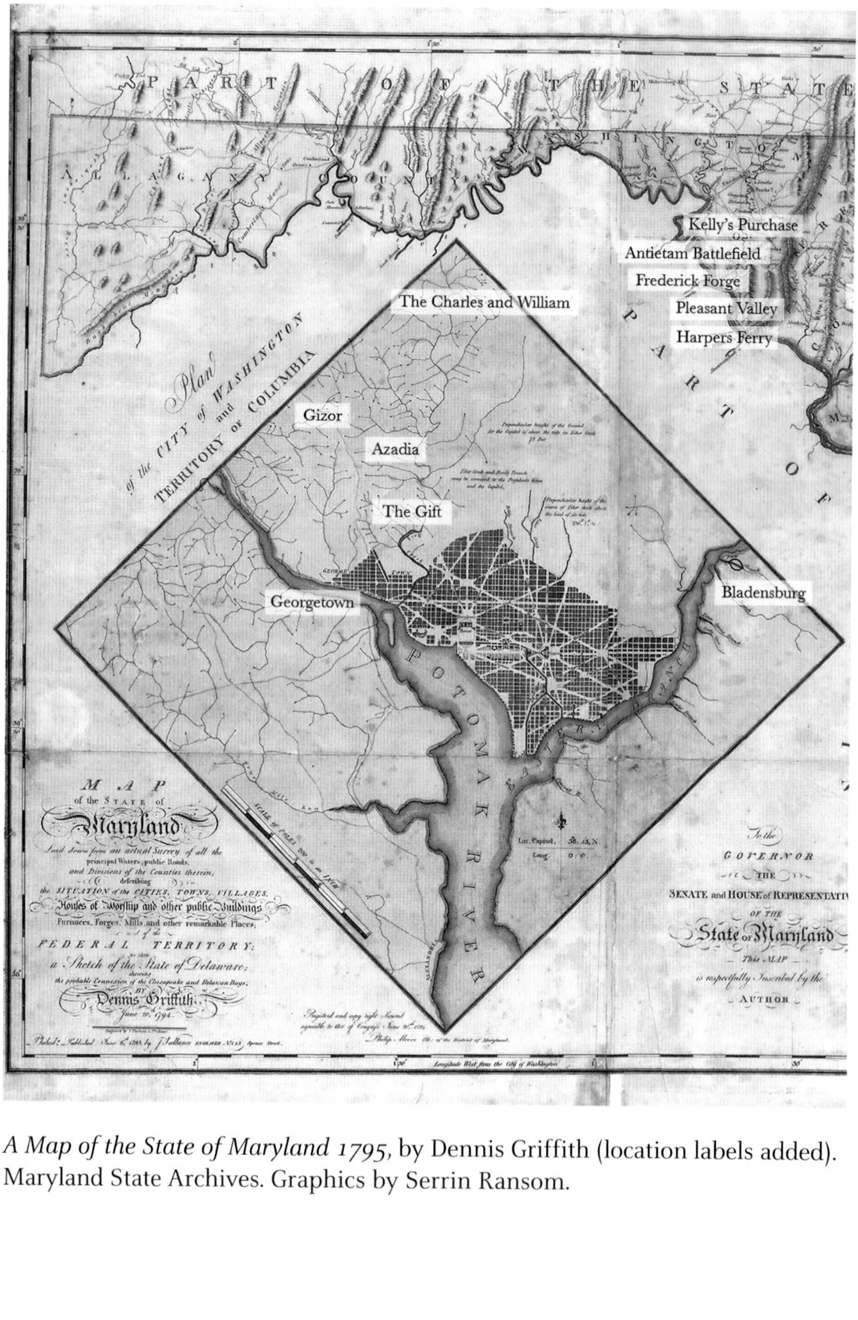

A Map of the State of Maryland 1795, by Dennis Griffith (location labels added). Maryland State Archives. Graphics by Serrin Ransom.

rederick
Rockville
Beallmount
Bladensburg
Georgetown
Annapolis
OF PENNSYLVANIA
NEW JERSEY
DELAWARE BAY
BALTIMORE COUNTY
HARFORD COUNTY
CECIL COUNTY
NEW CASTLE COUNTY
KENT COUNTY
QUEEN ANNS COUNTY
TALBOT COUNTY
DORCHESTER COUNTY
SUSSEX COUNTY
WORCESTER COUNTY
SOMERSET COUNTY
ANN ARUNDEL COUNTY
PRINCE GEORGES COUNTY
CHARLES COUNTY
KENT I.
POKOMOKE BAY
ATLANTIC OCEAN
EXPLANATION
SCALE of MILES 69½ to a DEGREE
East Longitude
North Latitude

Upton Beall, who signed Yarrow's manumission in Maryland. His grandfather Samuel and father, Brooke, had owned Yarrow. Sally Somervell Mackall, *Early Days of Washington* (1899), 65.

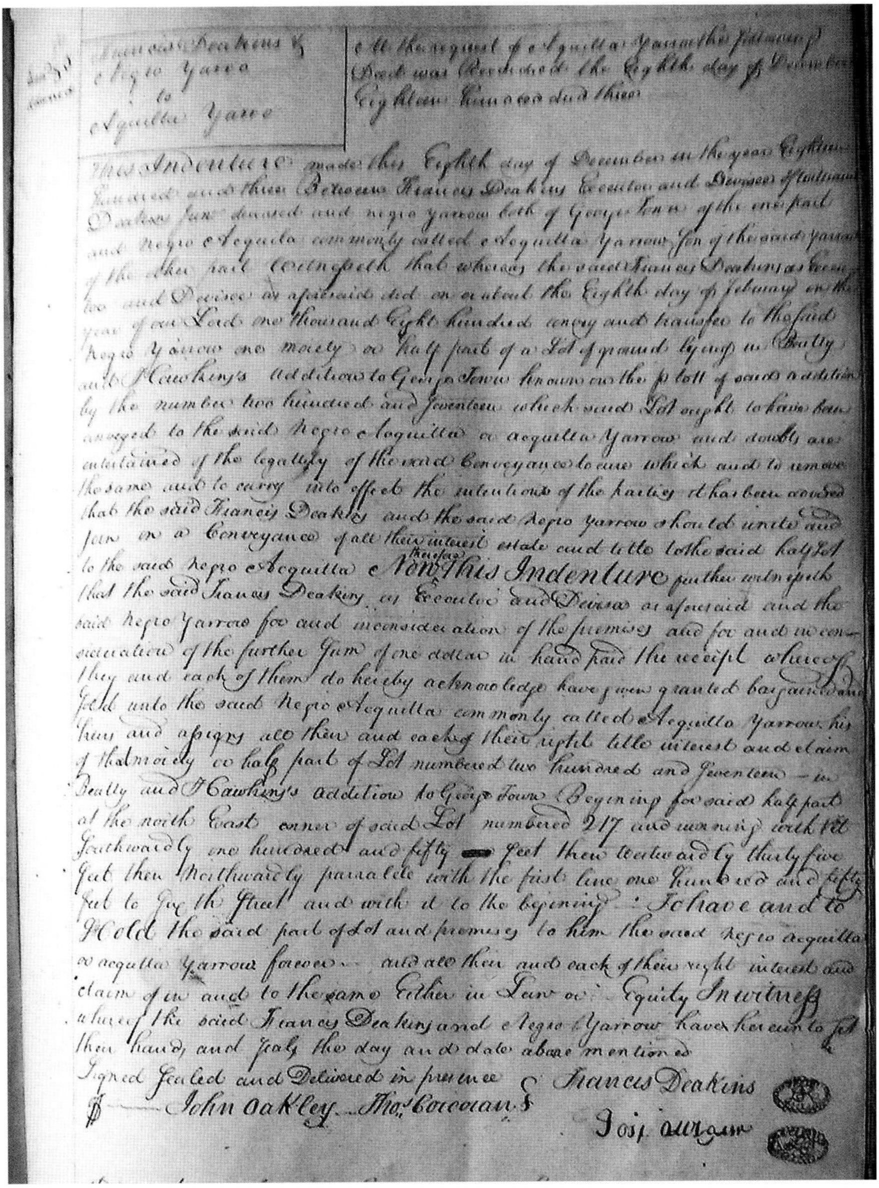
Francis Deakins &
Negro Yarro
to
Aquilla Yarro

At the request of Aquilla Yarro the following Deed was Recorded the Eighth day of December Eighteen hundred and three

This Indenture made this Eighth day of December in the year Eighteen hundred and three Between Francis Deakins Executor and Devisee of William Deakins Jun' deceased and negro Yarrow both of George Town of the one part and Negro Aquila commonly called Aquilla Yarrow Son of the said Yarrow of the other part Witnesseth that whereas the said Francis Deakins as Executor and Devisee as aforesaid did on or about the Eighth day of February in the year of our Lord one thousand Eight hundred convey and transfer to the said Negro Yarrow one moiety or half part of a Lot of ground lying in Beatty and Hawkins's Addition to George Town known on the plott of said addition by the number two hundred and seventeen which said Lot ought to have been conveyed to the said Negro Aquilla or Aquilla Yarrow and doubts are entertained of the legality of the said Conveyance to him which and to remove the same and to carry into effect the intentions of the parties it has been agreed that the said Francis Deakins and the said Negro Yarrow should unite and join in a Conveyance of all their interest estate and title to the said half Lot to the said Negro Aquilla Now this Indenture further witnesseth that the said Francis Deakins as Executor and Devisee as aforesaid and the said Negro Yarrow for and in consideration of the premises and for and in consideration of the further sum of one dollar in hand paid the receipt whereof they and each of them do hereby acknowledge have given granted bargained and sold unto the said Negro Aquilla commonly called Aquilla Yarrow his heirs and assigns all their and each of their right title interest and claim of that moiety or half part of Lot numbered two hundred and seventeen in Beatty and Hawkins's Addition to George Town Beginning for said half part at the north East corner of said Lot numbered 217 and running with [illegible] Southwardly one hundred and fifty feet then Westwardly thirty five feet then Northwardly parallel with the first line one hundred and fifty feet to Gay th Street and with it to the beginning To have and to Hold the said part of Lot and premises to him the said Negro Aquilla or Aquilla Yarrow forever and all their and each of their right interest and claim of in and to the same Either in Law or Equity In witness whereof the said Francis Deakins and Negro Yarrow have hereunto set their hands and seals the day and date above mentioned

Signed Sealed and Delivered in presence
of — John Oakley. Thos. Corcoran.

Francis Deakins

Yarrow's signature in Arabic. In 1803, Yarrow deeded his house in Georgetown to his son, Aquilla. This is the Recorder of Deeds' copy. National Archives and Records Administration.

The Artist at His Museum, by Charles Willson Peale. 1822. Oil on canvas. Joseph Harrison Jr. Collection, Pennsylvania Academy of Fine Arts, Philadelphia. Gift of Mrs. Sarah Harrison.

Portrait of Elizabeth Tasker Lowndes, Widow of Christopher Lowndes, by Charles Willson Peale. 1790. Oil on canvas. Collection of the Washington County Museum of Fine Arts; Gift of Edward Bowie Prentiss, Catharine Watkins Prentiss Plummer, and M. G. Louis Watkins Prentiss Jr. in memory of their mother, Helen Bowie Prentiss, 2007.

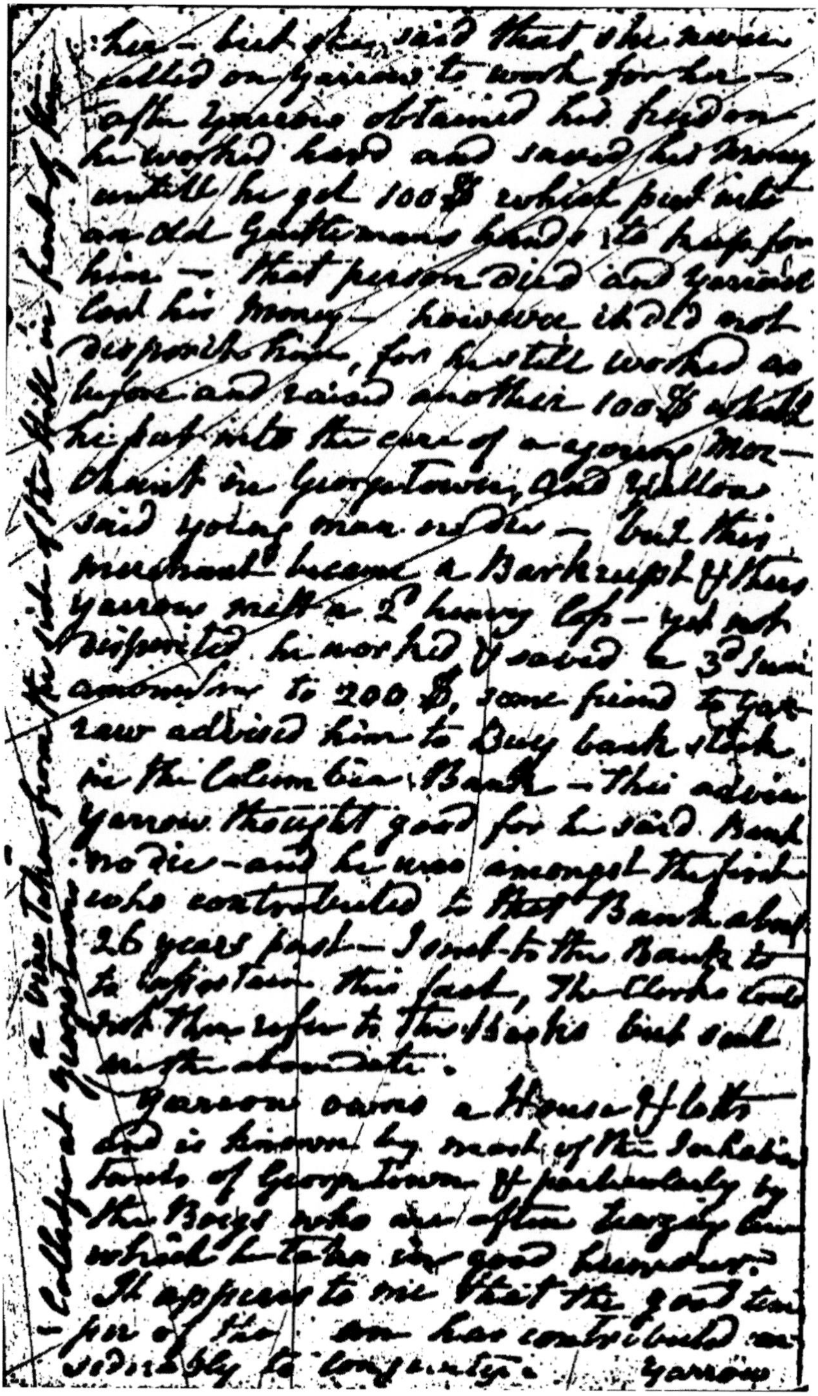
her — but she said that she never
called on Yarrow to work for her —
after Yarrow obtained his freedom
he worked hard and saved his money
untill he got 100$ which put into
an old Gentleman's hands to keep for
him — that person died and Yarrow
lost his money — however it did not
dispirit him, for he still worked as
before and raised another 100$ which
he put into the care of a young Merchant in Georgetown, and Yarrow
said young man as [illegible] — but this
merchant became a Bankrupt & thus
Yarrow met a 2d heavy loss — yet not
dispirited he worked & saved a 3d sum
amounting to 200 $, some friend to Yar-
row advised him to Buy bank stock
in the Columbia Bank — this advice
Yarrow thought good for he said Bank
no die — and he was amongst the first
who contributed to that Bank about
26 years past — I went to the Bank to
to ascertain this fact, the Clerks could
not then refer to the Books but said
[illegible] the [illegible] date.
Yarrow owns a House & lots
and is known by most of the Inhabitants of Georgetown & particularly by
the Boys who are often teazing him
which he takes in good humour.
It appears to me that the good tem-
per of this man has contributed considerably to longevity. Yarrow

Page from Charles Willson Peale's handwritten diary, recording the first day of his painting Yarrow's portrait. Original with American Philosophical Society.

Yarrow Mamout, by James Alexander Simpson. 1822. Oil on canvas. Peabody Room, Georgetown Branch, Washington, D.C., Public Library.

Hungerford's Tavern. Montgomery County Historical Society, Rockville, Maryland.

St. John's Catholic Cemetery, Frederick, Maryland. Unmarked graves in the African American cemetery around the Hillman marker in the foreground. Chief Justice Roger Taney's grave is beyond the tombstones above the obelisk in the foreground. Photograph by the author.

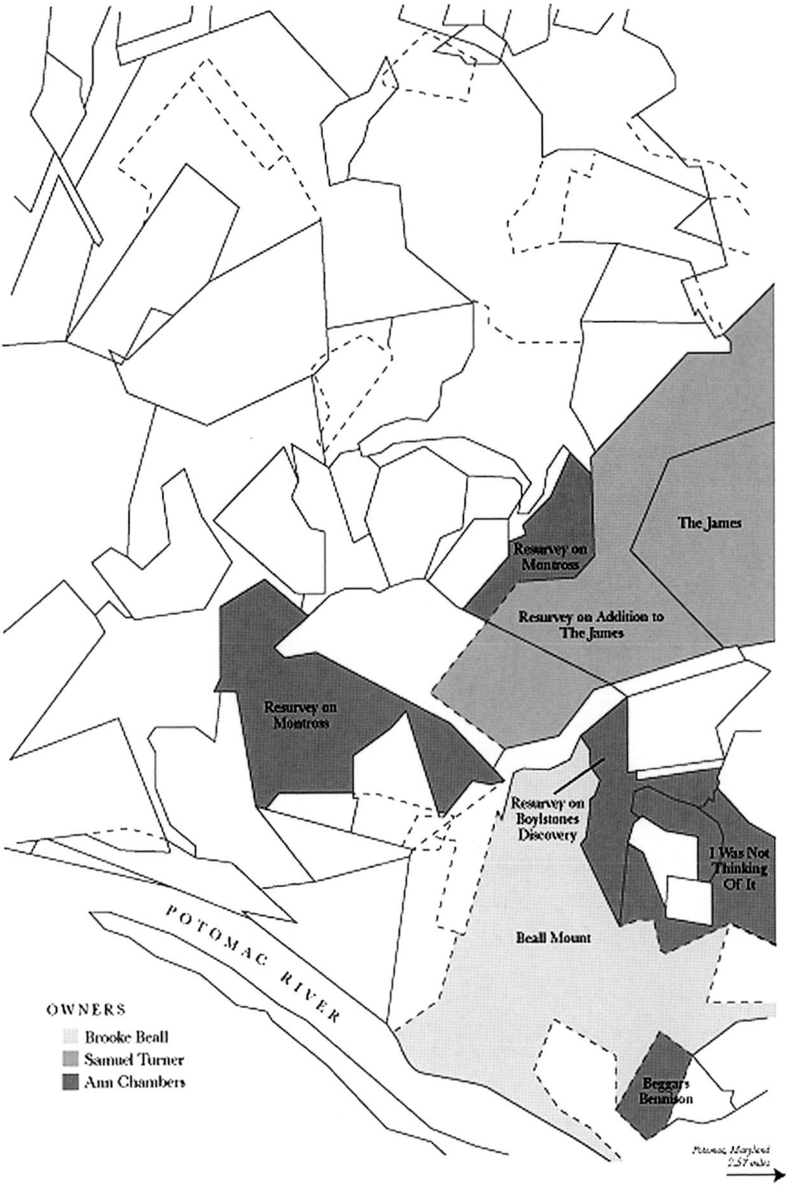

The Beall, Chambers, and Turner farms in Montgomery County, Maryland. Graphics by Serrin Ransom, based on original map by Sheila Cochran for the Montgomery County Historical Society.

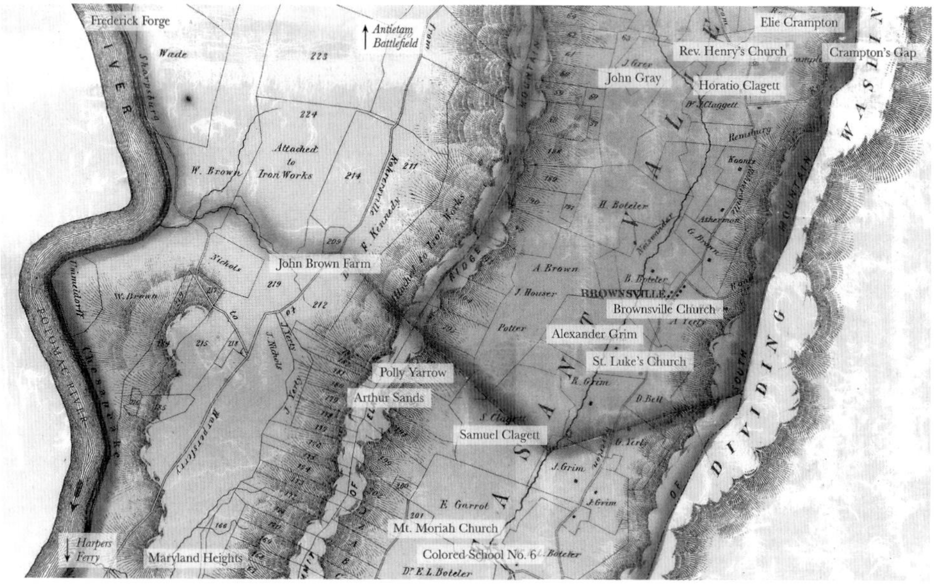

Pleasant Valley, from Thomas Taggart's *Map of Washington County, Maryland,* 1859 (location labels added). Geography and Map Division, Library of Congress. Graphics by Serrin Ransom.

Yarrowsburg Mennonite Church, 2005. Photograph by the author.

Springhouse, Elie Crampton farm in Pleasant Valley, believed to be the slave quarters where the Turner family lived. Photograph by the author.

Thirty-ninth Regiment, U.S.C.T., September 1864, the only known photograph of the unit. The tall, slender soldier in center background could be Simon Turner, although the photograph was taken after Turner had been injured at the Battle of the Crater. Prints and Photographs Division, Library of Congress.

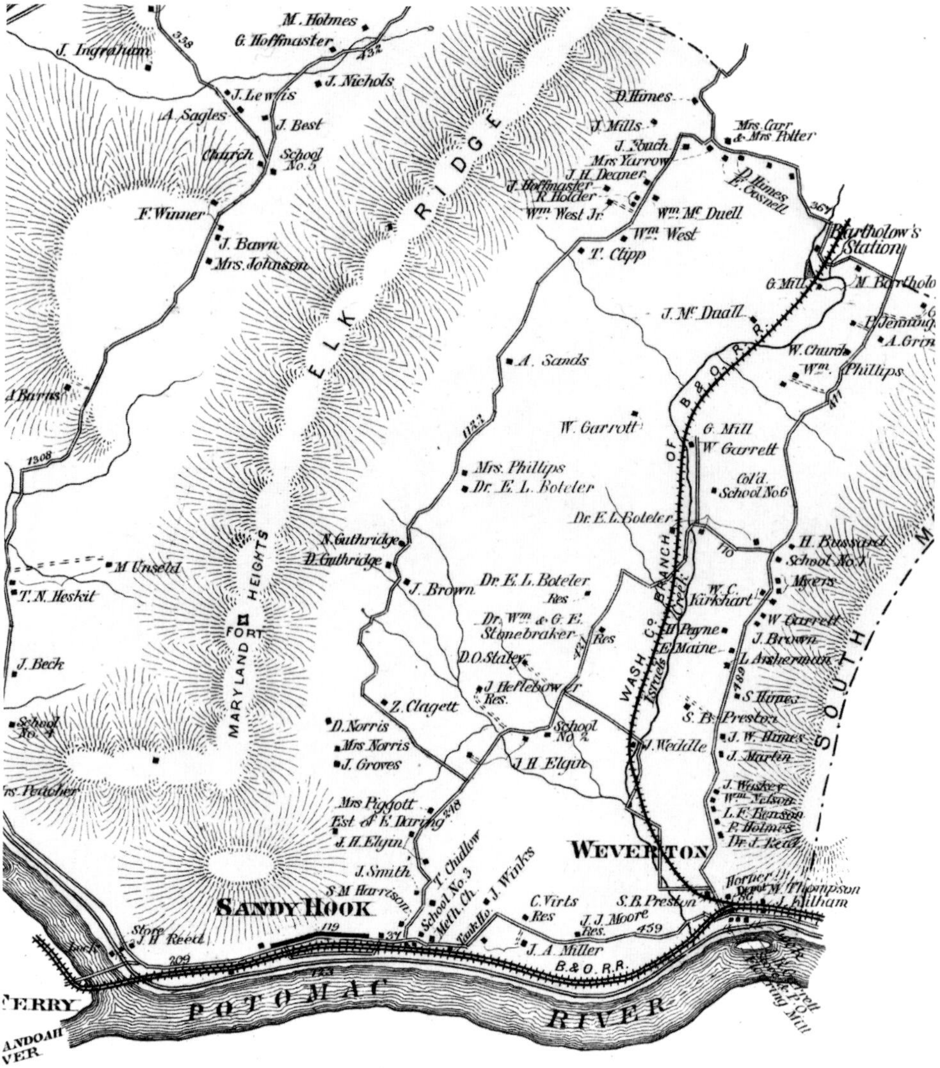

1877 map of Washington County by Lake Griffing and Stevenson, marking Mrs. Yarrow's house, Arthur Sands, and Colored School No. 6. From the Sheridan Libraries of The Johns Hopkins University.

Emma Turner Ford.

Robert Turner Ford.

(*Left to right*) Alice Truiett, Denise Dungee, the author, Cynthia Richardson, Emily Willis, and Gloria Dennis. A framed photograph of Emma Turner, the women's grandmother, is on the table.

Grave of Simon Turner in the Mt. Moriah Church Cemetery in Pleasant Valley, Maryland. The inscription reads, "He fought to save the Union." Photograph by the author.

In 1867, New England philanthropist John Storer became involved. He contributed $10,000 to add a normal school at Harpers Ferry to train black teachers. This became Storer College, and the Storer name was applied to both the preparatory school and the teachers college.[18] Howard College in Washington was another such college established for black students after the war. Indeed, this was how most of the "black colleges" were started.

Since Storer combined a high school with a teachers college, Emma stayed there long enough to get both her high school diploma and a teaching degree. College graduation must have been a heady experience for her, the daughter of former slaves, and an even headier one for her parents. So much had happened in such a short time. Simon and Lucinda were slaves in Pleasant Valley with two children when John Brown rented the Kennedy Farm just over Elk Ridge, raided Harpers Ferry, and called for a slave rebellion. Life for black people in the valley had been extremely tense in those days. The Maryland legislature had ended manumissions. Lucinda's father, Arthur Sands, had rushed to buy her freedom before the law took effect. Simon and Lucinda had seen the huge Union and Confederate armies pass through on the way to the deadly clash at Antietam in 1862. The Emancipation Proclamation had been issued. Simon himself had marched off to war and come home disabled. Yet here, in Harpers Ferry, less than forty years after John Brown's raid, their daughter was graduating from college up the hill from the firehouse where Brown was captured.

Trying to Get a Pension

While Simon was surely pleased with his daughter's accomplishments, life was not easy for him. He never felt fully recovered from his war injuries. In 1884, he applied for a disability pension. A doctor examined him to rule on his claim and concluded that the wounds had healed and that Simon was not disabled. The doctor wrote that although Simon said a bullet had passed through his upper arm, there was no evidence of this upon examination twenty years later. Likewise, the doctor found no visible marks to his side from the shell explosion.

Of course, it was his kidney that had been damaged, and the doctor could not see it. Simon was unsatisfied. A few years later, in 1887, he paid an attorney $10 to prosecute the pension claim. A second medical examination reached the same conclusion. The doctor's report said Simon was 5′11½″ tall, 186 pounds, and in good physical condition. The claim was eventually allowed, however.[19]

With Emma's departure for Storer in 1890, Simon and Lucinda's nest was nearly empty. According to the census that year, Emma's grandfather Arthur Sands was still alive and living on the farm with the Turners, but the only child left at home was her sister Martha, who was handicapped.

Simon and Lucinda's living descendants are great-granddaughters who did not know them. Still, they debate among themselves how well father-in-law Arthur Sands got along with son-in-law Simon Turner. Arthur always seemed to be putting up the money. He owned the farm and was trustee for the school; Simon lived on Arthur's farm under Arthur's roof. It was Arthur who had the money to buy Lucinda's freedom, not her husband Simon, who was still a slave. Thus, some of the great-granddaughters speculate that Arthur felt Simon was a drag. Others insist Simon was the brains in the family and behind all the clever decisions.[20] Whatever the truth may be, Arthur sold twenty acres of his farm to his grandson James, skipping over Simon.[21]

In one last community effort, Arthur Sands joined three other men as trustees to purchase land for Mt. Moriah Baptist Church in 1893. R. H. Boteler sold them the land.[22] He was a descendant of Dr. Henry Boteler, who had grown up on the Magnolia Plantation and was related by marriage to Charles Willson Peale. Of course, it is doubtful that any of these people in 1893 knew of the connection between Peale, Yarrow Mamout, and Polly Yarrow. Sands died a short time later. He may be buried in the church cemetery; if so, his grave is unmarked.

At first, the church building at Mt. Moriah consisted only of the covered basement that Robert Anderson had built; nevertheless, the colored school was moved there. Later, a proper church building was erected over the basement, and the classes moved upstairs. Isabel Johnson went to school there and remembers it was much drier upstairs in the church than it had been in the basement. The State of Maryland eventually paid for construction of a real school building next to the church.[23] This was the first school building for blacks in Pleasant Valley that the state had paid for. The building was still in use when the Supreme Court ordered all schools desegregated in its decision in *Brown v. Topeka Board of Education* in 1954. Soon thereafter, the colored school was closed forever. The building now serves the church as a community center.

In 1899, Simon Turner died from an infection resulting from an injury to his arm, not his old war wound.[24] He is buried in the cemetery at Mt. Moriah. Lucinda applied for a pension as the widow of a Civil War veteran. The government again seemed reluctant to pay and dragged its feet. The file on the case is now at the National Archives in Washington. The matter was assigned to an investigator who was given two questions. First, the Civil War muster rolls listed Simon as Samuel, and the Pension Bureau wanted an explanation of the discrepancy. This seemed to irritate the investigator as much as it did Lucinda, for he wrote in his report, "the question as to identity was evidently settled when soldier's claim was allowed, and it appears rather late in the day to raise that question in the absence of adverse testimony on that point."[25]

The second question was more problematic. Lucinda needed to prove she and Simon were married. There were two obstacles. One was that Maryland did not issue marriage licenses to anyone, black or white, in 1855 when Simon and Lucinda got married; the only records were those that churches might have kept. The other obstacle was that even if the state had kept records, slave marriages were not recognized. The investigator spent most of his time finding witnesses to vouch for Lucinda's claim that the Turners were married. Lucinda herself told the investigator:

> I was married at Brownsville, Washington Co Md May 14 1855 by Rev. Daniel Brown, a Dunkard Preacher who is dead. The witnesses as shown by my certificate of marriage in my Bible, were Absalom Brown, who died last spring, and Arthur Sands my father, who died eight years ago. (Bible containing record entries which appear to be genuine was published in 1883). I do not know of a person now living

who was present when we were married except Lucy Brown, Absalom Brown's widow, but she is so very old now her memory is all gave out she cannot remember dates. My husband and I were both slaves at the time. My husband belonged to Eli Crampton, and I belonged to Mr. John Gray. Both of our masters in slavery are dead, as are all the old people. A daughter of Eli Crampton lives in Hagerstown Md. She is as old as I am. Her name is Mrs. Jane Emmert, wife of Benjamin Emmert. . . . Being slaves, we did not get any license. Our masters gave us a written permit to get married and we got married on that permit. The preacher kept that permit. I reckon I never saw it again. I can refer you to Mr. John Hufflebower and his wife as to my being Simon Turner's wife, for they have known me all my life. . . . He enlisted in Frederick, Md. They were coming around drafting men, and he said he wanted not to be drafted so he went and enlisted. I did not see my husband from the time he enlisted until he came home. . . . I only know one man in this locality who was in the army with my husband. His name is Branson Mathews, he is blind. He lives across the valley from here in the mountain. Ezra P. Bush is dead and James K. Edemy lives on Bethel Street in Hagerstown Md with his daughter. There are a lot of my husband's comrades who live in Pennsylvania but I do not know where.[26]

The investigator met with Elie Crampton's daughter, and she said that Simon and Lucinda had been married. Fortunately, someone at the Pension Bureau had the common sense to issue a general ruling that widows of black Maryland veterans only needed to prove they cohabited with the veteran as husband and wife in order to be entitled to a pension. The investigator duly included the ruling in Simon's file together with affidavits from those who could attest to the fact.[27]

Lucinda was living in abject poverty. She told the pension examiner:

My tax receipt for 1898 shows that I am taxed on 50 acres of land valued at $200 and on 12 acres of land valued at $120 and on livestock valued at $50 and furniture and other property valued at $30. Also on $400 worth of improvements on land. In all $800 the tax being $7.02

> (Showing tax receipt to Examiner). . . . I have no money in bank and no income other than that which I get off the place which is not enough to keep me as if it were not for what my daughter in Washington [Hattie] does for me I could not get along. I did not get anything off the place this year to speak of, nothing to sell, and what I raised in the way of corn will hardly keep my old horse 23 years old. I have an invalid daughter living at home with me. She cannot do much to help. I will be present during the taking of the testimony in this immediate neighborhood.[28]

The examiner also took an affidavit from two neighbors, James Huffmaster and Thomas Spencer. The men said they had known Simon and Lucinda for more than thirty years and always regarded them as man and wife. Although Lucinda was only sixty-three years old, they added: "Lucinda Turner is old and feeble, and is not capable of making her living by manual labor, and cannot work the land, and can not afford to hire it worked; therefore her condition is a dependent one, and her support must depend largely upon charity."[29]

The examiner did his own inspection of Lucinda's house and land and described it in his report: "I went all over her place. The house and barn are in splendid condition, cleanly and well kept. The fields and wooded land, however clearly shows the lack of proper care, and attention, and is overgrown with bushes and brambles. What is said relative to the value and condition of the place [by others], ditto her income is borne out by the appearance of the place." He concluded by noting: "Every witness in this case excepting Jackson and Edemy, who have given testimony before me are white people and among the best citizens of Washington Co Md."[30]

Lucinda ultimately received the Civil War pension due her, but it was too little and certainly too late. The process had taken over a year. Only her handicapped daughter Martha was still living with her in the cabin on the mountain. Then the cabin burned down. Lucinda and Martha moved to Funktown, Maryland, near Hagerstown, where Lucinda died in 1903.[31]

Emma Turner had graduated from Storer College before her parents' deaths, so both Simon and Lucinda had the satisfaction of seeing their daughter graduate from college. She was the first in the Turner and Sands families and the only one of Simon and Lucinda's children known to have a college degree.

So few African Americans were in college at the time that they had trouble finding other college-educated blacks with whom to socialize. For this reason, Storer and Howard Colleges arranged weekend get-togethers where men from Howard would take the train from Washington to Harpers Ferry for dances and picnics. Black entrepreneur Thomas Lovett even built the Hilltop House hotel on the bluff overlooking the town of Harpers Ferry to serve visitors to Storer. It was at one of these get-togethers that Emma met Robert Ford, a theology student from Howard.[32] The couple was married in 1897. The stage was set for the next generation of the family to make a dramatic leap up the educational ladder.

15 From Harvard to Today

Judging by the photograph of her, you would never think that Emma Turner Ford was the daughter of slaves. She looks like any other middle-class woman of her day. Nor would you think she held such passionate beliefs about the inherent value of education, ones handed down through the family. These beliefs had served her in good stead in the one-room Colored School No. 6 in Pleasant Valley and then at the boarding school at Storer when she was only fifteen, and she was ultimately rewarded by seeing her son graduate from Harvard and five granddaughters earn college degrees.

Robert Turner Ford

The original intent of setting up black colleges such as Storer was to train black teachers, who would staff the elementary and secondary schools the Freedmen's Bureau had set up, and so Emma, first in the family to graduate from college, planned to devote herself to teaching others. This proved to be not as easy for her as she expected.[1] Her husband Robert had chosen to be a minister in the African Methodist Episcopal Church (A.M.E.), and she followed him. The church rotated young clergy from town to town almost every year, and the couple was constantly on the move.[2] Emma found that she was never in one place long enough to get her feet on the ground and teach.

The first of the Fords' six children, Robert Turner Ford, was born in 1905, eight years after the couple had married.[3] Having children did not stop the church transfers though. The family lived in Elkton, Berkley, and Conowingo, three small Maryland towns between Baltimore and the Pennsylvania border, and in Cecilton on the Eastern Shore.[4] Emma had five more children in the next nine years. She was forty-two years old when her last child was born.[5]

One of the rotations took the family to Hagerstown, and then to Pleasant Valley. In the words of Robert Turner Ford, in an interview years later by niece Cynthia Richardson, the family moved "to Mother's childhood home in Pleasant Valley."[6] Robert dated this to "before the outbreak of World War I."

In the Footsteps of Ancestors

Rev. Ford was pastor of the A.M.E. church near Knoxville, at the southern end of Pleasant Valley. Robert called it by an old name, "Weaverton Station," a stop on the rail line. Robert was walking in the footsteps of his ancestors in Weverton. His father's denomination, the A.M.E. Church, was an outgrowth of the Free African Society, started by Richard Allen and Absalom Jones in Philadelphia in 1787.[7] Charles Willson Peale's son, Rembrandt, had painted Absalom Jones's portrait in 1810, a work that was undoubtedly a factor in Peale's decision to paint Yarrow Mamout.

The Weverton church, as well as several others in Western Maryland, had been founded by Rev. Thomas Henry,[8] who had had the run-in with Constable Barnes in Pleasant Valley in 1835. Elie Crampton helped Henry out of the scrape, and Crampton owned Robert Turner Ford's grandfather, Simon Turner. If this were not enough personal history, in setting up the church in Weverton, Henry was helped by the prominent white landowner, Caspar Weaver, who had given his name to the community (albeit the spelling changed with time) and had been a neighbor of Ford's great-great-uncle Wesley Sands.[9] Of course, it is doubtful that either Robert Turner Ford or his father, the pastor, knew of all these family connections to the place.

The house the Fords were living in near Weverton burned down one winter, and the family had to move in with Emma's brother, whom Robert referred to as "Uncle Jim."[10]

Robert recalled that he attended one-room schoolhouses in the towns of Berkley and Conowingo. He said he went to school in Weverton, but since he did not say it was one-room, he presumably did not go Colored School No. 6 or the one-room school at Mt. Moriah. Both of those places are several miles from Weverton.

Frederick Douglass High School in Baltimore

After more than a decade of church rotations, Rev. Ford was finally rewarded with an assignment to Baltimore. He and Emma would live there the rest of their lives. Rev. Ford took over the Oak Street A.M.E. church. The family picked out a home on Druid Hill in Baltimore. It must have seemed the lap of luxury compared to all the places they had been living.

Robert had always been precocious, and he found urban Baltimore stimulating. Even though he been educated in small, rural schools, he was advanced enough in learning that the Baltimore schools let him skip three terms. At the time, the city's segregated school system had only one high school, Frederick Douglass, for its large African American population. Naturally, Robert went there. In his spare time, he participated in a science club that met in the students' houses, taught Sunday school, and worked in a grocery store.[11]

Carrington Lewis Davis, vice principal of Douglass and Robert's Latin teacher, recognized his student's academic talents and became his role model. Davis had graduated from Harvard University in 1904 and urged his gifted young protégé to apply there. Years later, in a speech at a Harvard reunion, Robert, with tongue in cheek, described his mentor: "Urbane, moderately scholarly, this man walked and talked in a manner that made him unique among his fellows. He never forgot that he was a Harvard man, nor, I am sorry to say, did he permit others to forget it."[12]

Harvard

Harvard was not a pioneer among New England colleges in the admission of African Americans. Colleges like Middlebury, Amherst, Bowdoin, and Dartmouth were. They were admitting black students in the

1820s when Yarrow Mamout was still alive and when slavery was at its full force in the southern United States.[13]

Harvard first tried to break the color barrier in 1850 by admitting three African Americans to its medical school. However, when white students objected, Harvard ended the experiment by expelling the three at the end of the first semester.[14] It was not until after the Civil War, in 1870, that an African American, Richard Greener of Massachusetts, graduated from Harvard. He distinguished himself by winning the Boylston Prize for oratory.[15] Yet despite such a successful outcome for its second experiment, the university continued a leisurely pace with black admissions.

In 1890, Harvard graduated two stellar black students: Clement Garnett Morgan and William Edward Burghardt (W. E. B.) Du Bois. Morgan had been born a slave in Virginia in 1859.[16] He too won the Boylston Prize for oratory. Du Bois, who went on to be a leader in the fight for civil rights, finished second in oratory, but he was chosen to deliver a commencement speech.[17]

Nonetheless, African Americans did not become regular attendees at Harvard graduations until 1899. Since then, only three graduations have had no black students. Robert Ford's mentor, Carrington Davis, was in the 1904 class.[18] Frederick Douglass's grandson graduated the next year. In 1908, Alain L. Locke graduated and became the first African American to be named a Rhodes Scholar. Indeed, Locke was the only African American to be so honored until the 1960s.[19]

With Carrington Davis filling his head with legends of these black achievements, Robert Turner Ford from Frederick Douglass High School in Baltimore, grandson of slave and Civil War veteran Simon Turner, applied for admission to Harvard for fall 1923. In his reunion speech, Robert looked back on his decision to apply. The voices of his great-grandfather Arthur Sands and his mother, Emma Turner Ford, can be heard in his views about education.

> In my youth I was attracted to Harvard because of what I believed an education at the oldest and most prestigious of American colleges could do in ensuring me a life of success and distinction. In the black segment of the segregated society in which I was born and bred there

> was an almost idologist faith in education as a means of obtaining social worth and economic freedom, a faith characterized by an inordinate emphasis upon the external and visible evidences of academic distinction. College graduates were rare in that society, and the possession of a diploma of any kind identified one as being a member of an elite group entitled to leadership and respect. A graduate of Harvard with all of its traditions and history, with all of its overwhelming roll of illustrious sons, and its numerous entries in "Who's Who in America," was viewed as the epitome of academic and social merit.

Racism and Anti-Semitism at Harvard

As Ford was soon to learn, he was viewing Harvard through rose-colored glasses in his high school days. The ivy-covered, ivory tower was going through its "Dormitory Crisis" the year before he entered, and it would leave him with a different perspective.

Harvard President Abbott Lawrence Lowell triggered it with the announcement in 1922 that incoming African Americans would not be allowed to live in the freshman dormitories. He compounded his mistake by imposing quotas on the admission of Jewish students. Lowell lamely suggested that these were not his own ideas; rather he was just caving into the racism and anti-Semitism that already existed at the university. In a famous letter to Roscoe Conkling Bruce, an African American alumnus of Harvard, Lowell explained: "We owe to the colored man the same opportunities for education that we do to the white man; but we do not owe it to him to force him and the white into social relations that are not, or may not be, mutually congenial." As for the quota, Lowell again suggested these were not his views but rather those of the men of Harvard. He was quoted in *Literary Digest* to say: "Anti-Semitic feeling is increasing, and it grows in proportion to the increase in the number of Jews."[20]

Of course, Robert Ford was not as naïve as his earlier remarks may suggest. In the same reunion speech, he went on to say:

> I'm certainly aware that there were young men who were literally born to be Harvard men, who were enrolled at birth or soon after for future

> matriculation. They grew up surrounded by Harvard parents and Harvard uncles and Harvard grandparents, and their coming to Cambridge was always a foregone conclusion. In my immediate community, Harvard men were a rarity.

Ford's saying Harvard men were a "rarity" in his community was a very careful choice of words. He was referring to his mentor, Carrington Davis, as perhaps the only Harvard man in his community. The true facts were that Ford's grandparents had been illiterate and that they and at least three of his uncles had been slaves.

Harvard President Lowell's discriminatory edicts did not stand. To many Harvard students and alumni, both black and white, Lowell seemed to be raising the very issues that the Civil War was supposed to have settled. Raymond Wolters captured the feeling in his essay covering the crisis, "The New Negro on Campus," in the compilation *Blacks at Harvard*:

> Du Bois was uplifted by the protest. "Deep as is the shame and humiliation of Harvard's recent surrender to the Bourbon South," he declared, "the spirited and whole-souled response that it has evinced is perhaps the most heartening sign of sanity on the race problem that has happened in fifty years. Not a single person of importance has yet dared to defend Lowell. . . ." Black and white liberals were convinced that Lowell had taken an "evil and indefensible position which, like a snake, must be scotched at once . . . or else it will, with its venomous bite, poison our entire educational system." Lowell's racist policy was thought to be as "bad as for what it portends as for what it immediately inaugurates."[21]

In January 1923, the Harvard board of overseers appointed a faculty committee to study Lowell's new policies. Later, based on the committee's recommendation that the university adhere to the principle of "equal opportunity for all regardless of race and religion," the overseers did their duty: They overruled Lowell and banned racial and religious discrimination at Harvard.[22]

This was the atmosphere at Harvard when Robert Turner Ford entered in the fall of 1923. Perhaps the turmoil was why in hindsight he did not see it as the "great Camelot on the Charles," which is how he characterized the view of mentor Davis. In his reunion speech, Ford continued:

> Camelot from within is never so enchanting as it appears when viewed from afar. Harvard afforded no secure harbor from what one experienced as evil and disturbing in the world from which I had come. I found that race and poverty were still the substantial barriers from the free enjoyment of college living, and that in reality the Harvard experience by a poor black lad differed greatly from that known to many other students. There were only 6 Negro members in the Class of 1927 [his], and of that number only one could afford to live in the [Harvard] Yard.

Robert certainly could not afford Harvard Yard. A minister's son did not have that kind of money. In fact, some of Emma's granddaughters say that one of her laments in life was that her husband chose the ministry, a calling that was not as remunerative as his talents might have commanded elsewhere. But the Turner family's historical commitment to education proved to be a different kind of wealth, and it came to Robert's aid. To help her nephew, "Aunt Hattie," Emma's older sister Elizabeth Turner Roach, pulled up stakes in New York City and moved to Cambridge. She found a minister there who needed a housekeeper. In exchange, she and nephew Robert got lodging.[23]

Yet, as Robert discovered, it was one thing for a poor black kid from Baltimore to get admitted to Harvard; it was another thing for him to be accepted socially. He told the reunion audience:

> Membership for blacks in many clubs and societies was not even thought of, and socialization with other students such as those met in classes was quite limited. This was, of course, before the institution of the house system provided framework for a modicum of close relationships. And the pursuit of membership in the elite group of [educated]

> men could be quite costly, even traumatically so, if one adds the [burdens of] keeping up with academic work while earning one's board and keep, [often] by some menial task, skrimping [*sic*] to meet term bills and [en]during the [loss] and deprivation of the normal social activities enjoyed by many of the students.[24]

Harvard in the 1920s was indeed a school of high privilege that paid no more than lip service to notions of diversity. It was a place where men from the South could openly object to sitting down to eat with African Americans and where their complaints about Jewish admissions would be echoed by the president. This was before the stock market crash in 1929 wiped out many a father's fortune, before the Great Depression threw even Harvard alumni out of work, before Harvard men were drafted for World War II, before a GI bill after the war paid for poor men to attend Harvard if they were veterans, and before the civil rights movement. Thus, while Robert's white classmates sailed off for tours of Europe in the summers, he worked as a Red Cap at Grand Central Station in New York City.[25]

Graduation and Reinvestment in Education

In 1927, Robert Turner Ford completed his studies and graduated. Commencement ceremonies in Harvard Yard must have been an extraordinarily emotional occasion for Emma Ford, mother of one of only six black graduates that year. Thirty some years earlier, she herself had been the first person in her family to graduate from college. At that graduation at Storer College in Harpers Ferry, she had stood in the shadow of John Brown. Both her parents had been slaves. Now here she was, seeing her son graduate from the most prestigious university in the county.

It was the dream come true of being rewarded for achievement and not punished for race. It was not just Emma's dream though. It was the dream of all those who had gone before. Like the dream of Hattie Roach, who had put her own life on hold to work as a housekeeper so that her nephew would have a place to live in Cambridge. Like the dream of Arthur Sands, who help start Colored School No. 6 in Pleasant Valley. Like the dream of Simon Turner, who had charged into the breach at the Battle of the Crater. Like the dream of the American Colonization Society and Horatio Clagett and Elie Crampton that blacks should be treated as human beings. Like the dream of Abraham Lincoln that African Americans should be free. Like Peale's dream of painting an accomplished black man. And, like the dream of Yarrow Mamout: "Must work again—worky, worky, get more dollar. . . . Oh Yaro—dollar breed now—every spring—every fall, Yaro get dollar—chichen now." Yarrow had come to America as a slave 175 years earlier, but in one sense, it was not that long before. Emma Turner Ford, who was sitting in Harvard Yard that day for the graduation, knew Yarrow's daughter-in-law, Polly Turner Yarrow. She and Polly lived a half-mile apart in Pleasant Valley until Polly died when Emma was ten.

With graduation ceremonies and celebrations at Harvard over, Robert Turner Ford packed his bags and returned to Baltimore. He followed the family ambition and reinvested his education in the education of the black community of Baltimore. He went back home and took a teaching job at his alma mater, Frederick Douglass High School, working alongside his mentor Carrington Davis. Having majored in the classics at Harvard, Ford taught Latin and German, among other things.[26] There were now two Harvard men at Douglass.

Robert Turner Ford Goes to War

Ford married Goldia Dennis, who gave them a daughter, Alice.[27] In 1941, when the United States entered World War II, Ford was thirty-six years old. He was too old to be drafted. However, like his grandfather Simon Turner, he enlisted. The army assigned him to the military police and promoted him to sergeant. He worked in educational units at Fort Lee, New Jersey, and Fort Leonard Wood, Missouri.

On occasion, Ford drew special duty. German prisoners of war were being sent to prison camps in the United States. Most of these men had been crews captured on the high seas from German submarines the Allies had destroyed. Ford was assigned to guard them and escort them on trains to the prison camps. Since he was fluent in German and a military policeman, he was a logical choice. But the military authorities also must have taken pleasure from the fact that the "master race" was welcomed to America by a black man serving as their guard, escort, and interpreter.

After the war, Ford returned home to Baltimore and Frederick Douglass High School. When Congress passed the GI Bill, which paid for college for veterans, he decided he wanted a master's degree. The closest university was the University of Maryland in College Park. But the school was still segregated even after World War II. Therefore, as Ford said later, he was able to enjoy the "picnic" of attending Columbia University in New York. His mother Emma, the daughter of slaves, died in 1957. She had lived long enough to see her son graduate from two Ivy League schools.[28]

Ford retired from teaching in 1973, but he did not retire from education. He went back to school and earned a degree in theology. It was the career that, he felt in hindsight, he should have chosen all along. But rather than following in his father's footsteps in the African Methodist Episcopal Church, Ford became Episcopalian. He died in 1984.

The Family Today

Ford's younger brother, George, stayed in Baltimore. He married and had four daughters: Gloria Ford Dennis, Emily Ford Willis, Cynthia Ford Richardson, and Denise Ford Dungee. He worked three jobs most of his life—postman, insurance agent, and printer—to put the four girls through college. In the 1960s, George Ford became active in the civil rights movement and encouraged his daughters to help.

Robert Ford's daughter, Alice Ford Truiett, and George's four daughters all live in Baltimore today. The five women have five bachelors' and three masters' degrees among them. The family sold off the mountain property in Pleasant Valley in 1984. When they get together, the five women debate the wisdom of their family's doing that. They also still debate whether they are related to Nat Turner of Southampton, Virginia, and lament that they did not ask their parents and grandparents, especially grandmother Emma, more questions about family history.

It was this generation that saw the last remnants of slavery begin to disappear. It was the slavery that had started more than three hundred years earlier on the tobacco plantations of Maryland and Virginia. In 1954, the Supreme Court ruled in *Brown v. Topeka Board of Education* that separate, segregated schools did not provide African Americans with the equal education to which they were entitled under the Constitution. As a result, all-black schools, such as Colored School No. 6 in Pleasant Valley and Storer College in Harpers Ferry, were closed, and segregation at the University of Maryland was ended. The civil rights laws and the civil rights movement came later. The United States was at last practicing the principles of equality that it had long preached.

Reflections at a Cemetery

Mt. Moriah Baptist Church is on Garretts Mill Road in Pleasant Valley. In the southwest corner of the cemetery is the grave of Simon Turner. The faded inscription on his tombstone reads, "He fought to save the Union." Next to him is the grave of his daughter, Hattie Roach. She had dropped everything to take a job as housekeeper to a minister in Cambridge to help put his grandson through Harvard. Mt. Moriah Church itself was built by stonemason Robert Anderson, cofounder of old Colored School No. 6. Anderson, too, had passed on to his descendants his belief in the importance of education. As Isabel Johnson said about his grandson: "I remember well how he pushed about education. It certainly ran in that family."

The cemetery at Mt. Moriah is hallowed ground. Harpers Ferry is just a few miles away, on the other side of Maryland Heights. That is where John Brown lit the spark for Civil War. That is where five hundred runaway slaves were captured by Confederate soldiers and marched back to their owners in Virginia. A few miles to the north is where the Battle of Antietam took place. It was the single bloodiest day in the Civil War, and indeed of any act of war in the United States.

Union victory there cleared the way for the Emancipation Proclamation. Antietam is also where Samuel Beall's Frederick Forge was and where Yarrow Mamout spent time.

Closer to the church is the community of Yarrowsburg, named for Polly, Yarrow Mamout's daughter-in-law. The church itself is on land that once belonged to the Botelers, one of whom married the granddaughter of Charles Willson Peale. The circle of this story is closed.

If you have imagination enough, you can see from this hallowed ground at Mt. Moriah all the way to Yarrow's home of Futa Jallon in West Africa. If you have imagination enough, you can see the slave ship *Elijah* bobbing at anchor in the Severn River at Annapolis. If you have imagination enough, you can see Harvard Yard in Cambridge, where Robert Turner Ford graduated. The Yarrows and Turners did not just have the imagination, though. They made the journey.

Epilogue: Guide to the Yarrows' and Turners' World Today

Many of the tangible things mentioned in this book—the art, the structures, and the documents—are still around. Each has its own story. Some are recognized in the context of traditional American history—that is to say, white history—but not considered part of black history. Most have never been connected to Yarrow, and certainly not to the other African Americans mentioned here. Anyone can visit the public sites, such as the parks and churches, but most of the houses are privately owned. The following twenty-nine items are arranged alphabetically within five geographic areas: Prince George's County, Washington (including Georgetown), Rockville, Washington County, and other places.

Prince George's County, Maryland

Benjamin Tasker Middle School, Bowie

Benjamin Tasker Jr. partnered with Christopher Lowndes in the slaving voyage of the *Elijah.* Tasker's father was acting governor of the colony at the time. This was probably why Lowndes brought the son in as a partner on the slaving voyage, although Lowndes also happened to be married to the junior Tasker's sister. The Benjamin Tasker Middle School is named for Benjamin Tasker Sr., the colonial governor. Maryland's tribute to the father of a slave trader seems insensitive in contemporary times, since the school is predominantly African American. Nonetheless, the insensitivity itself may be a lesson.

Bostwick House, Bladensburg

Bladensburg, Maryland, is located across the Anacostia River about five miles from the Capitol in Washington, D.C. It was the first permanent town in the area and is where Bostwick is. Slave trader and merchant Christopher Lowndes built Bostwick a few hundred yards from the old port. He also built the Port Masters house in Bladensburg. Both houses are still standing and are owned by the City of Bladensburg. The old port is now a park. Despite being surrounded by residential and industrial areas, the bucolic setting gives a sense for how the land and river might have looked to Beall, Ross, Lowndes, and other early settlers of the town although the flow of the now-polluted river is significantly reduced from what it was before the planters came.

Washington, D.C.

Forrest-Marbury House

Charles Willson Peale's in-laws lived in Georgetown. They were Joseph Brewer, who was the nephew of Peale's first wife, Rachel, and William Marbury, who was married to Rachel's niece. Marbury had purchased the Georgetown home of George Washington's friend Uriah Forrest. The house overlooked Analostan Island and the waterfront. It was a block downhill from where Forrest's friend Benjamin Stoddert lived. William Marbury's son, John, also lived in this house. He was supposed to protect Yarrow's loan on a warehouse in Georgetown. He failed to this, but Yarrow's niece Nancy Hillman collected on it.

During his three months in Washington, Peale stayed at a hotel and visited William Marbury on several occasions before his sessions with Yarrow. Marbury's bitter and famous lawsuit against President Thomas Jefferson over a trivial commission as a justice of the peace was a thing of the past. Marbury was extremely wealthy, and Peale elected to paint Yarrow to be like Marbury. But Peale knew Yarrow was not in Marbury's league. Indeed, not many people were in that league, which Peale described in his diary:

> We went to a Tea party at Coll. Marbury where there was about 3 Dozs. Ladies and not quite so many gentle-men—they danced Cotillion and country dances by the music of a Piana, which was distinctly heard as the company danced on Carpets. The intertainment was sumptous & Ellegant. Coll. Marbury is wealthy and can make such entertainments with perhaps (with) less expence than many others, having an abundance of fruit from his farms also Eggs, and his notable wife has the cakes made at home, however with the best economy such entertainments are very expensive, and the example too often followed by those whose circumstances are not in condition to bear the cost. With weak minds, fashion has too fascinating charms.[1]

The Forrest-Marbury House is now the Embassy of Ukraine. It is located just east of the Francis Scott Key Bridge on M Street in Georgetown. Ukraine has restored it to look as it did when Marbury owned it. A photograph of John Marbury is in the house. The embassy is not open to the public except by invitation on special occasions.

William Marbury's portrait, which is attributed to Peale's son Rembrandt, hangs in the Justices' Dining Room in the Supreme Court.

James Alexander Simpson Portrait of Yarrow Mamout

James Alexander Simpson's oil-on-canvas portrait of Yarrow Mamout belongs to the Peabody Room of the Georgetown branch of the District of Columbia public library. The date 1822 appears on the back. A fire in the library in 2007 resulted in water damage to the painting, but it has been completely restored.

A circuitous chain of custody suggests Simpson did the work on commission from Brooke and Margaret Beall's daughter, Christiana. She was wife of Benjamin Mackall. The key to reaching this conclusion is the library's note card for the provenance of the painting. It reads: "Yarrah or Yarrow. Oil Portrait painted by Simpson. Loan from Mrs. Hugh (Talcott) Barclay."

The chain of custody began with Christiana. Brooke and Margaret supposedly gave her and her sister each a large lot in Georgetown. Christiana's was known as "Mackall Square." Sally Somervell Mackall, writing in 1899 in her book *The Early Days of Washington,* described the property:

> [A] double square on Georgetown Heights; to Benjamin Mackall's wife [Christina Beall], part of the Rock of Dumbarton, known as Mackall Square, where quite a large frame house was built, where the family resided in winter. One hundred years ago this building was removed to another portion of the Beall estate on Congress street, where it still stands. . . . In its place on Mackall Square was built a handsome brick house of Colonial architecture, with large halls, and great square rooms on either side, lighted by four windows, situated on a high eminence overlooking the city of Washington, which spreads like a broad panorama to view. The Potomac flows just below [a half mile away] and in the sunlight appears like a great silver sheet, bordered on either side by the blue hills. In the distance the evening sun rests upon the dome of the new Congressional Library.[2]

Mackall Square was still in the family when *The Early Days of Washington* was published. The book included not only photographs of the two houses mentioned—they are still there today—but also family heirlooms which may or may not have been at Mackall Square, such as the "old Beall chair," the "Beall sword," a cane of William Whann, the "turban of Mrs. David Whann," and a miniature painting of Upton Beall. The portrait of Yarrow was not among the heirlooms photographed, but it was still in the house.

Not long after the book was published, the family moved out of Mackall Square, and the property was rented out, still furnished. In 1911, Herman Hollerith bought it.[3] Hollerith was the inventor of the tabulating machine and founder of one of several companies that were later merged into what became known as International Business Machines. He had another house built on the property and hired a designer from Wanamaker Department Store in Philadelphia to decorate it. (He chose Wanamaker because it was one of the first companies to use Hollerith's tabulating machines.)[4]

Hollerith was married to Lucia Beverly Talcott. The Talcotts lived at the Normanstone estate in Washington, D.C., built by Lucia's maternal grandfather Robert Barnard. In 1919 the British government acquired Normanstone and built its embassy on the site. The embassy is next to the Naval Observatory and the vice president's residence on Massachusetts Avenue in Washington.

In her 1931 book, *A Portrait of Old Georgetown,* Grace Dunlop Ecker after writing about Yarrow, noted that his portrait "is now owned by Mr. E.M. Talcott, who inherited it from Normanstone."[5] Thus, it appears that the portrait was still at Mackall Square when Hollerith bought the property and that at this time he transferred the painting to his in-law, Edmund Myers Talcott. Mrs. Hugh (Talcott) Barclay, who loaned the painting to the Peabody Room, was Mr. Talcott's daughter.[6]

In sum, Christiana Mackall commissioned Simpson to paint Yarrow Mamout, who had been her father's slave. The painting was handed down to later generations living at Mackall Square. When Hollerith bought the property in 1911, the painting was still there, and so Hollerith must have given it to his wife's family, the Talcotts of Normanstone. It was handed down through two generations of Talcotts before being given to the Peabody Room. The painting is on public view there.

Pierce Mill

The industrious Samuel Beall owned several water mills and other properties along Rock Creek. These included The Gift, Azadia, Gizer, and The Mill Seat. These properties extended from present day Tenleytown east into Rock Creek and north and south along Rock Creek. The Gift was located where the present Pierce Mill is in Rock Creek.

The stone mill there today is the one Pierce built, but Samuel Beall's mill probably was in the same location. Pierce had workmen's quarters opposite the mill on the east side of Rock Creek. They are gone today, but their location is shown on a marker at the site.

A survey of the tract when Beall owned it showed a mill, houses, and slave quarters. Yarrow Mamout may have lived in the slave quarters when he first came to America. Although the location of the slave quarters cannot be determined, they likely were in the same place where Pierce had workmen's quarters, that is, opposite the mill on the east side of the creek. The Pierce Mill site is in the National Park Service's Rock Creek Park and open to the public.[7]

Yarrow Mamout's House

Yarrow's house was in the Beatty and Hawkin's Addition to Georgetown on what is now Dent Place. The old Presbyterian Church, where the Reverend Bloomer Balch was pastor, was a few blocks south. The church is now a private residence. The graveyard of the church extended almost to Yarrow's backyard. The graves have since been relocated, and the graveyard has been paved over for the Georgetown Playground on Volta Place. There are markers to that effect at the playground. Yarrow's house is north of this. It was on the east half of his lot with a creek on the west half.

Tax assessment records indicate Yarrow's house was wood frame. There is an old, two-story frame townhouse on the lot today, but it does not appear to be the original house. The owner believes the house was moved there in the nineteenth century and that square nails are used in the construction.[8]

The present house sits on a brick cellar. While an expert has not inspected the house, photographs of the bricks were sent to William Kelso, an archaeologist, who opined that they looked handmade. If so, he said, they would date to before 1850, when making bricks by machine became common. Therefore, he speculated, the bricks date to the original house.[9] This raises the possibility that Yarrow made the bricks for his house, or that he used the bricks he had made for his late owner's house. If that house was on Mackall Square, Yarrow would have needed to move them less than half a mile. The cellar is small and probably would not have required more than a few wagonloads of bricks.

Yarrow's obituary said that he was buried in the yard where he went to pray. Assuming Yarrow faced toward Mecca and knew where it was, he was buried in the southeast corner of the lot. A swimming pool is in the backyard today, but the southeast corner is undisturbed, so Yarrow's remains may still be there. The house is private property and is not open to the public.

Yarrow's Signature, National Archives

In 1803, Yarrow arranged to put his house in the name of his son, Aquilla. Since Aquilla was only fifteen years old, Yarrow may have been attempting to prevent his creditors from seizing the house for the debts he owed them. The National Archives has the original record book from the office of the Recorder of Deeds for the District of Columbia.

The process for recording a deed in the United States is unchanged from Yarrow's day although the technology is different. Today, the Recorder of Deeds will scan the deed, put a digital image into a computer database, and may print a paper copy. In 1803, the Recorder of Deeds manually copied what was written on the original. It was supposed to be an exact copy. The Recorder of Deeds was in effect a human copying machine; he copied the mistakes and misspellings in the original.[10]

The 1803 deed on Yarrow's property is quite legible despite being more than two hundred years old. That is, it is quite legible except for one thing: Yarrow signature. The signature is not an "X," which Yarrow would have used if he were illiterate. And the signature certainly does not say "Yarrow Mamout." A photograph of the signature was emailed to Kevin Smullin Brown, an Arabic scholar in London. Brown was told that this was the Recorder of Deeds' copy of a signature by Yarrow Mamout. He opined that the original signature was a combination of English and Arabic. He thought the first word, which appears to be "Josi," was probably a copy of Yarrow's attempt to write "Jaro." The second word appears to consist of distorted Arabic characters and may read something like *Mamadou, daluh,* or *Bismillah,* with the last translating to "In the name of God." A devout Muslim might add Bismillah to his signature on an important document.

Rockville, Maryland

Beall-Dawson House

Upton Beall was the son of Yarrow's former owners, Brooke and Margaret, and signed Yarrow's manumission papers. Upton finished this all-brick home in Rockville 1814. Yarrow had made the bricks for his owner's Georgetown house nineteen years earlier, but he was seventy-eight years old when Upton's house was completed and surely too old to have made the bricks for it. However, his son, Aquilla, might have learned the skill from his father and done the work.

The Montgomery County Historical Society owns the Beall-Dawson House. It is open to the public. The Historical Society's library is in the wood frame building on the property.

Hungerford's Tavern

Hungerford's Tavern is generally thought to be the same as the old "Russell House" in Rockville that was occupied by Susan Russell. She was a descendant of Joseph Wilson, the man who owned Yarrow's sister. Although the Russell House was razed and replaced by an office building at the northwest corner of West Jefferson and South Washington Streets, photographs of it exist, and there is a plaque marking the site on the side of the present building.

The Russell House was a two-story frame house. Writing in a 1958 article, county history researcher Martha Sprigg Poole believed the structure clearly dated to before the Revolutionary War: "The man who razed the old house said that the logs of which it was built were 'chinked and dobed.' The wood was hand-hewed, mortised and put together with hand-made-nails. The chimney and dormers further identify it as being pre-Revolutionary and the huge fireplace with a pothook in it and the dirt floor of the back room further testify to its great age."[11]

Yarrow's sister may have worked in the tavern. If so, she and Yarrow could have gotten together frequently. His owner, Brooke Beall, was the clerk of the court near the tavern.

Josiah Henson, whose autobiography inspired the novel *Uncle Tom's Cabin*, was a slave in the Rockville area at this same time. He wrote of accompanying his owner while he spent weekends drinking and carousing with other young men of the county. Thus, Henson, too, may have spent time at Hungerford's Tavern and gotten to know Yarrow's sister.

Yarrow Drive

Joseph Wilson's will was written in 1790 and mentioned a slave named Yarrow living on the Two Brothers tract. This Yarrow must have been another male slave from Futa Jallon. Two Brothers was later acquired by the King family and remained a farm until the 1990s, when it was turned into a mixed-use development called King Farm. The name Yarrow Drive was given to a block-long street that dead-ends into a watercourse in the development.

The developer chose the street names in King Farm. The engineer responsible for the streets could not remember specifically how she came up with the name for this particular street. She said, however, she tried to name the streets for things related to the farm, such as its dairy business. She felt the name Yarrow Drive came from something she saw on the land or from one of the documents on the property. She might even have seen the name in Joseph Wilson's will.[12]

Washington County, Maryland

Alexander Grim House

Alexander Grim sold Aquilla Yarrow 1.25 acres of land in 1825. Grim's house is still there near Brownsville in Pleasant Valley. The house stayed in the Grim family until 1931. Because Grim's daughter married an Edwards, it is also called the Edwards house. Alexander Grim himself sometimes referred to the property by an early name, "King Cole."[13] The house is privately owned and not open to the public.

Antietam Iron Works (Frederick Forge)

In 1764, Samuel Beall, Dr. David Ross, Joseph Chapline, and Richard Henderson bought Frederick Forge from John Semple. The forge was located at the mouth of Antietam Creek in Washington County, Maryland. It was later called Antietam Iron Works. The National Park Service owns parts of the forge, which lie within the Chesapeake and Ohio Canal National Park. Thus, two of Samuel Beall's properties, The Gift

(Pierce Mill) and Frederick Forge (Antietam Iron Works), are in national parks.

The brick main house, lime kilns, and several outbuildings of the iron works are in private ownership, but other parts of the rambling facility fall within the boundaries of the Chesapeake and Ohio Canal, which the National Park Service controls and which is open to the public. A cemetery south of the main iron works site has graves marked with field stones, which some believe to be an indication they are slave graves although they could be of free blacks or poor Irish workmen.[14]

Clagett Houses

Two old houses along Rohrersville Road north of Brownsville are associated with the Clagett family. They are both at the intersections of Rohrersville and Gapland Roads. The Maryland Historical Trust identifies the one on the southeast corner as the "Claggett Farm." The farm includes the family cemetery. The other, which is on the northeast corner, is believed to be that of Dr. Horatio Clagett.[15] Rev. Henry wrote in his autobiography that he stayed with Dr. Clagett whenever he visited Brownsville. The houses are privately owned and not open to the public.

Elie Crampton's Descendant

Elie Crampton owned the slave Simon Turner. One of Elie's daughters, Mollie, was a teacher. She married John Otto, whose family owned a house damaged in the fighting at Burnside Bridge during the Battle of Antietam. Her descendant Charles Gardenhour has Mollie's autograph book with the signature of Elie Crampton, several of her letters, and a lock of her flaming red hair.

Elie Crampton House

Elie Crampton was a justice of the peace. He signed as witness on the deed from Grim to Aquilla Yarrow. He was the "Squire Crampton" in

Rev. Henry's story and rebuffed Constable Barn's attempt to stop a black church service. The Crampton family name has a place in Civil War history in the Battle of Crampton's Gap, which took place on South Mountain above the farm.

The original Crampton house is still around. The oldest part dates from the late eighteenth century. Part of the farm fell within the Keep Triest holdings of John Semple. The springhouse on the farm dates to around 1813 and has living space on the second floor. The current owner said the springhouse is believed to have once been the slave quarters. If so, this was where the Turners lived. Elie Crampton died in 1863. Daniel Mullendore purchased the property in 1868, and it has been in his family ever since. The house is on Townsend Road in Pleasant Valley.[16] It is privately owned and not open to the public.

John Gray House

John Gray owned Lucinda Sands and her children. His house is still there at the intersection of Yarrowsburg and Rohrersville Roads.[17] The house is privately owned and is not open to the public.

The current owner's parents bought the property from Gray's descendants in 1945. The house had remained in the Gray family until then. The owner said her parents tore down the slave quarters next to the house because the walls had rotted and the roof collapsed. Someone bought the foundation stones and hauled them away, but a few still dot the yard. The owner remembered a visit around 1970 by Lillian Gray, who had grown up in the house. The owner said her own father was from Yarrowsburg and went to St. Luke's Episcopal Church.

About twenty years ago, a bulldozer operating on the property uncovered the ruins of an old mill on Israel Creek. This would have been Bartholomew's Mill on Israel Creek. Treasure hunters have found bullets and equipment from the Civil War on the farm. The owner has a collection of these.[18]

Kennedy Farm

John Brown wanted a farm to use as a staging place for the raid he planned on Harpers Ferry, so in July 1859, he rented one from the estate of Robert F. Kennedy, a local doctor. It is located on Chestnut Grove Road just off Harpers Ferry Road and near Samples Manor. Brown packed twenty-four people, including two women, into the small two-story house. It had a tiny bedroom for the two women to share and an attic above it where the men slept. One advantage for Brown was that the house was back from the road and relatively secluded from curious eyes. However, Brown still made his men stay cooped up in the attic during the day in the summer to keep them out of sight.

When Brown lived on the farm, a road went over Elk Ridge through Solomon's Gap into Pleasant Valley. Polly Yarrow's house was just on the other side of the Gap, a mile and a half from the Kennedy Farm via this road. However, the only neighbor known to have been in contact with the raiders on the farm was a Mrs. Hoffmaster, who lived on the same side of the ridge as Brown did.

The Kennedy Farm is privately owned, but it was purchased for the purpose of preserving it. Tours of the restored house may be arranged.

Magnolia Plantation

Magnolia belonged to the Boteler family in Pleasant Valley. Dr. Henry Boteler grew up there. In 1814, he married Priscilla Robinson, daughter of Angelica Peale Robinson and granddaughter of Charles Willson Peale. After their marriage, the couple settled across the Potomac River in Shepherdstown, Virginia (now West Virginia).

Aquilla Yarrow's house was two miles from Magnolia as the crow flies. Thus, the artist's granddaughter and his sitter's son possibly ended up in the same tiny community in rural Maryland for a brief period, although they were probably not aware of their connection.

Henry and Priscilla Boteler had a son named Alexander. When Priscilla died, Alexander was sent to Baltimore and was raised by his maternal grandmother, Angelica Robinson, who was Charles Willson Peale's daughter. Boteler returned to Shepherdstown in 1835 and was eventually elected to Congress. Hearing that John Brown was in Harpers Ferry trying to start a slave rebellion, Boteler went there and talked to Brown after his capture.

Magnolia still stands, although it may not be the same house that Dr. Henry Boteler grew up in, since the house's nomination for the National Register of Historic Places dated it to circa 1835. The nominating papers also observed: "With somewhat more elaborate decorative detail in wood than is usually found in Washington County, Magnolia Plantation stands out as one of the finer houses of its period in the area. . . . The house shows mixing of stylistic influences from the late federal and early Greek Revival periods."[19]

The Boteler family cemetery is on the property. Although descendants sold the house and a part of the farm in 1853, the remainder of the plantation was still in the family in 1893, when they sold a parcel to Arthur Sands and several other men for Mt. Moriah Church.

Magnolia is south of Yarrowsburg on Valley Road in Pleasant Valley. It is privately owned and not open to the public.

Mt. Moriah Church and Cemetery

Arthur Sands and three other men acquired from Robert and Rebecca Boteler land for The Free Baptist Church of Pleasant Valley, later renamed Mt. Moriah.[20] A cellar was dug and finished by stonemason Robert Anderson, and church services were held there. Weekdays, the basement doubled as a school. As time went on, members of the congregation built a proper church over the cellar, and the classes were moved up there. Eventually, the state of Maryland funded construction of a one-room "colored school" on the property. That school was closed after the Supreme Court declared segregated schools unconstitutional, and the church acquired the school building.

The church cemetery contains the graves of Simon Turner, Hattie Roach, and Robert Anderson among others. Simon Turner was a veteran of the Civil War who served in the Thirty-Ninth Regiment, U.S.C.T. His tombstone reads, "He fought to save the Union." Hattie Roach was his daughter. She left New York City in 1923 and moved to Cambridge, Massachusetts, to work as a housekeeper for a minister there in exchange for room and board for herself and her nephew Robert Turner Ford while he attended Harvard University. Robert Anderson was a stonemason. In 1867, he had purchased land from John

Reed and later redeeded it to himself, Joseph Edemy, and Arthur Sands for the purpose of creating a school for the black families of Pleasant Valley.[21] It was later called Colored School No. 6 and located on Garrets Mill Road and Israel Creek. Classes were eventually moved to the church and then to their own building. Sunday services are still held in the church.

Polly Yarrow's Grave, Yarrowsburg

Yarrowsburg resident Bill Mullenix remembered being shown as a boy a stone marker said to be the grave of Polly Yarrow. It was north of Yarrowsburg Road near Israel Creek. Another resident, Robert Bowers, said there had been three markers in the area, and he was told they marked the graves of Polly Yarrow, her husband, and a boy. Bowers and I spent an hour searching through a bramble patch for the markers in August 2010 and found nothing. However, both Mullenix and Bowers described the markers as "field stones," which is how the graves of slaves and poor people were commonly marked. The purported site is on private land.

Samples Manor and Keep Triest

Before selling Frederick Forge, John Semple owned the land on both sides of the Potomac River. For this reason, an area on Harpers Ferry Road along the Maryland side of the Potomac River is still known as "Samples Manor." Semple called his property Keep Triest (also spelled Tryst). That phrase is on the Semple family crest and roughly translates as "always faithful." In Semple's day, Keep Triest referred to his large holdings on both sides of the Potomac, particularly his iron furnace on the West Virginia side north of Harpers Ferry. However, land on the Maryland side is also known as Keep Triest, and there is a Keep Tryst Road there.

Deeds from the early nineteenth century show the phrase Keep Triest was applied to an area in Maryland extending from the south end of Pleasant Valley to north of Yarrowsburg. Alexander Grim's farm, for example, was a part of Keep Triest.

St. Luke's Episcopal Church, Brownsville

The early settlers of Pleasant Valley were of English and German descent. The English settlers had generally come from the Maryland counties to the east and were Episcopalians. St. Luke's Episcopal Church in Brownsville served these families. It was built in 1839 on land purchased from Alexander Grim. The original congregation included Hezekiah Boteler, Emory Edwards, Dr. Horatio Clagett, Samuel Clagett, John Gray, and Caspar Weaver.

In September 1862, the church served as headquarters for Confederate General Lafayette McLaws during his occupation of the valley before the Antietam battle and as a Confederate field hospital. When Union forces took over, they burned the church. In a later remodeling, a wooden window arch singed in that burning was removed and is on display in the adjacent church hall. A visitor to the church in modern times came, he said, because he had a letter from an ancestor who was treated at the church during the Civil War and who wrote that severed limbs were stacked outside as high as the window sill.

The church is on Boteler Road in Brownsville. Alexander Grim is buried in the cemetery, as are Edwards, Grays, and Botelers. The construction of nearby Maryland State Highway 67 in the 1970s uncovered a number of unmarked graves that are believed to have been of slaves. The remains were reburied in the cemetery next to Alexander Grim's grave, and there is a marker to that effect. The church overlooks the Grim/Edwards house.[22] The small church still serves the Episcopal faith with regular services.

Yarrowsburg

Yarrowsburg is a collection of houses located at the intersection of Yarrowsburg, Reed, and Kaetzel Roads. Yarrowsburg Road itself is only a mile long, running west from Rohrersville Road or Route 67, which is the main north-south highway through Pleasant Valley, to Yarrowsburg.

Yarrowsburg has no signage to mark its location and no commercial buildings. Polly Yarrow's house was located on the south side of the intersection with Reed Road. It burned down more than a century ago and left no trace. Private homes are there now. The seventy-four-acre farm owned by Arthur Sands was a half-mile south of Polly's house along Reed Road.

Other Locations

Beallmount, Potomac, Maryland

Brooke Beall and his brother owned Beallmount (also called Beall Mount), an estate located west of Potomac, Maryland. At one time, it consisted of over 2,500 acres.[23] Both Yarrow and his son Aquilla undoubtedly spent time there. Some modern maps designate the area "Beallmont," and real estate listings use this word. Beallmont is generally bounded on the east by Beall Mountain Road at River Road and Watts Branch and on the west by Beall Springs Road.

There was a water mill located near where Watts Branch emptied into the Potomac River. A worksheet for the Maryland Historical Trust prepared in 1975 described the mill site:

> The ruins lie near the mouth of Watts Branch, on the south side of River Road. The race is visible both north and south of River Road, however. It has been filled in and cut in several places. The low area to the north probably contained the mill pond at one time.
>
> The actual mill ruins include a depression in the ground that may have been a wheel pit. Stone foundation visible. Stone piers nearby hint that there was a saw mill here also.[24]

Beggar's Bennison, belonging to Aquilla's owner Ann Chambers, was on the southeast side of Beallmount at Watts Branch. That property is now a water treatment plant belonging to the Washington Suburban Sanitary Commission. Another of Chambers's properties, Montross, was west of Beallmount. Directly north of Beallmount was Samuel Turner's tract, which was called The James. Turner owned Mary Turner, the future Polly Yarrow.

Beallmount stayed in the Beall family for several generations after Brooke Beall died. His son Upton, who signed Yarrow's manumission papers, was one of those who owned it.

Charles Willson Peale's Portrait of Yarrow Mamout, Philadelphia

Charles Willson Peale took the painting of Yarrow with him when he left Washington. It was not a commissioned work; otherwise, Yarrow or someone else would have kept it in Georgetown. Whether it was ever displayed at the museum in Philadelphia is not known. Peale died in 1829, but the museum stayed in operation until 1852. When it was closed, Peale's grandson labeled the painting "Billy Lee," and it went into storage. In 1948, Peale's biographer Charles Coleman Sellers compared the paintings in storage with Peale's diary and realized that the portrait must be Yarrow Mamout, not Billy Lee. Sellers apparently did not know of the Simpson portrait in Washington that would have confirmed his conclusion. Indeed, until comparatively recently, art historians apparently did not realize that there were two paintings of Yarrow. The portrait is owned by the Philadelphia Museum of Art.

The staff at the National Portrait Gallery spent years transcribing Peale's handwritten diary and eventually released it as a five-volume set together with annotations. One of the editors of that work, Sidney Hart, has called the depiction of Yarrow the most sensitive early portrait of an African American.

David Ross House, Cockeysville, Maryland

David Ross and Yarrow Mamout may have never met face-to-face, but still their lives were intertwined in odd ways. Ross was married to the niece of Vachel Denton's wife. He was the slave trader who handled the sale of the Muslim Ayuba Suleiman Diallo twenty-two years before Yarrow came. Ross's son was married to John Beale Bordley's daughter. She was the one who asked Peale to paint Christopher Lowndes's widow. Her father was Peale's protector, lawyer, advisor, and friend. Ross himself bought Samuel Beall Jr.'s lot in Bladensburg and was a business partner of Beall, Joseph Chapline, and Richard Henderson in Frederick Forge on Antietam Creek.

Originally in Bladensburg, Ross's house was large even by today's standards. In 1814, during the Battle of Bladensburg, the British commandeered it to serve as a hospital for their wounded. The house remained standing in Bladensburg into the 1980s when it was taken down and reconstructed brick by brick in Cockeysville, Maryland, north of Baltimore. The elegant Ross house is an example of how well the wealthy lived in Yarrow's time and stands in sharp contrast to the log cabins with dirt floors that slaves like Yarrow lived in. It is now in private ownership and not open to the public.

Shadrick Turner's Bible, Hyattsville, Maryland

Samuel Turner, who owned Mary Turner, had a brother named Shadrick. In the 1970s, researcher Theodore L. Bissell tracked down the family bible owned by Shadrick's wife Sarah.[25] A key discovery in the course of Bissell's search was a man who remembered a Turner family that lived on Edmonston Road in Prince George's County, Maryland. This meant that two hundred years after Samuel Turner married James Edmonston's widow, Turners were still living near where Edmonston had lived.

Sarah Turner's bible is now in the possession of the First United Methodist Church of Hyattsville, Maryland. In it, Sarah and later Turners recorded not only births and deaths in the Turner family but also ones in the families of their slaves. Although the earliest slave record was the death of a woman named Charity on October 15, 1820, which was well after Samuel Turner's death in 1809, the bible sheds light on the relationship between owners and slaves in the Turner family then.

St. John's Cemetery, Frederick, Maryland

St. John's Catholic Church in Frederick has used this cemetery since the cholera epidemic of 1832. Chief Justice Roger Brooke Taney is buried in the circle in the middle of the cemetery. He wrote the Supreme Court decision in the *Dred Scott* case. The southeast section of the cemetery was reserved for African American burials. Many of these graves are unmarked. Yarrow Mamout's niece, Nancy Hillman, was probably buried there. An obelisk marker in this section of the cemetery has the names of later Hillmans, who were presumably related to her by marriage. The cemetery is located between Third and Fourth Streets and North East Street.

Storer College, Harpers Ferry, West Virginia

Before the Civil War, West Virginia was part of Virginia. When the war broke out, delegates from the western part of the state met and voted not to secede. Hence, the new state of West Virginia was created and remained part of the Union, the town of Harpers Ferry included.

When George Washington was president, he decided to locate a federal arsenal and armory at Harpers Ferry to manufacture and store weapons. At the time, the town was surrounded by iron furnaces and forges, including the Keep Triest Furnace and the Frederick Forge. In fact, so connected was the forge with the arsenal that one of the early managers at the arsenal had come from Frederick Forge.[26]

John Brown fixated on the weapons stored at the federal armory at Harpers Ferry. He and his men seized it and its weapons briefly, and he called for slaves in Virginia to leave the plantations and come to the armory, where he would arm them. The rebellion never materialized, and John Brown was captured by federal troops and tried, convicted, and hanged by the state of Virginia. However, his actions made him a martyr to abolitionists and contributed to the Civil War.

Harpers Ferry was also a transportation hub. It was located at the confluence of the Shenandoah and Potomac Rivers, was across the Potomac from the C&O Canal, and sat at one end of the railroad bridge over the Potomac carrying trains from Washington, D.C., westward. Maryland Heights, the southern terminus of Elk Ridge, looms over the town from the east. Surrounded in all directions by higher ground, the town was impossible to defend during the Civil War yet was considered strategic by both sides. Hence, it changed hands seven times in the four years. Shelled repeatedly, Harpers Ferry was a shambles at the end of the war.

In 1867, New England philanthropist John Storer put up $10,000 "to found a school which might eventually become a College, to be located in one of the Southern States, at which youth could be educated without distinction of race or color; provided that the friends of the colored people in the Free Baptist denominations would raise an equal amount." The Baptists raised more than enough money. They chose Harpers Ferry as the site of the college and purchased a tract of land known as the Smallwood farm.[27]

Storer operated both as a preparatory school and a normal school or teachers college. Frederick Douglass became a trustee and in 1881 delivered at the school his noted oration on John Brown. Emma Turner entered Storer Preparatory School in 1890 and later earned her degree in education from Storer College.

Eighty-seven years after the creation of Storer, the Supreme Court in *Brown v. Topeka Board of Education* found that the policy of separating students by race was unconstitutional. Following the decision, Storer lost federal and state funding and closed. The National Park Service acquired the property and owns it now.[28]

United States Naval Academy, Annapolis, Maryland

Not many think of the United States Naval Academy as a slave port, but it was. From West Africa alone about 5,200 slaves came into Annapolis.[29] One example was Yarrow Mamout, who arrived on June 4, 1752 on board the *Elijah*. The ship was anchored in the Severn River where the Naval Academy is located today. While he was on the deck of the *Elijah* waiting to be sold, he would have gazed on the Academy grounds. After he was sold, he and Beall were probably ferried to the Annapolis city dock, the location of which has not changed significantly in 260 years.

Notes

Introduction

1. Some art history books refer to the Peale painting as "the chuckling Negro." The patronizing—or at least diminishing—expression does Peale as well as Yarrow an injustice. Peale intended the painting to make a statement about racial equality.

2. Polly was seventeen years older than Simon's father and forty years older than Simon. To keep the story as simple as possible, she is referred to as Simon's aunt in this book, but she might have been his great-aunt.

1. Yarrow Mamout, a West African Muslim Slave

1. While the historical record suggests only that Yarrow was from Guinea, the face in Charles Willson Peale's portrait seems clearly Fulani.

2. Henri Gaden "Du Nom Chez les Toucouleurs et Peuls Islamises du Fouta Senegalais," *Revue d'Ethnographie et de Sociologie* 3, nos. 1–2 (1912): 50, 53.

3. Joseph Earl Harris, *The Kingdom of Fouta-Diallon,* (Ph.D. diss. Northwestern University, 1965), 180.

4. Three other slaves named Yarrow have been found in estates. The will of John Garrett, who died in Frederick County in 1775, bequeaths a slave named Yarrow or Yarrone who was living on the "Merryland" tract along the Monocacy River. Frederick County MD Wills, Book 41, 179–181. The will of Thomas Gantt of Prince George's County in 1765 also bequeaths a slave named Yarrow. Leslie and Neil Keddie, *Prince George's County Wills, No. 1, 1761–1770, folios 523–632* (Family Tree Bookshop, 2001), 6:40–41 (folio 575). As will be detailed later, Joseph Wilson of Rockville also owned a slave named Yarrow.

5. Becaye Traore, cultural affairs office of the Embassy of Senegal in Washington, D.C., telephone interview, September 23, 2010.

6. Tierno Bah, research associate, National Museum of African Art, Washington, D.C., interview, November 15, 2010.

7. Thomas Bluett, *Some Memoirs of the Life of Job, the Son of Solomon the High Priest of Boonda in Africa* (London: Richard Ford, 1734).

8. Diallo, also Jiallo, is an anglicized form.

9. Bluett, *Some Memoirs of the Life of Job*, 18.

10. Karen Mauer Green, *The Maryland Gazette 1727–1761, Genealogical and Historical Abstracts* (Galveston: The Frontier Press, 1989) 2, citing *Maryland Gazette*, 21 January 1728–29, No. 71.

11. Ibid., 31; *Maryland Gazette*, 19 February 1747, No. 94.

12. Ibid., 96; *Maryland Gazette* 25 December 1751, No. 348.

13. Bluett, *Some Memoirs of the Life of Job*, 19–20.

14. Ibid., 21.

15. The details about the life of Abdul-Rahman are from Terry Alford, *Prince Among Slaves, the True Story of an African Prince Sold into Slavery in the American South* (New York: Oxford University Press, 2007).

16. On one of his journeys, Newton sailed out of Liverpool on August 11, 1750 bound for Africa in the snow *Duke of Argyle*, arriving off the coast of West Africa about a year before Yarrow left. Marcus Rediker, *The Slave Ship: A Human History* (New York: Viking, 2007), 164.

17. Although the verse of "Amazing Grace"—"I once was lost, but now am found"—could be interpreted to refer to the experience of the slaves on his ships, the hymn is about the spiritual journey that transformed Newton from slave ship captain to clergyman.

18. John Newton, "Thoughts upon the African Slave Trade," *The Posthumous Works of the Late Rev. John Newton* (Philadelphia: W. W. Woodward, 1809), 247–248.

19. Marcus Rediker, *The Slave Ship: A Human History* (New York: Viking, 2007), 41.

20. Vaughn W. Brown, *Shipping in the Port of Annapolis, 1748–1775* (Annapolis, Md.: United States Naval Institute, 1963), 22.

21. Robert F. Marx, *Shipwrecks in America* (Mineola, N.Y.: Dover, 1987), 174; Trans-Atlantic Slave Trade Database, www.slavevoyages.org. For the genealogy of the Lowndes family, see Christopher Johnston, "Lowndes Family," *Maryland Historical Magazine* 2 (1907): 276, 277.

22. Rediker, *Slave Ship,* 164.

23. Ibid., 270.

24. When interviewed by Charles Willson Peale, Yarrow's former owner, Margaret Beall, said that Yarrow was fourteen or slightly older when he was brought to America. Since he was in fact sixteen, Yarrow must have looked young for his age even as a teenager.

25. The age of Yarrow's sister is arrived at by deduction. According to the 1850 census, her daughter, Nancy Hillman, was eighty-one years old. This means Hillman was born around 1769. Yarrow was born in 1736 and would have been thirty-three years old in 1769. Although it is possible his sister was older and had a child when she was thirty-four or thirty-five years old, it seems more likely that she was younger than Yarrow.

26. Rediker, *The Slave Ship,* 69.

27. Anita Jo Harrison, "Rascals Family Page," http://tiny.cc/ajharrison (accessed September 2010).

28. This may have been the *Chesterfield,* captained by William Earle. According to the Trans-Atlantic Slave Trade Database, it left Africa on March 30, 1750. Its owners included two of the owners of the *Elijah,* William Whaley and Edward Lowndes.

29. Samuel Beall's daughter-in-law, Margaret, told Peale that Beall "had purchased him from the Ship that brought him from Afreca." Charles Willson Peale, Lillian B. Miller, Sidney Hart, David C. Ward, and Rose S. Emerich, ed., *The Selected Papers of Charles Willson Peale and His Family* (New Haven: Yale University Press, 1991), 3:651.

30. John Ridout to Horatio Sharp, July 27, 1784, "Ridouts Return from England & France," Ridout Papers, Maryland State Archives, Special Collections, D504, item 600.

31. For the proposition that it was common practice to sell servants, convicts, and slaves from on board the ship, see Silvio A. Bedini, *The Life of Benjamin Banneker* (New York: Charles Scribner's Sons, 1972), 12–13. Bedini quotes from the announcement of a sale of convicts in the *Maryland Gazette* of June 29, 1767: "Just imported from Bristol, in the Ship Randolph, Capt. John Weber Price, One Hundred and Fifteen Convicts, men, women, and lads: Among whom are several Tradesmen, who are to be sold on board the said Ship, now in Annapolis Dock."

32. The figures in the text on the number of slaves and ships for which an investor was responsible were derived from the Trans-Atlantic Slave Trade Database.

2. Tobacco and the Importation of a Labor Force

1. Maryland Online Encyclopedia, "The Voyages of the *Ark* and the *Dove,*" http://tiny.cc/ark-and-dove (accessed March 2010).

2. Arthur Pierce Middleton, *The Tobacco Coast: A Maritime History of the Chesapeake Bay in the Colonial* Era (Newport News, Va.: Mariners Museum, 1953), 93–94.

3. Thomas F. McIlwraith and Edward K. Muller, *North America: The Historical Geography of a Changing Continent* (Lanham, Md: Rowman & Littlefield, 2001).

4. Middleton, *Tobacco Coast,* 95.

5. James Rogers, telephone interview, November 3, 2009.

6. Email from Jean Russo, associate general editor, Archives of Maryland Online, August 12, 2010. Ms. Russo's study covered the period April 6, 1756, to October 6, 1775. There were a total of 17,650 arrivals, of which 7,620 were servants, 6,783 were convicts, and 1,918 were slaves. The remaining 1,329 were "redemptorists" or passengers.

7. McIlwraith, *North America,* 105.

8. Middleton, *Tobacco Coast,* 148–149.

9. Ibid., 150.

10. *Maryland Gazette,* October 4, 1753.

11. George Ely Russell, *The Ark and the Dove Adventurers: By the Society of the Ark and the Dove* (Baltimore: Genealogical Publishing Company, 2005) 121, 138–139.

12. Middleton, *Tobacco Coast,* 139.

13. Ibid., 154.

14. Ibid., 10.

15. Ibid., 154–155.

16. Ibid., 101.

17. The latter area is now the counties of St. Mary's, Charles, Prince George's, Calvert, and Anne Arundel. Like the Tidewater region of Virginia, this part of Maryland was prime tobacco country, with a temperate climate, good soil, and ready water access to ocean-going vessels. There was a difference between Maryland and Virginia tobacco that caused the plantation systems in the two colonies to take divergent paths. Maryland tobacco was a variety known as Oronoco. It had coarse fibers and a strong flavor. The Tidewater region of Virginia, particularly along the York and James Rivers, had soil

suited to growing a milder, finer tobacco called "sweetscented." Sweetscented tobacco was preferred in England and commanded a higher price. Hence, although tobacco could be grown in many parts of the two colonies, the plantations along the York and James Rivers were generally larger, more prosperous, and more luxurious because they grew the sweetscented variety. Middleton, *Tobacco Coast* 97.

18. Under the consignment system, the planter retained ownership of the crop from harvesting through transport until sale in England. If the crop was lost at sea, the planter bore the loss. A consignment agent in London received the shipment and made the final sale, crediting the planter's account. Rather than sending cash back across the Atlantic, the London merchant commonly bought, at the direction of the planter, whatever goods the planter wanted from England and shipped them back across the ocean to his client. In this way, tobacco was exchanged directly for English goods sent to the colonies. This is how the planters obtained the nails, axes, and tools needed to build their houses and work the fields and the paper, fabrics, furniture, books, carriages, and clothing needed for their elegant lifestyles. Middleton, *Tobacco Coast*, 104–105.

The consignment system was more suitable for the larger plantations whose owners had the bargaining power and business savvy to use it. George Washington was an example that proved both the merits and perils of the consignment system. His plantation, Mount Vernon, was located on the Potomac River where the tobacco could be transferred directly from field to ocean-going ship. Washington had no need of tobacco warehouses and middlemen. He would give the captain of the ship written instructions to be delivered to Washington's agents in London as to what he wanted them to buy with the proceeds from the sale of the tobacco. They would then have the purchases shipped to him. One year, Washington sent detailed instructions for his agents to have a carriage—"chariot" was the term he used—built to his specifications and sent to him. The London agent did this, but when the chariot arrived at Mount Vernon, Washington discovered it had been made with green, uncured wood and was unusable. He had been swindled. Henry Wiencek, *An Imperfect God: George Washington, His Slaves, and the Creation of America*, (New York: Farrar, Straus and Giroux, 2003), 114.

19. The price for the tobacco might be lower than if it were sold in England, but the merchant bore the risk of loss on the passage across the Atlantic. This system was well suited to the smaller planters, though, and they were

by far the more numerous in Maryland. The factors were men they could meet and do business with face-to-face, not just faraway, impersonal correspondents. The consignment agents also typically imported goods from Europe and operated stores to sell the imports to the planters. This meant that the goods could be inspected before purchase, thus avoiding experiences like Washington's with his chariot.

20. Middleton, *Tobacco Coast*, 107.

21. Jackson Day, *Descendants of Robert "the Scotsman" Beall, Immigrant* (Portland, Ore.: Beall Family Association, 1994), 18a; Prince Georges County Genealogical Society Library, Prince Georges County, Maryland.

22. Henry F. Thompson, "Maryland at the End of the Seventeenth Century," *Maryland Historical Magazine* 2 (1907): 163, 165.

23. Historians Joseph Smith and Philip Crowl studied the court records of Prince George's County, Maryland for the years 1696 to 1699 and reached a similar conclusion: "Negro slavery had yet to establish its absolute sway over the plantation economy of Maryland. The number of slaves in the province in 1700 probably did not greatly exceed 3,000, largely employed as domestic servants; of this number there were probably not more than 300 in Prince George's County. There was no mass importation of Negro slaves into the colony at this time." Joseph H. Smith and Philip A. Crowl, *Court Records of Prince George's County, Maryland 1696–1699* (Washington, D.C.: American Historical Association, 1964) 10. See also Thompson, "Maryland at the End of the Seventeenth Century," 166.

24. City of Bowie, Maryland, "A Brief History of the City of Bowie," http://tiny.cc/historyofbowie (accessed July 2008).

25. Martha Sprigg Poole, "Ninian Beall," *The Montgomery County Story* 3, no. 3 (May 1969): 2.

26. Ruth Beall Gelders, "Colonel Ninian Beall," http://tiny.cc/ninianbeall (accessed 7 November 2011).

27. Ibid., 5; Prince George's County MD, Will Book, Liber 1, folio 92; John Bedell, Stuart Fiedel, Charles Lee Decker, "Bold, Rocky, and Picturesque," Archeological Overview and Assessment and Identification and Evaluation Study of Rock Creek Park District of Columbia, Prepared for National Capital Region, National Park Service, I, The Louis Berger Group Inc., (August 2008), 24, referencing Christoph von Graffenried's map, page 25.

To avoid confusion, modern place and county names are used for locations. For example, when Ninian Beall came to Maryland, the place he lived was called Calvert County. Later, Calvert was divided in two, with the northern part renamed Prince George's County. Later still, the western part of Prince George's was lopped off and renamed Frederick County, and even later Montgomery and Washington Counties were cut from Frederick.

28. Gelders, "Colonel Ninian Beall"; The Bell-Beall Family of Scotland and Maryland, http://tiny.cc/bell-beall (accessed October 21, 2007). By the time of the first United States census in 1790, there were eighty-six Bealls in the thirteen states, with seventy-three of those in Maryland. By 1920, the last census that is available in full at the time of this writing, there were 1,735 Bealls in the United States, with 242 of those in Maryland and ninety-eight in the District of Columbia.

29. Prince George's County Historical Society, "Prince George's County: Over 300 Years of History," http://tiny.cc/prince-georges (accessed May 1, 2011).

30. Jackson H. Day, *Maryland Beall Families Pre 1800*, Draft (October 24, 1994), 22.

31. Eleanor Vaughn Cook, *The Brooke Beall and the Johns Family*, unpublished (July 1986), 65.

32. Ibid., 66; *Maryland Beall Families Pre 1800*, 15; Eleanor M. V. Cook, "The Story of Burnt Mills," *The Montgomery County Story* 35, no. 4 (November 1992): 225; Patent Certificate 486, Prince George's County Circuit Court, Land Survey, Subdivision and Condominium Plats, Maryland State Archives S1203.

33. 1783 Montgomery County Tax assessment card file, Sarah Beall, Montgomery County Historical Society, Rockville, Md. The Charles and William had been divided up by this time. The assessment counted 612 acres, whereas the original tract had 1,100.

34. Priscilla McNeil, "Pretty Prospects: The History of a Land Grant," *Washington History*, 14, no. 2 (Fall–Winter 2002–3): 6–25. A map on page 8 shows Samuel Beall's property along Rock Creek as well as "Addition to the Rock of Dumbarton" to the north of Georgetown. The Montgomery County Historical Society also has map overlays with the old tract names. Beall's Azadia and Gizer were roughly where Tenleytown is today.

35. Day, *Maryland Beall Families Pre 1800*, 23.

36. Port of Bladensburg, http://tiny.cc/bladensburg (accessed May 2010).

37. Thomas Cramphin was also one of these men. Although his name was spelled "Crampton" on at least one deed, he was probably not related to Thomas Crampton of Washington County, Maryland, a man who later played a significant role in this saga.

38. Anita Jo Harrison, "Rascals Family Page," http://familytreemaker.genealogy.com/users/h/a/r/Anita-J-Harrison/GENE1-0010.html (accessed September 2010).

39. George Washington letter to David Ross, June 25, 1757, George Washington Papers, Library of Congress, http://tiny.cc/gw-letter (accessed February 2011).

40. Papers of George Washington, The Road to Revolution 1765–1775, George Washington to George Mason 5 April 1769, Alderman Library, University of Virginia. http://tiny.cc/gmason.

41. Email from John Heller, February 25, 2009. The Hellers owned the David Ross house in 2009.

42. Elise Greenup Jourdan, *Early Families of Southern Maryland* (Berwyn Heights, Md.: Heritage Books, 2007), 7:27; Charles Willson Peale, *The Selected Papers of Charles Willson Peale and His Family*, ed. Lillian B. Miller, Sidney Hart, David C. Warden, and Rose S. Emerich (New Haven: Yale University Press, 1991), 3:697.

43. Prince George's County, Md., Inventories 1777–1780, pages 155–157, Maryland State Archives, CR 34,690–3, CM809–8.

44. Lowndes was the son of Richard Lowndes of Bostock House in Cheshire, England. He had come to America and married Benjamin Tasker Sr.'s daughter Elizabeth. His sometime partner in the slave trade, Benjamin Tasker Jr., was his brother-in-law. By 1748, Lowndes was doing business in Bladensburg as Christopher Lowndes and Company with his younger brother Edward and with John Hardman and William Whalley as partners in Liverpool, the main English port in the slave trade.

45. Town of Bladensburg, http://tiny.cc/bladensburg-bostwick (accessed May 25, 2011). The source of this information may be a compilation from the *Maryland Gazette* by Louise Joyner Hienton, "Items from Maryland Gazette 1745–1785 Concerning Christopher Lowndes of Bostwick," Prince George's Historical Society library; Market Masters House http://tiny.cc/townofbladensburg. In the September 2, 1762, *Maryland Gazette,* Lowndes advertised the launch and sale of a ship at Bladensburg. The vessel, fifty-eight feet long, and twenty-three feet wide, was designed for the shallow water work of transporting tobacco from plantations to the warehouse—"she will draw but little Water, and take the ground very easy"—and could carry 350 hogshead. *Maryland Gazette,* (September 2, 1762) 3.

46. Christopher Johnston, "Lowndes Family," *Maryland Historical Magazine* 2 (1907): 276–277.

47. Prince George's County Inventories, 1781–1787, pages 177–196; Maryland State Archives Microfilm CR 34,690–4 CM 809–9.

48. John Glassford and Company Records, Manuscript Division, Library of Congress, Washington D.C., Reel 1 Part 3 (1753).

49. Middleton, *Tobacco Coast*, 137, 14.

3. Welcome to America

1. The data here are from the Trans-Atlantic Slave Trade Database, ships sailing from the Gold Coast or Senegambia to Maryland between 1700 and 1773. The database shows that during its entire history the slave trade brought a total of 158,427 slaves into the Chesapeake region, which included both Maryland and Virginia.

2. An excellent summary of the warfare in West Africa between Muslims and non-Muslims who sent Muslim slaves to America can be found in Michael Gomez, "Muslims in Early America," *Journal of Southern History* 60, no. 4 (1994): 671–710.

3. Proceedings and Acts of the General Assembly of Maryland, 1751–1754, Archives of Maryland Online, http://tiny.cc/mdassembly, 1–2.

4. Ibid., 32.

5. Eleanor M. V. Cook, "The Story of Burnt Mills," *The Montgomery County Story* 35, no. 4 (November 1992): 225, 226.

6. Eleanor M. V. Cook, "Newport Mill," *The Montgomery County Story* 34, no. 1 (February 1991): 141, 142; "Early Water Mills in Montgomery County," *The Montgomery County Story* 33, no. 4 (November 1990): 129, 133; "Georgetown Jewel of Montgomery County—Part 2," *The Montgomery County Story* 41, no. 4 (November 1996): 49, 56.

7. Theodore Hazen, email of July 15, 2010. Hazen, a third-generation millwright, was employed by the National Park Service at Pierce Mill in Washington for eleven years. He operates Pond Lilly Mill Restorations and is a millwright, millstone dresser, and milling consultant.

8. Proceedings and Acts of the General Assembly of Maryland, 1751–1754, 34.

9. Inventory of Estate of Christopher Lowndes, Prince George's County MD Inventories, 1781–1787, 177. Maryland State Archives CD 34, 690–4, CM 809–9.

10. Inventory of Estate of Colonel Jeremiah Belt, Prince George's County MD Inventories, 1763–1777, 144, Maryland State Archives, CR 34, 690–1, CM 809–7.

11. Inventory of Estate of Richard Chew, Anne Arundel County MD Prerogative Court Inventories, Liber 102I, folio 114–123, Maryland State Archives SR 4365.

12. Inventory of Estate of Joseph Galloway, Anne Arundel County MD Prerogative Court Records, Liber 57I, folio 133–137, Maryland State Archives, SR 4350–2.

13. Inventory of Estate of Walter Stoddert, Charles County, Charles County MD Inventories 1766–1773, 520–522, Maryland State Archives CR 39, 592–1, CM 386–5.

14. Inventory of Estate of David Ross, Prince George's County MD Inventories, 1777–1780, 155. Maryland State Archives, CR 34,690, CM 809–8.

15. The four Foula ethnic surnames were Diallo, Bah, Sow, and Barry. Common Muslim given names for men were Mamadou, Amadou, Abdoul, Alou, Boubaka, Ibrahima, Omar, Seikou, Ismaila, and Saliou. For women, the given names were Aissatou, Mariama, Faimatou, and Kadiatou. Joseph Earl Harris, *The Kingdom of Fouta-Diallon.*

16. Mark Walston, "Slave Housing in Montgomery County," *The Montgomery County Story* 27, no. 3 (1984): 111.

17. Patent 1578 Frederick County MD survey 11 Nov. 1760, Patented 20th March 1762, B.C. & G. S. No. 14 folio 601.

18. Hazen email, July 15, 2010.

4. Slavery and Revolution

1. David Bailles Warden, *A Chorographical and Statistical Description of the District of Columbia the Seat of the General Government of the United States* (Paris: Smith, 1816), 49.

2. Perhaps the best-known body servant from this time was Billy Lee, who served George Washington in this capacity. Lee took care of myriad details in Washington's personal life, even riding into battle with him during the Revolution.

3. Warden, *A Chorographical and Statistical Description*, 49–50.

4. "Keep Triest" is the Semple family motto in Gaelic and is on the Semple family crest. It translates roughly to "keep being trustworthy." The name may

still be found on a road near Harpers Ferry, although the spelling has changed to "Keep Tryst." Samples Manor is also a place name on the Maryland side of the Potomac, opposite where Semple's furnace was and obviously derived its named from Semple. Many deeds along Israel Creek in Pleasant Valley (presumably named for pioneer Israel Friend) recite that the land was originally part of Keep Triest, so Semple's properties must have extended there. The spelling once mutated to "Keep Trice" in an 1825 newspaper. "Sheriff's Sale," *Hagerstown Torch Light*, March 1, 1825.

5. Michael D. Thompson, "The Iron Industry in Western Maryland, Baltimore," unpublished manuscript, 22.

6. Eleanor M. V. Cook, "The Brooke Beall and the Johns Family," unpublished manuscript, 71, citing agreement of January 17, 1763, Frederick County MD Land Records Book J Folio 793, recorded October 1765.

7. Jackson Day, "Maryland Beall Families Pre 1800," unpublished manuscript, 25; *Maryland Gazette*, August 21, 1766.

8. Day, "Maryland Beall Families Pre 1800," 23.

9. William Hand Browne ed., *Proceedings of the Council of Maryland 1761–1769* (Baltimore: Maryland Historical Society, 1913), 32:112–113; Cook, "The Brooke Beall and the Johns Family 70.

10. Day, "Maryland Beall Families Pre 1800," 23.

11. Cook found that in 1770, Beall sold 124 acres of The Benjamin, 413 acres at Mattapony and Turkey Island, 139 acres of the Charles and William, 20 acres of the Addition to Mill Seat, 70 acres of the Enlargement, 500 acres of Benjamins Inspection, 13 acres of Supply, 98 acres of Gleening, and 125 acres of Azadia. Cook, "The Brooke Beall and the Johns Family," 67–69.

12. Day, "Maryland Beall Families Pre 1800," 23–24.

13. Declaration of the Association of the Freemen of Maryland, July 26, 1775. The accompanying note by the Maryland Historical Society indicates the original is "preserved under glass at Annapolis, consists of two pieces, apparently torn apart, and pasted down on card-board" and suggests there may be a page missing. It therefore assumes that Samuel Beall's signature and others were on the missing page.

14. Joseph Theophilus Singewald, *The Iron Ores of Maryland: With an Account of the Iron Industry* (Baltimore: Johns Hopkins Press, 1911), 133–134. The citizens of Alexandria, Virginia, also wanted to buy cannon, saying in a letter that the Hughes were "the only persons in this part of the continent to be depended on for cannon."

15. J. Thomas Scharf, *History of Western Maryland, Being a History of Frederick, Montgomery, Carroll, Washington, Allegany, and Garrett Counties* (Baltimore: Regional Publishing Company, 1968), 1:127–128.

16. Thompson, "The Iron Industry in Western Maryland," 32.

17. Will of Samuel Beall Washington County MD Register of Wills, Book TS2 Page 19 executed 15 October 1774, filed 10 January 1778.

18. Conceivably, Jarro could have been Yarrow's son, but there is no other evidence that Yarrow had a son at this time. Jarro was surely not another similarly named slave of Beall's. The chances that he owned a second slave with an African-sounding name like Jarro, but who was not Yarrow Mamout are too remote. George Washington is known to have referred to his body servant Billy Lee as his boy, writing: "I went to Colo. Cresaps leaving the Doctr. At Pritchards with my boy Billy who was taken sick." Donald Jackson and Dorothy Twohig, eds, *George Washington Papers at the Library of Congress, 1741–1799: The Diaries of George Washington,* (Charlottesville: University of Virginia Press, 1976), 278. Billy Lee was in his late teens or early twenties.

5. Yarrow of Georgetown

1. National Park Service, "The Patowmack Canal," http://tiny.cc/patowmack (accessed October 17, 2008). Years later, the longer and better-known Chesapeake and Ohio Canal was constructed on the Maryland side and stretched along the Potomac 184 miles from Georgetown to Cumberland, Maryland. The C&O Canal is, of course, still there.

2. Forrest and Stoddert owned much of the land in what is now northwest Washington. They bought additional land that fell within what would become the District of Columbia for resale to the government before word of the intended use leaked out. One of the most precise accountings of who owned the land that became the District of Columbia is Priscilla W. McNeil's "Rock Creek Hundred: Land Conveyed for the Federal City," *Washington History* 3, no. 1 (Spring/Summer 1991). McNeil did a similar study of the lands that made up Pretty Prospects, the land Forrest and Stoddert owned in what was to become northwest Washington. Pricilla W. McNeil, "Pretty Prospects: The History of a Land Grant," *Washington History* 14, no. 2 (Fall/Winter 2002–3). The Beall and Edmonston families also owned parcels of the future Washington, D.C.

See "Fight for Millions, Beall and Edmonston Heirs Seek Title to Lands," *The Washington Post,* February 1, 1911.

3. David Bailles Warden, *A Chorographical and Statistical Description of the District of Columbia* (Paris: Smith, 1816), 159–160. Warden visited the 1,500-acre Riversdale plantation of George Calvert near Bladensburg and saw firsthand how far tobacco had fallen. An acre of tobacco, he wrote, yielded about one hogshead, worth between six and ten dollars, whereas an acre planted in wheat yielded eleven to thirty-three dollars. "Wheat is now more profitable than tobacco," he wrote, while a single cow was worth twelve to forty dollars.

4. The business of getting the iron to Georgetown eventually paid off. David Warden reported that for the eleven month period ending in July 1811, some twenty-five tons of bar iron and 1,313 tons of pig iron were transported by river to Georgetown. Ibid., 10.

5. Michael D. Thompson, "The Iron Industry in Western Maryland," unpublished manuscript, 29.

6. Ibid., 32, citing the agreement between Alexander Clagett and Richard Henderson, settling Samuel Beall's affairs with Frederick Forge filed June 6, 1783, Washington County MD Land Record Book C Vol C Page 83.

7. Eleanor M. V. Cook, "The Brooke Beall Family and the Johns Family," unpublished manuscript, 2.

8. Ibid., 83. In 1804, Brooke's sons, Upton and Aquilla, divided the Beallmount property. According to Cook, Brooke took 643.5 acres while Aquilla got 1,250 acres plus additional tracts totaling 113 acres.

9. Michael F. Dwyer, Senior Park Historian, National Capital Parks and Planning Commission, "Beall's Mill Site," Nomination Form for the National Register of Historic Places, National Parks Service, Maryland Historical Trust Worksheet (Feb. 28, 1975). The worksheet noted: "The actual mill ruins include a depression in the ground that may have been a wheel pit. Stone foundation visible. Stone piers nearby hint that there was a saw mill here also." When I visited the site in early 2011, it looked as Dwyer described and indeed what appeared to be the long millrace was still there.

10. Cook, "The Brooke Beall Family and the Johns Family," 11.

11. Sally Somervell Mackall, *Early Days of Washington* (Washington, D.C.: Neale Company, 1899), 54.

12. Cook, "The Brooke Beall Family and the Johns Family," 18. A copy of George Washington's handwritten diary is online from the Library of Congress at http://tiny.cc/gwhome (accessed March 6, 2008).

13. Cook, "The Brooke Beall Family and the Johns Family," 11. Brooke Beall died intestate in 1795. In 1803, his heirs divided up his property by agreement. The document, which was recorded, refers to "the Warehouse lot" and house where Brooke Beall resided in Georgetown and to the "Mills Plantations" at or near Watts Creek. Montgomery County MD Land Records, Book L, pages 16–18 (August 11, 1803).

14. Cook, "The Brooke Beall Family and the Johns Family," 11.

15. John Thomas Scharf, *History of Western Maryland* (Philadelphia: L. H. Everts, 1882), 94.

16. Cook, "The Brooke Beall Family and the Johns Family," 15.

17. Ibid., 79. The 1790 census enumerated free whites, slaves, and all other persons separately.

18. Ibid., 26.

19. Ira Berlin, *Generations of Captivity: A History of African-American Slaves* (Cambridge, Mass.: Harvard University Press, 2003), 78.

20. Warden, *A Chorographical and Statistical Description of the District of Columbia*, 45–46.

21. Warden's book, published in Paris, was aimed at informing European readers about life in the new American capital. Warden did his research in 1811. The fact that John Mason had spent almost four years in France, from 1788 to 1792, may explain why Warden relied so much on him. Gunston Hall, "Children of George Mason," http://tiny.cc/gunston-hall (accessed May 28, 2011).

22. Maryland, 1793–1803 Collection, Papers of John Mason, Gunston Hall Library & Archives, Gunston Hall, Mason Neck, Virginia. The collection includes insurance papers on the *Maryland*, accounting records, and cargo for some voyages.

23. Brooke Beall Summary Ledger, Call No. MS 111, Q9700000003309, Maryland Historical Society, Baltimore MD.

24. Cook, "The Brooke Beall Family and the Johns Family," 26.

25. Ibid.

26. Warden, *A Chorographical and Statistical Description of the District of Columbia*, 48.

27. Cook, "The Brooke Beall Family and the Johns Family," 100.

28. Montgomery County MD Land Records, G, 285 (August 22, 1796).

29. District of Columbia, Recorder of Deeds, R17, 201 (1807).

30. National Archives and Records Administration, Washington DC, District of Columbia, Recorder of Deeds Liber E page 80 old page 67 new (1800).

The original ledger books are now at the National Archives and Records Administration in Washington, D.C. The Recorder of Deeds for the District of Columbia has record books in which the old deeds were reentered by typing. Hence, deeds are cited by Liber and by the original (old) and the typed (new) page number.

31. Georgetown Tax Assessments, 1800–1803, 1807, 1815, 1818, 1819, microfilm, Washingtoniana Room, Martin Luther King Jr. Public Library, Washington D.C.

32. Ibid.

33. When Charles Willson Peale visited Georgetown in 1818, he was told that Yarrow owned the house, but that is not what is reflected in the deed books.

34. National Archives and Records Administration, Washington DC, District of Columbia, Recorder of Deeds Volume 10 of Liber K, 7 (1803).

35. Interview with Sulayman Nyang, January 2006.

36. According to the Georgetown University student newspaper, the *Hoya*, university archives held a worn, miniature Quran in 1964. However, it has since disappeared, and there are no other records about it. John Druska, "Lost Treasurers—The Archives," *The Hoya*, October 23, 1964.

37. Emails from Kevin Smullin Brown, January 2006 and September 2010.

38. Warden, *A Chorographical and Statistical Description of the District of Columbia*, 49–50.

39. Thomas Peter and Martha Parke Custis bought Tudor Place in Georgetown in 1805 from Francis Lowndes, the son of Christopher Lowndes. http://tiny.cc/tudor-place. Custis was the granddaughter of Martha Washington.

40. Warden, *A Chorographical and Statistical Description of the District of Columbia*, 50–51.

41. Grace Dunlop Ecker, *A Portrait of Old Georgetown* (Richmond, Va.: Garrett and Mossie, 1933), 170–171.

42. Warden, *A Chorographical and Statistical Description of the District of Columbia*, 50.

43. Quoted in Ecker, *A Portrait of Old Georgetown*, 180.

6. The Portraits: Peale, Yarrow, and Simpson

1. Charles Coleman Sellers, *Charles Willson Peale: A Biography* (New York: Charles Scribner's Sons, 1969), 6–8.

2. Ibid., 9–11.

3. Ibid., 18.

4. Charles Willson Peale, *The Selected Papers of Charles Willson Peale and His Family,* ed. Lillian B. Miller, Sidney Hart, David C. Warden, and Rose S. Emerich (New Haven: Yale University Press, 1991), 1.

5. Sellers, *Charles Willson Peale,* 19–29.

6. Ibid., 44–47.

7. Peale, *The Selected Papers of Charles Willson Peale and His Family,* 3:617.

8. Sellers, *Charles Willson Peale,* 53–64.

9. Ibid., 75–82.

10. Ibid., 87.

11. Ibid., 100.

12. Ibid., 111.

13. Ibid., 119.

14. Ibid., 109.

15. Ibid., 137, 156.

16. Ibid., 180, 182.

17. Ibid., 230.

18. Ibid., 294–301.

19. Ibid., 297–298.

20. Society members were progressive on race issues, as was Peale. The president of the Society at this time, David Rittenhouse, was asked to review an almanac that was prepared by Benjamin Banneker, an African American. Rittenhouse approved it and added: "Every Instance of Genius amongst the Negroes is worthy of attention, because their oppressors seem to lay great stress on their supposed inferior mental abilities." Silvio A. Bedini, *The Life of Benjamin Banneker* (New York: Scribner, 1972), 148.

21. Sellers, *Charles Willson Peale,* 254.

22. Ibid., 251.

23. Peale, *The Selected Papers of Charles Willson Peale and His Family,* 3:566.

24. Ibid., 1:697.

25. Sellers, *Charles Willson Peale,* 288.

26. Peale, *The Selected Papers of Charles Willson Peale and His Family,* 3:628.

27. Ibid., 2:829, 2:629.

28. Marbury has gone down in history as the man who sued Secretary of State James Madison in 1801 for the seemingly petty reason of wanting him to deliver a commission as a justice of the peace for Georgetown that outgoing President John Adams had signed. Marbury lost, but the lawsuit, *Marbury v. Madison,* established the important legal principle that the Supreme Court is the final arbiter of the Constitution. The Forrest-Marbury house is now the Embassy of Ukraine, located near the Francis Scott Key Bridge in Georgetown. Peale was impressed by Marbury's wealth and social standing, writing in his diary: "We went to a Tea party at Coll. Marbury where there was about 3 Dozs. Ladies and not quite so many gentlemen—they danced Cotillion and country dances by the music of a Piana, which was distinctly heard as the company danced on carpets. The intertainment was sumptuous & Ellegant." Ibid., 3:648.

29. Ibid., 2:617.

30. Kathleen M. Lesko, Melissa Babb, and Carroll R. Gibbs, *Black Georgetown Remembered: A History of Its Black Community from the Founding of "The Town of George" in 1751 to the Present Day* (Washington, D.C.: Georgetown University Press, 1991) 3; Georgetown Assessments 1815 pages 43 and 84, Microfilm, District of Columbia Public Library, Washingtoniana Room; Brooke Beall Summary Ledger, MS 111, Q9700000003309, Maryland Historical Society, Baltimore.

31. David Bailles Warden, *A Chorographical and Statistical Description of the District of Columbia* (Paris: Smith, 1816), 119.

32. Peale, *The Selected Papers of Charles Willson Peale and His Family,* 3:650.

33. Ibid., 3:649.

34. Ibid., 651.

35. Today, some Bealls pronounce the name to rhyme with "real."

36. The Riggs Bank of Washington was a successor of the Columbia Bank of Georgetown. In researching this book, I reviewed the records that Riggs then kept in its archives. The records of at least some of the stockholders, including George Washington, were extant at that time. Subsequently, PNC Bank acquired Riggs.

37. There is a photograph of the house in Sally Mackall's *Early Days of Washington* (Washington, D.C.: Neale Company, 1899), 157.

38. Peale, *The Selected Papers of Charles Willson Peale and His Family,* 3:651–652.

39. Ibid.

40. Ibid., 652. The fact that Peale spelled it "Yallow" instead of Yarrow once in this paragraph suggests he may sometimes have heard Yarrow say his name with an "L" sound, more like Diallo, and is evidence, albeit thin, that Yarrow's name was derived from the Futa Jallon surname Diallo rather than from Yero.

41. Ibid.

42. Fritz Hirschfeld, *George Washington and Slavery: A Documentary Portrayal* (Columbia: University of Missouri Press, 1997), 109.

43. Charles Coleman Sellers, "Charles Willson Peale and Yarrow Mamout," *The Pennsylvania Magazine of History and Biography* (1947): 99–102.

44. Vivian Raynor, "A Display of Four Illustrious Families," *New York Times*, January 1, 1984.

45. The only known writing on Simpson's life is Kenneth C. Haley, "A Nineteenth Century Portraitist and More: James Alexander Simpson," *Georgetown Day* (May 1977). Haley was assistant professor of fine arts at Georgetown University when he wrote the article and noted: "Facts about Simpson's life are drawn from the letters of Francis A. Barnum." Barnum was the first archivist at the university, according to Lynn Conway, the archivist. She said that much of what is known about the university in the nineteenth century comes from Barnum's letters, which contain his recollections. However, Conway could not then locate the letters Haley relied upon. His article may be the only existing source of biographical information about Simpson. Interview with Lynn Conway, April 2003. Conway was also the source for the information about the old Georgetown College uniforms.

46. Sellers, "Charles Willson Peale and Yarrow Mamout," 99.

47. *Gettysburg Compiler*, February 23, 1823.

48. Captain Christopher Lowndes, Prince George's County, Maryland Land Patents, Certificate 1940 (June 9, 1766).

7. Free Hannah, Yarrow's Sister

1. Hannah was a very common name, and several men mentioned in this narrative owned slaves with that name. None, however, could have been Yarrow's sister. For example, Samuel Turner, who owned the future wife of Yarrow's son, had a slave named Hannah. She was thirty-five years old in 1809 and so could not possibly have been Yarrow's sister. Likewise, William Worthington, the husband of Joseph Wilson's daughter, had a slave named Hannah. This could not have been the same slave Hannah that Wilson owned,

who was named in his will in 1790, since the Hannah that Worthington named in his 1834 will had three young children. Will of William Worthington, Montgomery County MD Will Book V, 183 (September 12, 1831).

2. Martha Sprigg Poole, "Early Rockville Taverns," *The Montgomery County Story* 1, no. 3 (May 1958): 1.

3. 1783 Tax assessment records, Joseph Willson, card file at Montgomery County Historical Society Library, Rockville, Md.; Joseph Wilson genealogy, Wilson family folder at Montgomery County Historical Society. The historical society maintains genealogical folders contributed by researchers on county residents. The contributor of Wilson's is not identified.

4. Poole, "Early Rockville Taverns" 3; Anne W. Cissel, "The Families of a Derwood Farm Through Two Centuries," *The Montgomery County Story* 27, no. 2 (May 1984): 1, 2–4.

5. Montgomery County MD, Deed Book F-6, 270.

6. Will of Joseph Wilson, Montgomery County MD, Register of Wills, Wills B, 433 (February 1791).

7. Henri Gaden, "Du nom chez les toucouleurs et peuls islamisés du Fouta Senegalais," *Revue d'Ethnographie et de Sociologie* 3 (1912): 3.

8. *Montgomery County Sentinel*, February 20, 1880. Although the article referred to "Mr. Crampton's Bob," this probably was a man named Cramphin. The Cramptons of Washington County, Maryland, did not own property in Montgomery County. However, a man named Cramphin did, and he was well known in Montgomery County. His name was incorrectly spelled Crampton in at least one of the country's tax assessment rolls and in Brooke Beall's accounting ledger. Thus, Nugent's ancestor was probably Mr. Cramphin's Bob.

9. A further connection between Nugent and the Yarrows was that George Graff, Nugent's owner, lived on the Two Brothers tract, which Joseph Wilson had bequeathed to his daughter Sarah. Graf had purchased the land from George Riley, who was married to Wilson's daughter, Sarah. John Thomas Scharf, *History of Western Maryland* (Philadelphia: L. H. Everts, 1882), 1:683–684.

10. Hungerford Tavern in Montgomery County served as courthouse and meeting place for revolutionaries. Poole, "Early Rockville Taverns" 3.

11. Ibid.

12. John Suter operated the tavern but the property was owned by Robert Peter. Oliver W. Holmes, "Suter's Tavern: Birthplace of the Federal City," *Records of the Columbia Historical Society* 49 (1973–74): 1, 8. John Suter was

Joseph Wilson's nephew by marriage. The two were close enough that Suter went to Georgia and South Carolina with Wilson when the latter purchased his Rockville farms. Cissell, "The Families of a Derwood Farm Through Two Centuries" 2.

13. Holmes, "Suter's Tavern," 3, 15–16.

14. David Bailles Warden, *A Chorographical and Statistical Description of the District of Columbia Seat of the General Government of the United States* (Paris: Smith, 1816), 47.

15. Josiah Henson, *An Autobiography of the Rev. Josiah Henson ("Uncle Tom"). From 1789 to 1881. With a Preface by Mrs. Harriet Beecher Stowe, and Introductory Notes by George Sturge, S. Morley, Esq., M.P., Wendell Phillips, and John G. Whittier* (Ontario, Calif.: Schuyler, Smith, & Co., 1881), 14.

16. Anne W. Cissell, "Public Houses of Entertainment and Their Proprietors 1750–1828," *The Montgomery County Story* 30, no. 3 (August 1987): 279, 281.

17. Henson, *Autobiography of the Rev. Josiah Henson*, 6.

18. Ibid., 23.

19. According to the lawsuit Nancy Hillman brought in 1843 to collect on Yarrow's loan to William Hayman, she was the daughter of Yarrow's sister and lived in Frederick, Maryland. The 1850 census for Frederick shows Nancy Hillman to be eighty-one years old, meaning she was born in 1769.

20. Will of Joseph Wilson. Of these, only Wager was named in the will of William Worthington. Montgomery County MD, Register of Wills, Will Book V, 183 (September 12, 1831).

21. Robert Shean Riley, "The Colonial Riley Families of the Tidewater Frontier, I, A History of Several Riley Families of Maryland and Virginia" (Salt Lake City: Family History Library), copy in Montgomery County Historical Society Library, genealogical collection. Isaac Riley's father, Hugh, owned at least two lots in Beatty and Hawkin's Addition in Georgetown that were only a few blocks from Yarrow's lot, which was in the same addition.

22. Cissell's "The Families of a Derwood Farm Through Two Centuries" notes oral traditions to the effect that Riley owned a tavern on the Valentines Garden tract, generally the same location as Owen's Ordinary. She found no supporting evidence. However, Andrew Graff, who purchased the property from Riley in 1820, held a license for an ordinary house. Judy Christensen and Gail Littlefield, "King Farm, Draft 1" Draft Environmental Impact Statement, Food and Drug Administration Consolidation, Montgomery County Campus

(December 9, 1994) in possession of C Historic Preservation, City of Rockville, Md.; Scharf, *History of Western Maryland.*

23. Henson, *Autobiography of the Rev. Josiah Henson,* 10.

24. Ibid., 37–38.

25. Will of Joseph Wilson.

26. Brooke Beall's ledger entry in 1790 lists Charles Hungerford, "Interest for 11 years."

27. A runaway would be jailed and sold at public auction if unclaimed. The Reverend James W. C. Pennington had been a slave in western Maryland and wrote about running away. Walking along the National Turnpike toward Baltimore, he met a man with whom he had this exchange:

> Are you travelling any distance, my friend?
> I am on my way to Philadelphia.
> Are you free?
> Yes, sir.
> I suppose, then, you are provided with free papers?
> No, sir. I have no papers.
> Well, my friend, you should not travel on this road: you will be taken up before you have gone three miles. There are men living on this road who are constantly on the look-out for your people; and it is seldom that one escapes them who attempts to pass by day.

Pennington, James W. C., *The Fugitive Blacksmith: or, Events in the History of James W.C. Pennington, Pastor of a Presbyterian Church, New York, Formerly a Slave in the State of Maryland, United States* (London: Charles Gilpin, 1849), 19–20.

28. The Washington County book may still be seen at the Maryland State Archives in Annapolis.

29. Yarrow had manumission papers filed in both the District of Columbia and Montgomery County.

30. Letitia Woods Brown, *Free Negroes in the District of Columbia, 1790–1846* (New York: Oxford University Press, 1972), 92.

31. Ann Worthington's estate was not inventoried when she died, so it is not possible to see whether the Hannah she inherited was owned at her death. All her property, including her slaves, must have gone to her husband William. He died much later. His will, which is dated in 1831, included the names of some of the slaves Ann inherited, but Hannah was not among these. Will

of William Worthington, Montgomery County MD Will Book V, 183 (September 12, 1831).

32. Censuses do not show street addresses for the people counted, so it is impossible to be absolutely certain that the Free Hannah in the 1800 census and the Hannah Peale in the 1820 census were living in exactly the same place. However, the names of several people near Hannah in the two censuses are the same, making it very likely that the two Hannahs were the same woman.

33. Henson, *Autobiography of the Rev. Josiah Henson*, 38.

8. Nancy Hillman, Yarrow's Niece

1. The 1850 census for Frederick County, Maryland listed Nancy Hillman as eighty-one years old.

2. The deed of sale of the tavern property from Leonard Davis to Joseph Wilson in 1786 recorded that Hannah had a child named Callaby. Nancy was not mentioned. She would have been seventeen then. Joseph Wilson's will in 1790 names Hannah but not Callaby. There are several possibilities. First, the assumption that Hannah was Nancy Hillman's mother is wrong. Second, Nancy and Callaby were the same woman, but she changed or modified her name. Third, Nancy had left home by 1786, and Callaby was her sister.

3. Frederick County MD Certificates of Freedom 1806–1827, Maryland State Archives, CM 1198–1, Microfilm Reel CR 47246–3, August 20, 1811.

4. John Thomas Scharf, *History of Western Maryland* (Philadelphia: L. H. Everts, 1882), 1:1047.

5. Brooke was obviously saying things about which he had no personal knowledge, and so there is no reason to put much stock in his assertion that Negro Nancy was twenty-eight. This woman might have been Nancy Hillman—and therefore forty-two years old. But if Brooke said that, then his lie would be apparent on its face. Moreover, since Maryland law prohibited freeing older slaves, perhaps Brooke thought it best to say Nancy was younger. On the other hand, if Negro Nancy was twenty-eight, then she could not have been Nancy Hillman.

6. In addition to the two Supreme Court justices named in the text, the court of appeals judges were Roger Nelson, Upton Sheredine, Richard Potts, Abraham Shriver, William Claggett, Robert Martin, Richard Marshall, and Madison Nelson. John Nelson served as attorney general.

7. *Dred Scott v. Sandford,* 60 U.S. 393 (1856). Taney had freed his own slaves years earlier, and the racist language in his opinion is always used in the context of referring to the views of others rather than Taney himself. That is, the opinion does not say that African Americans were in fact inferior. It merely says that at the time the Constitution was written, people thought they were. But many people even then, including Charles Willson Peale, thought that blacks and whites were equal in ability. It is inconceivable that Taney did not know this. Therefore, his attempt to shift the blame of racism to others appears disingenuous.

8. Jacob Englebrecht, *The Diary of Jacob Engelbrecht,* ed. William R. Quynn (Frederick, Md.: Historical Society of Frederick County, 2001), 23. Several other black men are mentioned in this entry, most in connection with men who were lawyers in Frederick, including "Beall's Robert Magruder." Since several men named Beall appear in the 1820 census of Frederick County, this may refer to one of them. However, it could also refer to Upton Beall, who was clerk of the Montgomery County court, since a later entry in Engelbrecht's diary notes Upton Beall's death. Ibid., 259.

9. William Ross was an attorney in Frederick in 1820. His son, also named William, had been born in 1806. The younger Ross went to Princeton and graduated in 1825. He returned to Frederick to study law under his father and was admitted to the bar in 1828. William Ross obituary, *Frederick Examiner,* March 21, 1883.

10. "Reich's mountain land above Bartgis's paper mill, the residence of Ignatius Hillman, is hereby declared to [be] named 'Black Heath' and must be respected as such. Witness our hands this 25th day of September AD 1823 Philip Reich." Jacob Engelbrecht, *Diary* 146. However, since Frederick County land records include no deed for this transaction, it must have been just an informal arrangement between Reich and Hillman.

11. "Died yesterday on 'black heath' (Reichs Mountain Land) Negro Ignatius Hillman formerly 'Pottss Eagy' aged about 60 years Buried today on the Roman Catholic Cemetery P. Reich author. Thursday October 11, 1827 9 o'clock AM." Engelbrecht, *Diary* 281.

12. Ibid., 368. The entry credited to Aaron Hillman as author is clearly in the same handwriting as other entries in the original diary. However, a scrawled "X" appearing after Hillman's name suggests that Engelbrecht had written this in his presence and then asked him to sign it.

13. Jacob Engelbrecht, *The Jacob Engelbrecht Death Ledger of Frederick County, Maryland 1820–1890,* ed. Edith Olivia Eader and Trudie Davis-Long

(Monrovia, Md.: Paw Prints, 1995), 86. The same ledger recorded Ignatius Hillman's death in 1827. Ibid., 85.

14. Interview with William H. Mohan, member of the board of directors of St. John's cemetery, July 11, 2011. Mohan added that there are several tombstones dating in the latter part of the nineteenth century for Hillmans in a section of the cemetery set aside for African Americans.

15. Engelbrecht, *Diary*, 418.

16. Ibid., 416–422.

17. *Niles Weekly Register* (Baltimore: William Ogden Niles, 1833), vol. 7, 4th series, 71.

18. Richard Plummer Jackson, *The Chronicles of Georgetown, from 1751–1878*, (Washington, D.C.: R.O. Polkinhorn, 1878), 287.

19. Mary Mitchell, The "Potomac Insurance Company of Georgetown, 1831–1841," *Records of the Columbia Historical Society* 69–70: 102–113.

20. "An Act to Incorporate a Fire Insurance Company in Georgetown in the District of Columbia," *Register of Debates in Congress, Second Session, 21st Congress* (Washington, D.C.: Gales & Seaton, 1831) 7:58.

21. Hillman first had to file with the probate court in Washington in order to be appointed Yarrow's representative. She then intervened into the ongoing lawsuit over the proceeds from the public sale.

22. Judge Morsell, State of the Proceeding and Opinion, *Eliza M. Moshier v. John Marbury, & William Redin*, Chancery Court of the District of Columbia (circa December 1849), National Archives and Records Administration, Washington DC, RG 21, Entry 115, Old Series Administration Cases Files, 1801–78, #2472.

23. Biographical information from the Historical Society of the District of Columbia Circuit, "Morsell, James Sewall," http://tiny.cc/biosalpha (accessed April 27, 2011).

24. The procedural aspects of the case were somewhat complicated. There had been no probate of Yarrow's estate. Therefore, Hillman's lawyer, John A. Smith, first had to get the probate court to begin a proceeding and name him the administrator. He then apparently had to get that court to find that Nancy Hillman was Yarrow's heir and certify the fact to the court handling the lawsuit over the loans. The court found that the prior deed of trust had been filed and was therefore a matter of public record that could have been found by the later lender. Judge Morsell's notes recite the facts, but his written opinion is confined to the challenge to Hillman's right to sue and to her claim's being

stale because of the passage of time. The court's ruling was narrow, holding only that because there was insufficient money to pay the last creditor, this creditor's claim was to be dismissed.

25. William Ross was not descended from the David Ross, who had been Samuel Beall's friend and business partner, but he was the son of the Ross mentioned in Jacob Engelbecht's diary about Frederick Hillman, and, ironically, connected to the waning Beall network. When Ross's daughter Juliana married Rev. John Hoff of Georgetown in Frederick in 1839, the Rev. Upton Beall presided. The pastor was the nephew of the Upton Beall who had signed Yarrow's manumission. He went on to become so well known that the Sinclair family named their son for him. This is how the writer Upton Beall Sinclair got his name.

26. Accounting of Nancy Hillman, Frederick County MD Register of Wills, 1851, Accounting Docket G.H. 1–22.

27. Mohan interview. Mohan also noted that African Americans typically were buried only in a shroud. Indeed, no purchase of a coffin is recorded in Hillman's accounting.

28. Will of Nancy Hillman, Frederick County MD Register of Wills, 1851, Will Docket T.S. 1–152.

29. Nonetheless, the fact remains that there were African Americans named Hillman who continued to live in Frederick after Nancy Hillman's death. Likely her in-laws, they are buried in St. John's Church Cemetery. It is surprising that she did not make any provisions for them in her will.

9. Aquilla Yarrow

1. 1783 Tax Assessments, William Chambers, Card File, Montgomery County Historical Society Library, Rockville, Maryland. Beggar's Bennison is also spelled Beggar's Benison in the assessments.

2. It literally means beggar's prayer, but Beggar's Benison also was and is the name for a secret Scottish sex society, and whoever gave the place that name may have intended the double meaning.

3. Volunteers at the Montgomery County Historical Society went through the painstaking process of determining the boundaries of old county land tracts such as Beallmount and Beggars Bennison and drawing these onto sheets of plastic designed to be overlaid on a modern county map. The overlays and maps are kept at the Montgomery County Historical Society library.

Sheila S. Cochran prepared the overlay for the Beallmount and Beggar's Bennison area.

4. Brooke Beall Summary Ledger, Call No. MS 111, Q9700000003309, Maryland Historical Society, Baltimore.

5. Montgomery County MD Land Records, Book G Page 147–48 (March 16, 1796). If Aquilla was eight years old in 1796, he was conceived about 1787. If Yarrow was born in 1736, he was about fifty-one when he sired a son. On the other hand, if Yarrow were born in 1679, as Peale initially heard, then Yarrow was fertile into his 108th year!

6. District of Columbia Deeds, Book R17 Page 201. Researcher Diane D. Broadhurst first discovered Aquilla's manumission. See "An Examination of Slaves and Slavery in the Beall Family Household," unpublished report for the Montgomery County Historical Society, September 25, 2001, 16.

7. Montgomery County Maryland MD Land records, Book K, Page 342, MSA WK 318–19.

8. Frederick Douglass, *Narrative of the Life, My Bondage, and My Freedom, Life and Times* (New York: Literary Classics of the United States, 1994), 41.

9. David Bailles Warden, *A Chorographical and Statistical Description of the District of Columbia* (Paris: Smith, 1816), 119.

10. Photographs of the bricks in an exterior cellar wall were emailed to William M. Kelso, director of archaeology for the Association for the Preservation of Virginia Antiquities. Kelso wrote that one of the bricks looked handmade and hence probably dated to before 1850 and urged the bricks be inspected in person by a qualified person. Email from William Kelso, June 21, 2010.

11. District of Columbia Deeds, Liber E page 80 old, page 67 new. The original ledger books are now at the National Archives and Records Administration in Washington. "Old" refers to the page number in original, handwritten ledgers. "New" refers to the page number in typed, transcribed ledgers at the Recorder of Deeds office.

12. Montgomery County MD, Register of Wills, will, Will Book F, page 184 (October 13, 1807); inventory Will Book F, page 443 (December 7, 1807).

13. Account of Sale of Property of the estates of Sarah and Ann Chambers, Montgomery County MD, Register of Wills, Will Book F, page 287 (April 12, 1808).

14. Warden, *A Chorographical and Statistical Description of the District of Columbia*, 48.

15. Yarrow's property was sold for taxes in 1837. The deed of sale recited that the taxes had not been paid since 1832. This was the year Aquilla died; hence, it is logical to assume that he had continued to pay the taxes after Yarrow's death, but that there was no one to do that after Aquilla died. Tax assessment on heirs of Yarrow, National Archives and Records Administration, Washington DC. Record Group 351, Records of the Government of DC entry 184, Assessment Books 1835–1839, p. 101.

16. Washington County MD, Land Records, Book HH 26 page 248 (March 26, 1825).

10. Mary "Polly" Turner Yarrow

1. Mary Turner and Polly Yarrow was the same person. The 1832 sheriff's list and the 1840 census referred to her as Mary Turner. In the 1850 census she was Mary Yarro. In the 1860 census she was Polly Yaner. An 1877 map named the location of her house as "Mrs. Yarrow's." She was called Polly Yarrow in her obituary. Present-day residents refer to her as Polly Yarrow. The inventory of Aquilla's estate has the annotation "(Polly)" in the margin, but the itemization of the estate sale refers to one buyer as Mary Turner.

2. In order to simplify the relationships, the family tree at the beginning of this book suggests Mary may have been descended from the slave Nick and that Nick was on the *Elijah*. It also shows Samuel as Mary's brother. Neither of these facts is certain.

3. The proof that Mary Turner and Turners, who were slaves of Elie Crampton, were related is circumstantial but strong. First, for the last twenty-five years of her life, Mary "Polly" Turner Yarrow lived less than a mile from Simon Turner, a former slave of Crampton, and his family. Second, Simon Turner's family believed they were related to Nat Turner. Since Nat's owner was Samuel Turner of Southampton, Virginia, Simon may have heard his family had once belonged to a Samuel Turner, but this was surely the same Samuel Turner of Montgomery County who seemed to have owned Mary. Third, there were only two families, black or white, named Turner in Pleasant Valley: Mary Turner and Simon Turner and his family. Fourth, there were only two white men named Turner in Washington County at this time—Jonathan who died in 1818 and Edmund who died in 1822. According to estate inventories at the Maryland State Archives, only Edmund owned slaves. But

he did not live in Pleasant Valley; none of his slaves was named Samuel; and none of the buyers at his estate sale was from Pleasant Valley. Therefore, it seems unlikely that the Cramptons acquired the Turner slaves from him. Fifth, the only plausible explanation for Aquilla's moving to Pleasant Valley is that he and Mary wanted to be near her relatives.

4. The *Hagerstown Herald*, which was read in Pleasant Valley, Maryland, carried the story of Nat Turner's rebellion on August 31, 1831, with the headline "Insurrections of the Blacks" and began with "I have a horrible, heart-rendering tale to relate." *Hagerstown Herald*, August 31, 1831.

5. "An act relating to the People of Color in this state" was passed by the Maryland legislature on March 12, 1832. It is reprinted in, Jerry M. Hynson, *Free African Americans of Maryland 1832* (Westminster, Md.: Family Line Publications, 1998), introduction.

6. Ibid., 131.

7. Interview with Denen Mullendore, June 3, 2010.

8. Nat Turner's father ran away from Samuel Turner's plantation in southern Virginia around 1800, when Nat was but a boy. Stephen B. Oates, *The Fires of Jubilee: Nat Turner's Fierce Rebellion* (New York: Harpers & Row, 1975), 13. For the family story to be true, something like this had to happen. After escaping, Nat's father was recaptured and shipped two hundred miles away to Pleasant Valley, where he started a new family, thus giving Nat a half-brother. Nat's father would have had to tell this boy that he had a half-brother named Nat back in Southampton. And then, thirty-one years later, when Nat's name got in all the papers for leading the rebellion, the half-brother would have had to make the connection. The possibility is too remote, and there is no evidence whatsoever that this happened.

9. There were other connections between Turner and the Yarrows. For example, Samuel Turner's father, John, bought land in Prince George's County from Hugh Riley in 1698. Hugh was the grandfather of the Isaac Riley who owned Josiah Henson. Harry Wright Newman, "John Turner of Anne Arundel County," *Maryland Genealogical Society Bulletin* 33, no. 2 (Spring 1922): 345. Thus, the chain of connection was: the Turners knew the Rileys, the Rileys knew the Wilsons, and the Wilsons owned Yarrow's sister. Similarly, Samuel Turner sold land in Prince George's County to James Low in 1754. This could be the same James Lowe who captained the *Elijah*; there is no way to be certain. When Samuel Turner became Register of Wills in Montgomery County in 1779, he took the oath of office from Joseph Wilson. Ibid., 346. And

when Aquilla's owner, Ann Chambers died, Turner was both a neighbor and the Register of Wills who recorded her will.

10. "Sir Archibald Edmonstone 3rd., The Family Edmonstone of Duntreath, 1875," edited and with additions by Mary McGrigor, 1996, http://tiny.cc/duntreath.

11. Unknown author, "Archibald Edmonston, Maryland, Revised to include his Father Robert Edmonston, the Immigrant," 1990, Prince George's Genealogical Society Library, Prince George's County, Md.

12. "Fight for Millions," *Washington Post*, February 10, 1911.

13. *Town of Bladensburg Minute Book 1742–1789*, Prince George's Historical Society, Prince George's County Md., transcribed from Maryland State Archives, transcriber and date of transcription unknown.

14. Email from Susan Pearl, November 5, 2009. Pearl is a historian and the author of several books on Prince George's County history.

15. Robert E. Oshel and Marilyn S. Slatick, "The Development of Silver Spring," http://tiny.cc/silverspring (accessed October 12, 2010).

16. The value placed on Nicholas in the inventory of Edmonston's estate in 1754 suggested he was a teenager. That is, his value was lower than other male slaves. Prince George's County Circuit Court Records, DD2, 428 (November 27, 1754).

17. Newman, "John Turner of Anne Arundel County," 351.

18. Ibid.

19. Volunteers for the Montgomery County Historical Society prepared acetate overlays to be used with county maps to show the location of the old land patents. These are kept at the society's library in Rockville. Overlay map of old land patents of Montgomery County, F. Howard, Early Montgomery County Land Patents & Survey #12 (1997), Montgomery County Historical Society Library.

20. 1783 Montgomery County Tax Assessment, Samuel Turner, card file, Montgomery County Maryland Historical Society Library. The library also has copies of the original pages of the assessment.

21. Samuel Turner, Inventory, May 1809, Montgomery County MD, Register of Wills, Will Book G page 11. In a document of May 12, 1752, Edmonston pledged slaves as security for a loan to Charles Carroll. The male slaves were Cook, Sharper, Ben, Tom, Peter, and Anthony, and the female slaves were Bab, Dill, Candys, and a child named Clary. This list was made a month before the *Elijah* anchored at Annapolis. Indenture James Edmonston to Charles Carroll,

Prince George's County MD Land Records Book NN page 76 dated May 12, 1752, recorded October 3, 1752. The 1754 inventory of Edmonston's estate showed that he still owned the same ten slaves he had in May 1752 plus Nick. Prince George's County MD Circuit Court Records, DD2, 428 (November 27, 1754). Since Edmonston acquired Nick between May 1752 and his death in late 1753, Nick may have arrived on the *Elijah* along with the teenaged Yarrow Mamout in June 1752 and may have even been from the same part of Africa. In addition, at his death Turner owned Dilly and a fifty-seven-year-old slave named Anthony, who surely were the slaves Dill and Anthony who had belonged to Edmonston.

22. Samuel Turner, Inventory, May 1809, Montgomery County MD, Register of Wills, Will Book G page 11.

23. A bible owned by Samuel Turner's brother, Shadrick, who lived near Greenbelt has been preserved. In it are recorded not only events in the life of Shadrick's family but also of his slaves. The First United Methodist Church of Hyattsville, Md., has this book. Susan Pearl of the Prince George's County Historical Society inspected and photographed the pages. Samuel Turner may have also have kept such records in a bible that is now lost.

24. Samuel Turner, Will, March 1809, Will Book F page 445; Sale, November 1809, Will Book H page 403.

25. The first Clagett in America was Thomas Clagett. His maternal grandfather was Sir Thomas Adams, Lord Mayor of London in 1645 and Member of Parliament. Brice Clagett, unpublished and untitled manuscript, in Clagett family folder, Montgomery County Historical Society library, Rockville, Md. The late Brice Clagett was a gifted Washington lawyer who thoroughly researched the Clagett and related families and was the local authority on them. He reportedly had thousands of pages, but he never published.

26. The Clagetts were also friends of Samuel Turner. He had done business with various members of the family for years, purchasing some of his Montgomery County land from them. In 1763, Turner borrowed £80 from Thomas Clagett of Prince George's County and pledged three slaves as security for the loan. "John Turner of Anne Arundel County," 351. The slaves were Thomas Cooke, age eight; Anthony, age six; and William, age four. The security agreement included a heartless clause providing that the three boys would be sold at public auction if the loan were not repaid. Prince George's County Maryland Land Records TT, 25 (May 25, 1763). The slaves were treated as commodities, like horses or sewing needles, to be auctioned off as security for

a debt. Cooke and Anthony were also the names of the slaves that had been pledged to Carroll in 1752, but their ages in 1763 suggest they were not the same people. Perhaps they were the sons of the men named in the 1752 document, or perhaps the ages were wrong.

27. He had grown up in Montgomery County and, when he moved to Pleasant Valley, he sold his Quince Orchard estate in Montgomery County to Joseph.

28. Brice Clagett manuscript, 1. See also Ann Harris, "Clagetts of Potomac, Part I," *Potomac Gazette*, April 12, 1989; copy in Clagett family folder, Montgomery County Historical Society.

29. Documents suggest three possible routes for how Mary Turner ended up married to Aquilla by 1830 and how Simon Turner ended up a slave to Elie Crampton. Although Simon was not born until later, there is reason to believe his father was named Samuel, a name that shows up in the documents. First, there is a slave named Samuel in the inventory of the estate of Elie's grandfather, Thomas, who died in 1819 and in the estate of Elie's father, Elias, who died in 1825. Elias Crampton Inventory, Washington County MD, Executors and Administrators Accounts 8, 230. Under this scenario, after Samuel Turner died, the Clagetts may have arranged the sale of the family of the slave Samuel to Thomas Crampton. These slaves were then passed along to Thomas's son and grandson by inheritance. The second possibility comes from the inventory of Joseph Clagett's estate in 1829. He had handled Turner's estate. Clagett's inventory lists a "Polly and child." Joseph Clagett Inventory, Montgomery County MD Will Book Q, page 515 (September 1829). Although Polly was a common name, this might have been Polly Yarrow. They were valued at only $30, whereas other women with a child were valued at far more. The probate record further showed that she and the child were sold to Joseph's son, but for only five dollars. That suggests a token sale that might have been done for purposes of freeing them. Perhaps, Polly had already joined Aquilla in Pleasant Valley by the time Clagett died but was still counted as a slave in the inventory of his estate. Third, in 1828, Horatio Clagett sold an eighty-six-acre farm in western Montgomery County to Elie Crampton. He also sold a slave named Samuel at the same time but the record does not list the buyer. It might have been Crampton. Frederick County MD Equity Court Liber JS-8, 536–554, (February 1825), Dorinda Davis Shepley, "Equity Records at Mid Maryland Roots, http://tiny.cc/equity-court. Although these documents suggest possibilities, none is definitive.

11. Aquilla and Polly in Pleasant Valley

1. Interview with Gary Himes, September 20, 2010. Himes is a source of local history, color, and good humor.

2. The Scots and English families included the Clagetts and Botelers, who had come from Montgomery and Prince George's counties to the east, while the Germans, like the Hoffmasters and Mullendores, came from Pennsylvania.

3. George Ross, *American Freedmen's Inquiry Commission Interviews, 1863*, Slave Testimony, 405, 406. Ross was born in 1817 and interviewed in 1863 when he was forty-six. He said he came from Hagerstown.

4. Federal Writers' Project 1936–38, *Slave Narratives, A Folk History of Slavery in the United States From Interviews with Former Slaves* (Washington, D.C.: Library of Congress, 1941), volume 8, Maryland Narratives 44.

5. John Thomas Scharf, *History of Western Maryland* (Philadelphia: L. H. Everts, 1882), 1:1047.

6. Yarrow's lot was sold for unpaid taxes in 1837. The deed of sale recited that the taxes had not been paid since 1832, which was the year Aquilla died, so presumably Aquilla was the one who paid the taxes between Yarrow's death in 1823 and his own death in 1832. National Archives and Records Administration, Tax Assessment, Record Group 351, Records of the Government of the District of Columbia entry 184, Assessment Books 1835–1839, p. 101; Deed from Corporation of Georgetown to Henry Trunnell; Record Group 351 Deed Books, Vol. 68 page 198; Deed from Henry Trunnell to Francis Dodge, Record Group 351, Liber WB No. 62 382 old, 287 new.

7. Several residents of Pleasant Valley spoke of existing buildings or ruins on the eastern slope of Elk Ridge near Yarrowsburg that they thought might be slave cabins. Interviews with John Eaton, April 26, 2007; Alice Kelly, April 25, 2007; William Wadbrook, April 27, 2007; and Judy Wolf, May 2, 2007.

8. Richard Grim vs. Elizabeth Grim at the Maryland State Archives, MSA T450–1, SC 4239–32–22, involved litigation over slaves belonging to Alexander Grim's estate. Grim is buried in the graveyard at St. Luke's Episcopal Church in Brownsville.

9. *Hagerstown Torch Light*, February 22, 1825; ibid., March 1, 1825. The latter specified one hundred acres of Grim's "King Kole" and "Keep Trice" properties, together with two slaves.

10. Reverend Edward T. Helfenstein, Editor, "Consecration of St. Luke's," *The Church News*, November 1, 1894, copy in church history file at St. Luke's Episcopal Church, Brownsville, Md.

11. During the Battle of Antietam, St. Luke's Church was converted into a field hospital for Confederate wounded. Once the Confederates had cleared out, Union troops came and burned the church. The church is in use today, and the burning is still in evidence. According to the church's present pastor, Rev. Charles Holder, painters working there recently noticed charred wood behind the walls and asked him if there had been a fire. "Yes," he replied, "in 1862." Charles Holder interview, May 7, 2011.

12. William Mullenix and John Bowers interview, October 22, 2005.

13. Thomas W. Henry, *Autobiography of Thomas W. Henry, of the A.M.E. Church,* (Baltimore: 1872) electronic edition, University of North Carolina, page 25. Indeed, manumission records in Washington County show several manumissions of people at the iron works. Marsha Lynne Fuller, *African American Manumissions of Washington County, Maryland* (Westminster, Md.: Heritage Books, 2007).

14. Richard D. Raymond, Museum Curator, Harpers Ferry National Historical Park, September 29, 2008.

15. Interview with Robert Bowers, August 31, 2010. According to Bowers, a local Mennonite group slaughters and quarters the hogs. Bowers and others buy the meat and make other products from it.

16. Harlan D. Unrau, *Historic Resource Study: Chesapeake & Ohio Canal* (Hagerstown, Md.: U.S. Department of the Interior, National Park Service, C& O National Historical Park, 2007), 121.

17. Since there was a fee for recording manumissions, free blacks may not have done that. A delegate to the American Colonization Society convention in this time period found "that in Washington County the number of newly freed Negroes allowed to remain in the state without permits from the Orphans' Court far exceeded the number which complied with the law in this respect. . . . He thereupon contacted county officials and in every case found either total neglect of the law or so little attention to it that it might as well not have existed. Evidence confirmed earlier speculation that manumitted slaves frequently remained unnoticed in the community, keeping the fact of their freedom as quiet as possible and relying upon their own insignificance for exemption from the law." Penelope Campbell, *Maryland in Africa: The Maryland State Colonization Society 1831–1857* (Urbana: University of Illinois Press, 1971) 177.

18. Estate of Aquilla Yarrow, Washington County Register of Wills, Letter of Administration, Book I, page 310 (October 2, 1832), Appraisal Book I page

554, Debts Book A page 61, Sale of Personal Property Book L, page 159, Accounts Book 9 page 441 and Book 10 page 4.

19. *Virginia Free Press*, September 6, 1832; September 20, 1832; September 27, 1832; October 4, 1832; *Hagerstown Mail*, July 27, 1832. The papers did advise cooking food and not eating fruits or vegetables, such as watermelons, that lay on the ground.

20. "The Board of Health, organized in Hagerstown, deem it a duty which they owe to the town, and the adjacent country, under the present state of excitement and alarm, to state that although the prevailing epidemic has made its appearance in this place, and proved fatal to three of our citizens, and two strangers from the line of the canal, yet there has been no case of cholera in town since Saturday last." *Hagerstown Mail*, September 28, 1832.

21. Unrau, *Historic Resource Study*, 121–127. The check registers for the Canal Company have been preserved. There is no record of a payment to Aquilla Yarrow or indeed to any individual workman. Instead, the construction was done under contract. The check registers only show the payments to the contractors, who in turn hired the workers. National Archives and Records Administration, Records of the National Park Service (Record Group 79), Register of Requisitions and Checks, 1828–70 (Entry 349) (Location: Archives II, 150/36/19/1).

22. Pleasant Valley resident Robert Bowers remembered three stone markers in the field next to Yarrowsburg Road. He was told they were Polly Yarrow's, her husband's, and a boy's. However, the area is now covered with brush and brambles, and he and I were able to find only flat stones during a visit on August 30, 2010.

12. Traces of Yarrow

1. National Archives and Records Administration, Tax Assessment, Record Group 351, Records of the Government of the District of Columbia entry 184, Assessment Books 1835–1839 p. 101; Deed from Corporation of Georgetown to Henry Trunnell; Record Group 351 Deed Books, Vol. 68 page 198; Deed from Henry Trunnell to Francis Dodge, Record Group 351, Liber WB No. 62 382 old, 287 new.

2. In researching this book, I met Gloria Edmonson of the District of Columbia in the congregation of Mount Moriah Church. Her husband, Glenwood, said his ancestors got their name because they were slaves of James Edmonston of Berkeley Springs. This was the same James Edmonston that Samuel Beall knew. Edmonson also said that he thought he might be related to the Edmonsons on the *Pearl* because he heard family stories about relatives that got into trouble on a ship and that were imprisoned for an escape. The *Pearl* was not mentioned. He read about it later and made the connection. Glenwood Edmonson also said he saw pictures of the Edmonsons who were on the *Pearl* and, they reminded him of his grandfather's relatives. Interviews, August 8, 2008, and February 12, 2009.

3. Mary Kay Ricks, *Escape on the Pearl: The Heroic Bid for Freedom on the Underground Railroad* (New York: Morrow, 2007).

4. Daniel Drayton, *The Flight and Capture of the Pearl, Personal Memoir of Daniel Drayton* (1855), excerpts reprinted in John R. Wennersten and Robert S. Pohl, *Abraham Lincoln and the End of Slavery in the District of Columbia* (Washington, D.C.: Eastern Branch Press, 2009), 41, 46.

5. Thomas Bloomer Balch, "Reminiscences of Georgetown, Second Lecture Delivered in the Methodist Protestant Church, Georgetown D.C.," March 9, 1859.

6. Thomas Bloomer Balch, "Reminiscences of Georgetown, A Lecture Delivered in the Methodist Protestant Church, Georgetown D.C.," January 20, 1859.

7. Balch, "Reminiscences of Georgetown, Second Lecture," 13.

8. "A Montgomery County Negro 119 Years Old," *Maryland Sentinel*, 1879, in John Thomas Scharf, *History of Western Maryland* (Philadelphia: L. H. Everts, 1882), 684–685.

9. Ibid.

10. Ibid.

11. Charles Willson Peale, *Selected Papers of Charles Willson Peale*, ed. Lillian B. Miller, Sidney Hart, and Toby A. Appel (New Haven: Yale University Press, 1983), 3:651.

12. Eleanor M. V. Cook, "The Four Beall Women and Their Slaves," *The Montgomery County Story* 45 (February 2002): 1.

13. "The Legal Record, *Washington Post*, October 5, 1911.

14. Grace Dunlop Ecker, *A Portrait of Old Georgetown* (Richmond, Va.: Garrett & Massie, 1933), 171.

13. Unpleasant Valley

1. Edward L. Adams Jr., Thomas Crampton of Gapland, Washington Co., MD, and family http://tiny.cc/my-families-va (accessed May 10, 2011). Interview with Adams, descendant who researched the family.

2. Conceivably, Thomas Crampton acquired the additional six slaves by purchasing them from Samuel Turner's estate in 1809, meaning the Turners arrived in Pleasant Valley about that time. When Crampton died in 1819, the inventory of his estate listed four slaves with the same names as ones in Samuel Turner's estate: George, James, Isaac, and Harry. But since these were common names, this fact alone does not mean much. More significant was the fact that Thomas also owned a slave named Samuel, who would be passed through Thomas's son, Elias, to his grandson, Elie Crampton, and who may have been Simon Turner's father. Simon was sometime referred to by the name Samuel, as though his father's name was Samuel. Simon's father may have been born around 1816, because the 1860 slave schedule showed Elie Crampton owned a forty-four-year-old male slave, who was probably Simon's father. Simon's manumission referred to him as Samuel alias Simon Turner. Washington County MD Land Records Book IN 17, page 596 (April 19, 1864). Simon enlisted in the army as Samuel Turner. However, he was listed in the census as Simon and applied for a veteran's pension as Simon.

3. Jacob Engelbrecht, *The Diary of Jacob Engelbrecht*, ed. William R. Quynn (Frederick, Md.: Historical Society of Frederick County, 2001), 811.

4. Charles Varle, *A Map of Frederick and Washington Counties* (Philadelphia: Francis Shallus, 1806).

5. For a history of African Americans in Washington County, see Eddie B. Wallace, "Reclaiming Forgotten History: Preserving Rural African-American Cultural Resources in Washington County, Maryland," M.A. thesis, Goucher College, 2003.

6. The 1840 census shows Mary Turner and Samuel Clagett separated by fifteen names.

7. Other delegates to the American Colonization Society's convention from the valley were sufficiently important that they are place names now: Peter Beelar, for whom Beeler's Summit is named; Edward Garrett, whose name is associated with Garretts Mill; and Caspar W. Weaver, who gave his name to the community of Weverton. James Hall, ed., *Maryland Colonization Society Journal* 1, no. 1 (1841): 12.

8. Ibid., 5.

9. Grimm was of German descent and a member of the Church of the Brethren. He was not related to the Alexander Grim, an Episcopalian, who had sold Aquilla his land.

10. Thomas Henry, *Autobiography of Reverend Thomas W. Henry, of the A.M.E. Church* (Baltimore: Thomas Henry, 1872), 27–28. The "white church" was located at what is now the intersection of Rohrersville Road and Trego Road south of Rohrersville.

11. Interview with William Mullenix, October 11, 2005.

12. Allen Sparrow diary in George Brigham Jr. Library, quoted in Kathleen A. Ernst, *Too Afraid to Cry: Maryland Civilians in the Antietam Campaign* (Mechanicsburg, Pa.: Stackpole Books, 1999), 14.

13. George Ross, *American Freedmen's Inquiry Commission Interviews*, 1863, Slave Testimony, 405.

14. Interviews with Dennis Hammond, March 20, 2010; Rev. Charles Holder, April 13, 2010; Ellen Hammond, March 22, 2010. All three said the story of slaves being whipped was about the Grim/Edwards house, which still is standing to the west of St. Luke's Episcopal Church.

15. Interview with John Frye, March 23, 2007.

16. Ross, *American Freedmen's Inquiry*, 406.

17. Even George Ross noted that life as a slave in Washington County for him personally was not too bad. His fear was that he had no control over his own destiny, since he might be sold. Indeed, when his owner ran into financial difficulties and failed to pay his debts, Ross and the other slaves were treated as mere property on which creditors levied. Ross said he and seven others were jailed until their owner could pay his debts: "We were treated first rate in jail. . . . [S]eeing we were trusty servants, [the jailer] let us out to wait on tables, sweep the yard, and so on. I was married, & he said, 'you may go home every night at 7 o'clock, and come back at 7 in the morning,' and so I did. The other fellows drove the jailer's wife all over town, & walked round the streets smoking segars, and came back to the jail to sleep night. If I could not have been sold, you may be sure I would not have left, because I could not expect to be any better off in slavery." Ibid. 407–408.

18. Wesley and Arthur must have been brothers. The 1860 census showed Wesley as sixty-years old, so he was born in 1800. The same census showed Arthur as forty-eight, suggesting he was born in 1812. However, the 1870 and 1880 census gave ages for Arthur that would put his birth around 1802. In

any event, he was younger than Wesley. They were obviously related because descendants of Arthur have preserved a document signed by Wesley.

19. Handwritten promissory note from Wesley Sands to John Gray, administrator of the estate of Thomas Clagett, January 23, 1847, in possession of Arthur Sands's descendant Gloria Ford Dennis of Baltimore.

20. Written in pencil on the back of the document is, "Important History My Grandfather pays slave owner for his Daughter." This note was obviously added by someone later; Wesley Sands was illiterate. The note does not square with the facts though. It was probably written by Emma Turner. She was in the first generation of the family that could write. She was the granddaughter of Arthur Sands, not Wesley. The purpose of the promissory note may have gotten confused by the time the story reached her. John Gray did not own Wesley Sands's daughter. He owned the wife and daughter of Arthur, who did indeed buy his wife's and children's freedom from Gray, but in 1860 not 1847. In other words, while the promissory note was rightly handed down as an important family document, the story behind it got twisted in the telling. By the time it was passed on to Emma, she may have concluded that this was the document by which her grandfather had purchased her mother's freedom from Gray. The family also has a bill of sale of May 18, 1849, reciting that a Henry Duvall sold Wesley Sands to Sands's own wife, Henrietta. Duvall did "grant, bargain, sell, alien, release, and confirm unto the said Henrietta Sands a negro man named Wesley (husband of said Henrietta Sands)." This means that Sands was married to a free woman. The document undercuts the penciled suggestion that Wesley used the promissory note to purchase his daughter's freedom. If Wesley's wife was free, then his daughter should have been free as a matter of law because she was born of a free woman.

21. Arthur was a slave to John Mullendore, according to his manumission. Washington County MD Land Records IN 5 page 596 (March 22, 1857).

22. Jane Emmert affidavit in support of Lucinda Turner pension application. Case of Lucinda Turner, No. 709030. Simon Turner, Company D, 39th Regiment USCT, Civil War Pension Records, National Archives and Records Administration, Washington DC. (Hereafter "Turner Pension File"). Actually, in the affidavit Crampton's daughter was confused and said Arthur Sands was owned by a Clagett, but such confusion about events that happened forty years earlier is understandable.

23. Interview with Rev. Charles Holder, May 7, 2011.

24. Lucinda Turner affidavit, Turner Pension File.

25. Washington County MD Deed Book IN page 425 (September 7, 1858).

26. Interview with John Frye, May 12, 2011.

27. A former Pleasant Valley resident did meet Brown. In fact, the man was in Harpers Ferry during the raid, met Brown after he was captured, and wrote about it. This was Alexander Boteler. He was the son of Dr. Henry Boteler of Pleasant Valley and his wife Priscilla, the granddaughter of Charles Willson Peale. The younger Boteler was a congressman from Shepherdstown, an office he gave up to become a general in the Confederate Army.

Years later, Boteler wrote an article about the meeting. In October 1859, he was at his home in Shepherdstown when his daughter brought news from town of "a negro insurrection at Harper's Ferry." She reported hearing that Negroes there had been issued guns and were shooting people in the streets. Boteler immediately set out to see for himself. As he rode to Harpers Ferry, he was calmed somewhat by seeing "the negroes were at work as usual" on the farms along the way. By the time Boteler got to Harpers Ferry, Brown and his men had retreated to the firehouse in the town to make their stand. Eventually, U.S. Marines under the command of Colonel Robert E. Lee broke into the firehouse and captured Brown and his raiders. Boteler went inside a short time later and briefly questioned the firebrand but to no purpose or effect. Still, the mere fact he spoke to Brown got the article published. Biographical Directory of the United States Congress. http://tiny.cc/arboteler. Alexander Boteler "Recollections of the John Brown Raid by a Virginian Who Witnessed the Fight," *Century Magazine*, 26 (July 1883), 399–411.

28. Osborne P. Anderson, *A Voice from Harper's Ferry* (Boston: Osborne P. Anderson, 1861) 53; Ralph Keeler, "Owen Brown's Escape from Harper's Ferry," *Atlantic Monthly*, (March 1874). In Keeler's article, Owen Brown recounted how his group took "a new road" into Pleasant Valley. Present-day resident and valley historian John Frye said that was surely not the road at Solomon's Gap but another road, no longer there, that led from Chestnut Grove Road over Elk Ridge and into Rohrersville. Frye said that since Elk Ridge is about six hundred feet lower in elevation there than at Solomon's Gap, it would be a much easier route. Interview with John Frye, May 12, 2011. Anderson was less specific about his route.

29. The Maryland Code: Public General Laws and Public Local Laws, 1860, Volume 145, page 458 [Art. 66. Free Negroes. Manumission. 42].

30. Washington County MD Deed book, IN 15 pages 41–42 (May 30, 1860). On the same day, a manumission was filed for Henrietta Sands. Washington County MD Deed book IN 14 page 643 (May 30, 1860). However, this

manumission was dated ten years earlier, August 1850. The Henrietta Sands in this earlier manumission was described as a thirty-five-year-old Negro slave and the daughter-in-law of Henrietta Sands. Elie Crampton witnessed it. Given that it was filed on the same date as the manumission that Arthur Sands filed, Henrietta was presumably related to him. To add further confusion, both Arthur's and Wesley's wives were named Henrietta. Conceivably, this was a manumission of Arthur's wife in 1850 by Wesley's wife, but if that were true, then Arthur did not need to buy his wife's freedom. Besides, if the census data is believed, Wesley was only a few years older than Arthur and so Arthur's wife could not have been his wife's daughter-in-law. Perhaps, this woman was yet a third Henrietta Sands.

31. Washington County MD Deed book, IN, 710–711 (October 22, 1861).

32. Ernst, *Too Afraid to Cry.*

33. Reports of Maj. Gen. Lafayette McLaws, C.S. Army (October 18, 1862), Commanding Division, of Operations September 10–17, The Maryland Campaign, September 3–20, 1862, Official Records, Series I, Volume XIX/1.

34. Doris Kearns Goodwin, *Team of Rivals* (New York: Simon & Schuster, 2005), 468.

35. Less than a year after the Battle of Antietam, in July 1863, the threat of war came to the valley again. The Confederates were fleeing from their defeat at Gettysburg while Union forces were trying to prevent Lee's army from crossing the Potomac River to get back on Virginia soil. This time, however, only Union troops occupied the valley. The beaten Confederate Army passed farther west and crossed the river unmolested. The valley was at peace for a bit longer.

36. *Hagerstown Herald and Torchlight*, October 7, 1863; Washington County MD Appraisals Book U, 724, 727 (November 9, 1863).

37. W. O. Tobey and Milton Wright were editors of a pamphlet called "Religious Telescope." Bishop Wright's tribute to Tobey appeared in *The Christian Conservator* periodical of January 17, 1917, p. 2. Wright wrote that William Otterbein Tobey was born near Burkittsville and grew up on his father's farm in Washington County.

38. *Minutes of the Annual Meetings of the Church of the Brethren: Containing All Available Minutes from 1778–1909* (Elgin, Ill.: Brethren Publishing House, 1909), 135, 142–143.

39. Lucinda Turner affidavit, Simon Turner Pension File.

40. Washington County MD, Land Records, Book IN 17, 586.

41. Washington County MD, Accounts Book 22, 341.

42. Interview with Isabel Johnson, November 16, 2005.

43. Biographical Directory of the United States Congress. http://tiny.cc/ozora.

44. "Field and Staff of 39th U.S. Colored Inf. In front of Petersburg, Va., Sep 1864. Library of Congress. Reproduction number LC-DIG-cwpb-04364, Call number LC-B817-7052 (glass negative; lot 4187 [photographic print]).

45. L. Allison Wilmer, J. H. Jarrett, W. F. George Vernon, State Commissioners, *Maryland Volunteers, War of 1861–5* (Baltimore: Press of Guggenheimer, Weil & Co., 1899), 2:261.

46. His manumission referred to him as "Samuel alias Simon Turner." Washington County MD Land Records Book IN 17, 586 (April 19, 1864).

47. "Account of the Rebel Raid through Middletown Valley," *Middletown Valley Register*, July 8, 1864.

48. Interview with Isabel Johnson, May 26, 2010.

49. Interview with Regina Jones, August 1, 2010.

50. Congressional Medal of Honor Society, http://tiny.cc/dorseydecatur.

51. Wilmer, *Maryland Volunteers*, 262–289.

52. Lucinda Turner affidavit, Simon Turner Pension File.

14. Freedom

1. Mollie Crampton letter, June 9, 1864, in possession of Charles and Ann Gardenhour, Cheverly, Maryland. Charles Gardenhour is a descendant of Elie Crampton.

2. Simon Turner, pension application form, Simon Turner Pension File; Lucinda Turner affidavit, December 22, 1899, Simon Turner Pension File.

3. Slave Codes of the State of Georgia, 1848, Section II, 11. http://tiny.cc/slavecodes (October 1, 2010).

4. James Edemy affidavit, undated, Simon Turner Pension File.

5. Interviews with Mary Gross, July 19, 2010, and Isabel Mariah Johnson, July 16, 2010.

6. Washington County MD Deed Book, Book IN 19, 714–715 (March 12, 1867). Anderson bought the land from John H. Reed. The 1860 census showed Reed ran a boarding house in Sandy Hook, Maryland. The 1870 census listed him as a "ret. [retail] merchant." The Sands property was on what is now

called "Reed Road," but former resident Isabel Johnson said the road names are relatively new. When she lived in Yarrowsburg in 1926, the back roads had no names. What is more, she said that a family named Reed had a house on Israel Creek and what is now Garretts Mill Road. The same road is called "Reed Road" on other maps. Interview with Isabel Johnson, May 26, 2010.

7. Washington County MD Deed Book, Book WmCKK 1 page 78 (September 7, 1868).

8. Hamilton Keys, Teacher's Monthly School Report for the Month of August 1868, Pleasant Valley, Freedmen's Bureau Records, National Archives and Records Administration.

9. Ibid., January 1868.

10. Lizzie Lovett, Teacher's Monthly School Report for the Month of February 1869, Pleasant Valley, Freedmen's Bureau Records, National Archives and Records Administration.

11. *An Illustrated Atlas of Washington County, Maryland* (Philadelphia: Griffing, Lake, and Stevenson, 1877).

12. Interview with Isabel Johnson, May 26, 2010.

13. Interview with William Mullenix, October 26, 2005.

14. *Hagerstown Herald and Torch Light*, November 26, 1885.

15. Simon Turner application for pension, Simon Turner Pension File.

16. Interviews with John Frye, March 22, 2010; Judy Wolf, May 5, 2007; Isabel Johnson, March 16, 2007; Mary Gross, July 19, 2010.

17. Lucinda Turner affidavit, Simon Turner Pension File; email from Richard Raymond, National Park Service historian, Harpers Ferry, March 27, 2007, with attachment StorCollege Stdnts. The file was described as a "loosely documented" student list that the Park Service had prepared from Storer College Records. Emma Turner was listed with the date 1890. Since she was only fifteen years old, this was most likely the date she entered rather than graduated. The National Park Service acquired the Storer College campus. Most of the college's records were reportedly turned over to the University of West Virginia.

18. Vivian Verdell Gordon, "A History of Storer College, Harpers Ferry, West Virginia," *Journal of Negro Education* 30, no. 4 (Autumn 1961): 445–449.

19. Simon Turner's Pension File contains his applications for pensions and the medical examinations. Although the file suggests that his second pension application was also disallowed because of the medical examination, the special examiner who investigated Lucinda's request for a widow's pension,

wrote "the question as to identity [of Simon and Samuel Turner] was evidently settled when soldier's claim was allowed." Letter W. E. Clapp, Special Examiner to Hon. H. Clay Evans, Commissioner of Pensions, Washington, D.C., October 30, 1900, Simon Turner Pension File.

20. Interview with Cynthia Richardson, Denise Dungee, Emily Willis, and Alice Truiet, August 15, 2010.

21. Washington County MD Land Records Book GBO 99, page 530 (January 6, 1893).

22. Washington County MD Land Records Book GBO 95, page 55 (May 1, 1890).

23. Interview with Isabel Mariah Johnson, May 26, 2010.

24. Simon Turner death certificate, Simon Turner Pension File.

25. Clapp Letter, Simon Turner Pension file.

26. Affidavit of Lucinda Turner before W. E. Clapp, October 29, 1900, Case of Lucinda Turner, No. 709030, Simon Turner Pension file.

27. Simon Turner Pension File.

28. Lucinda Turner affidavit, Simon Turner Pension File. According to the affidavit, Hattie Turner had purchased twenty acres of the farm from Lucinda, although this was not reflected in a deed. At the time, Hattie was keeping house for, as Lucinda described them, "two wealthy widows" at 1735 Q Street NW in Washington. The 1900 census confirms this, although it shows her keeping house for three sisters.

29. James Huffmaster and Thomas Spencer affidavit, November 25, 1899, Simon Turner Pension File.

30. Clapp Letter, Simon Turner Pension File.

31. Interview with Cynthia Richardson, October 17, 2010. The 1900 census shows Lucinda and Martha in Funkstown with a lodger named Jerry Ruffin. Richardson believes that Ruffin and Martha married.

32. Interview with Cynthia Richardson, August 31, 2006.

15. From Harvard to Today

1. Interview with Cynthia Ford Richardson, March 3, 2007.

2. Cynthia Ford Richardson, "Interview with a person over 50 years of age about the highlights of the times in which he lived," Robert Turner Ford, 1979.

3. Maryland Census 1910.

4. Richardson, "Interview."

5. Maryland Census 1920.

6. Richardson, "Interview."

7. African Methodist Episcopal Church, History http://www.amechurch.com.

8. The church building is not the same, of course. Not only did it burn down in Rev. Henry's day, but it also burned down since Rev. Ford was pastor. The church's current edifice has a cornerstone dated 1869, but it was a Methodist church, converted to an A.M.E. one in 1986. Rev. Jonathan Davis telephone interview by author October 17, 2010.

9. Thomas W. Henry, *Autobiography of Thomas W. Henry, of the A.M.E. Church* (Baltimore: Privately printed, 1872), 29–30.

10. "Uncle Jim" was James Turner, who was still living in Washington County in the early 1900s. Only George and Robert Ford's descendants are known. The Turner family still owned the farm on Elk Ridge, but the house there had burned down by this time.

11. Richardson, "Interview."

12. Robert Turner Ford, "What Harvard Has Meant to Me," Harvard University Class Reunion (1984).

13. Werner Sellers, Caldwell Sitcom, and Thomas A. Underwood, eds., *Blacks at Harvard: A Documentary History of African-American Experience at Harvard and Radcliff* (New York: New York University Press, 1993), 2.

14. Randall Kennedy, "Blacks and the Race Question at Harvard," in ibid., xix.

15. Ibid., xxi.

16. Sellers, *Blacks at Harvard,* 59.

17. Kennedy, "Blacks and the Race Question at Harvard," *Blacks at Harvard,* xxi.

18. Harvard Alumni Office, *Harvard Alumni Directory (*Boston: Harvard Alumni Associaton, 1919), 177.

19. Kennedy, "Blacks and the Race Question."

20. Wolters, *Blacks at Harvard,* 195, citing A. Lawrence Lowell to Roscoe Conkling Bruce, *New York Age,* 20 January 1923; *Literary Digest* 74 (July 8, 1922): 28–29.

21. Wolters, *Blacks at Harvard,* 198.

22. Ibid., 201.

23. Richardson, "Interview."

24. The family only has a photographic copy of Ford's speech. Several words in the quoted portion are illegible, and words have been substituted that seem to keep the meaning.

25. Richardson, "Interview."

26. Ibid.

27. Interview with Alice Ford Truiett, the daughter of Robert and Goldia Ford, August 15, 2010.

28. Richardson, "Interview."

Epilogue: Guide to the Yarrows' and Turners' World Today

1. Charles Willson Peale, *The Selected Papers of Charles Willson Peale and His Family,* ed. Lillian B. Miller, Sidney Hart, and Toby A. Appel (New Haven: Yale University Press, 1983), 3:648.

2. Sally Somervell Mackall, *Early Days of Washington* (Washington, D.C.: Neale Company, 1899), 159.

3. Virginia Hollerith, "Oral History Interview" by Mary Jo Dearing, May 1, 1981, Barnard-Talcott Hollerith Family Papers, Special Collections Research Enter, The George Washington University, Gellman MS2088, 5; *Washington Post,* October 5, 1911.

4. Virginia Hollerith Oral History, 43.

5. Grace Dunlop Ecker, *A Portrait of Old George Town* (Richmond, Va.: Garrett & Massie, 1933), 171.

6. The *Washington Post* of October 11, 1915, announced the engagement of Mr. and Mrs. Edmund Myers Talcott's daughter, Dorothy Lawrence, to Hugh Gaylord Barclay.

7. Steve Dryden, *Peirce Mill: 200 Years in the Nation's Capital* (Washington, D.C.: Bergamot, 2009).

8. Interview with Margaret Cheney, November 8, 2005.

9. Email from William Kelso, Preservation Virginia Foundation, June 21, 2010.

10. Interview with Larry Todd, Recorder of Deeds for the District of Columbia, February 1, 2006.

11. Martha Sprigg Poole, "Early Rockville Taverns," *The Montgomery County Story* 1, no. 3 (May 1958): 5.

12. Interview with Mary Fertig, July 11, 2008.

13. Paula Stoner, Architectural Historian, "King Cole," "Grim Farm," "Edwards Farm," WA-III-010, Maryland Inventory of Historic Properties, District 8, Map 86, parcel 88, 11, Maryland Route 67, Brownsville (June 1978), www.mdihp.net.

14. Interview with John Frye, October 1, 2005.

15. Paula Stoner, Architectural Historian, "Claggett Farm," WA-III-055, Maryland Inventory of Historic Properties, District 8, Map 84, Parcel 84 (July 1978), www.mdihp.net. John Frye, valley resident and historian at the Washington County Free Library, believes the house on the northeast corner of Rohrersville and Gapland Road was Horatio Clagett's. Indeed, that would fit with Rev. Thomas Henry's description of Clagett living near the AME church in Pleasant Valley. However, Horatio Clagett's house is not included on the Inventory of Historic Properties.

16. Paula Stoner, Architectural Historian, "Crampton-Mullendore Farm," Maryland Inventory of Historic Properties, WA-III-008. District 8, Map 84, Parcel 10, Reedsville (July 1978), www.mdihp.net. Denen Mullendore owns the farm today.

17. Paul Stoner, Architectural Historian, "19th Century Brick Farmhouse," WA-III-011, Maryland Inventory of Historic Properties, District 8, Map 86, Parcel 39, Brownsville (July 1978), www.mdihp.net.

18. Interview with Regina Jones, August 1, 2010.

19. Paula Stoner Dickey, Consultant, "Magnolia Plantation, WA-III-014, Maryland Inventory of Historic Properties, Knoxville, Maryland (July 1974), www.mdihp.net.

20. Deed by Robert and Rebecca Boteler to Ezra Bush, Arthur Sands, Reuben Brockett, Daniel Bush, and Jerry Brown Trustees of Free Baptist Church of Pleasant Valley. Washington County MD Land Records, GBO 95, p. 55 (December 4, 1893).

21. Ibid., IN 19, p. 714 (March 12, 1867); ibid., WMcKK 1, page 78 (September 7, 1868).

22. History, Saint Luke's Episcopal Church, Brownsville, Maryland, www.stluke.ang-md.org; interview with Rev. Charles Holder, May 7, 2011.

23. Eleanor Vaughn Cook's manuscript on the Bealls and Johns families indicated Beallmount was about 1,900 acres. However, an 1895 profile of descendant Margaret Beall stated that even after she had sold off four farms, Beallmount still had 2,500 acres. *Portrait and Biographical Record of the Sixth Congressional District, Maryland* (New York: Chapman Publishing, 1895), 674.

24. Michael F. Dwyer, Senior Park Historian, "Beall's Mill Site, M: 25–16, Maryland Inventory of Historic Properties (2/28/75), www.mdihp.net. I visited the site in 2011. The stonework for two watermills is still visible, as is other stonework. A large millrace can also be seen.

25. John Turner of Anne Arundel County, *Maryland Genealogical Society Bulletin* 347; Theodore Bissell, "Tracing Shadrick and Sarah Turner, Pioneer Methodists of Bladensburg," *Prince George's Historical Society, News & Notes* 1, no. 10 (December 1973). Copy in Turner family file, Montgomery County Historical Society Library, Rockville, Md.

26. Ray Jones, *Harpers Ferry* (Gretna, La.: Pelican Publishing, 1992) 58; Merritt Roe Smith, *Harpers Ferry Armory and New Technology* (Ithaca, N.Y.: Cornell University Press, 1980).

27. Vivian Verdell Gordon, "A History of Storer College, Harpers Ferry, West Virginia," *Journal of Negro Education* 30, no. 4 (Autumn 1961): 445. Quotations from Storer College catalogue of 1870.

28. National Park Service, Camp Hill & Storer College, http://tiny.cc/storer-college.

29. Trans-Atlantic Slave Trade Database, www.slavevoyages.org.

Bibliography

Adams, Edward L. Jr. "RootsWeb's WorldConnect Project." http://tiny.cc/my-families-va (accessed May 10, 2011).

Alford, Terry. *Prince Among Slaves.* Oxford: Oxford University Press, 2007.

Anderson, Osborne P. *A Voice from Harper's Ferry.* Boston: Osborne P. Anderson, 1861.

Balch, Thomas Bloomer. "Reminiscences of Georgetown D.C." Lecture delivered at the Methodist Protestant Church, Georgetown, D.C., March 9, 1859.

Bedell, John, Stuart Fiedel, and Charles Lee Decker. *Bold, Rocky, and Picturesque: Archaeological Overview and Assessment and Identification and Evaluation Study of Rock Creek Park District of Columbia, Prepared for National Capital Region, National Park Service.* Washington, D.C.: National Park Service, 2008.

Bedini, Silvio A. *The Life of Benjamin Banneker.* New York: Scribner, 1972.

Berlin, Ira. *Generations of Captivity: a History of African-American Slaves.* Cambridge, Mass.: Belknap Press of Harvard University Press, 2003.

Bissell, Theodore. "Tracing Shadrick Turner and Sarah Turner, Pioneer Methodists of Bladensburg." *Prince George's Historical Society, News & Notes,* December 1973.

Blassingame, John W., ed. *Slave Testimony.* Baton Rouge: Louisiana State University Press, 1977.

Bluett, Thomas. *Some Memoirs of the Life of Job the Son of Solomon the High Priest of Boonda in Africa, Who Was a Slave about Two Years in Maryland, and Afterwards Being Brought to England, Was Set Free and Sent to His Native Land in the Year 1734.* London: Printed for Richard Ford, 1734.

Boteler, Alexander. "Recollections of the John Brown Raid by a Virginian Who Witnessed the Fight." *Century Magazine* 26 (July 1883): 399–411.

"Boteler, Alexander Robinson." Biographical Directory of the United States Congress. http://tiny.cc/boteler (accessed June 6, 2011).

Broadhurst, Diane D. "An Examination of Slaves and Slavery in the Beall Family Household." September 25, 2001. Unpublished manuscript, Montgomery County Historical Society Library, Rockville, Md.

Brown, Lettia Woods. *Free Negroes in the District of Columbia, 1790–1846*. New York: Oxford University Press, 1972.

Brown, Vaughan W. *Shipping in the Port of Annapolis, 1748–1775*. Annapolis, Md.: United States Naval Institute, 1965.

Browne, William Hand, ed. *Proceedings of the Council of Maryland 1761–1769*, vol. 32. Baltimore: Maryland Historical Society, 1913.

Campbell, Penelope. *Maryland in Africa: The Maryland State Colonization Society, 1831–1857*. Urbana: University of Illinois Press, 1971.

Cissel, Anne W. "The Families of a Derwood Farm Through Two Centuries." *The Montgomery County Story* 27, no. 2 (1984): 1–10.

———. "Public Houses of Entertainment and Their Proprietors 1750–1828." *The Montgomery County Story* 30, no. 3 (August 1987): 279–287.

Clagett, Brice. Selected Clagett Family Genealogy. Unpublished manuscript, Montgomery County Historical Society Library, Rockville, Md.

Cook, Eleanor M. V. "The Brooke Beall and the Johns Family." July 1986. Unpublished manuscript.

———. "The Four Beall Women and Their Slaves." *The Montgomery County Story* 45 (February 2002): 213–223.

———. "Georgetown Jewel of Montgomery County—Part 1." *The Montgomery County Story* 41, no. 4 (1996): 49–60.

———. "Newport Mill." *The Montgomery County Story* 34, no. 1 (1991): 141–151.

———. "The Story of Burnt Mills." *The Montgomery County Story* 35, no. 4 (1992): 225–235.

Day, Jackson. *Descendants of Robert "the Scotsman" Beall, Immigrant*. Portland, Ore.: Beall Family Association, 1994.

———. "Maryland Beall Families Pre 1800." October 24, 1994. Unpublished manuscript.

Douglass, Frederick. *Narrative of the Life, My Bondage, and My Freedom, Life and Times*. New York: Literary Classics of the United States, 1994.

Dryden, Steve. *Peirce Mill: 200 Years in the Nation's Capital*. Washington, D.C.: Bergamot, 2009.

Ecker, Grace Dunlop. *A Portrait of Old George Town.* Richmond, Va.: Garrett & Massie, 1933.

Engelbrecht, Jacob. *The Diary of Jacob Engelbrecht.* Edited by William R. Quynn. Frederick, Md.: Historical Society of Frederick County, 2001.

Engelbrecht, Jacob, Edith Olivia Eader, and Trudie Davis-Long, eds. *The Jacob Engelbrecht Death Ledger of Frederick County, Maryland 1820–1890.* Monrovia, Md.: Paw Prints, 1995.

Ernst, Kathleen. *Too Afraid to Cry: Maryland Civilians in the Antietam Campaign.* Mechanicsburg, Pa.: Stackpole Books, 2007.

Federal Writers' Project. *Slave Narratives: A Folk History of Slavery in the United States from Interviews with Former Slaves,* vol. 7. Washington, D.C.: Library of Congress, 1941.

Ford, Robert Turner. "What Harvard Has Meant to Me." Speech, 1984 Reunion, Harvard Class of 1927, Cambridge, Massachusetts.

Fuller, Marsha Lynne. *African American Manumissions of Washington County, Maryland.* Westminster, Md.: Heritage Books, 2007.

Gaden, Henri. "Du nom chez les toucouleurs et peuls islamisés du Fouta Senegalais." *Revue d'Ethnographie et de Sociologie* 3 (1912): 50–56.

Gelders, Ruth Beall. "Colonel Ninian Beall, A Paper for the Daughters of the American Revolution." http://www.krystalrose.com/kim/BEALL/ninian1.html

Gomez, Michael. "Muslims in America." *Journal of Southern History* 60, no. 4 (1994): 671–710.

Goodwin, Doris Kearns. *Team of Rivals: The Political Genius of Abraham Lincoln.* New York: Simon & Schuster, 2005.

Gordon, Vivian Verdell. "A History of Storer College, Harpers Ferry." *Journal of Negro Education* 30, no. 4 (Autumn 1961): 445–449.

Green, Karen Mauer. *The Maryland Gazette, 1727–1761: Genealogical and Historical Abstracts.* Galveston, Tex.: Frontier Press, 1989.

Haley, Kenneth C. "A Nineteenth Century Portraitist and More: James Alexander Simpson." *Georgetown Day,* May 1977.

Hall, James. *Maryland Colonization Journal: New Series, July 15, 1841, Vol. I, No. 2.* Baltimore: John D. Toy, 1841.

Harris, Joseph Earl. "The Kingdom of Fouta-Diallon." Ph.D. dissertation, Northwestern University, 1965.

Henry, Thomas W. *Autobiography of Thomas W. Henry, of the A.M.E. Church.* Baltimore: Thomas W. Henry, 1872.

Henson, Josiah. *An Autobiography of the Rev. Josiah Henson ("Uncle Tom") From 1789 to 1881. With a Preface by Mrs. Harriet Beecher Stow, and Introductory Notes by George Sturger, S. Morles, Esq., M.P., Wendell Phillips, and John G. Whittier.* Ontario, Calif.: Schuyler & Smith, 1881.

Hirschfeld, Fritz. *George Washington and Slavery: A Documentary Portrayal.* Columbia: University of Missouri Press, 1997.

Holder, Charles. "History, St. Luke's Episcopal Church, Brownsville, MD." http://www.stluke.ang-md.org (accessed June 7, 2011).

Holmes, Oliver W. "Suter's Tavern: Birthplace of the Federal City." *Records of the Columbia Historical Society* 49 (1973–74): 1–34.

Hynson, Jerry M. *Free African Americans of Maryland 1832: Including: Allegany, Anne Arundel, Calvert, Caroline, Cecil, Charles, Dorchester, Frederick, Kent, Montgomery, Queen Ann's, and St. Mary's Counties.* Westminster, Md.: Family Line Publications, 1998.

An Illustrated Atlas of Washington County, Maryland. Philadelphia: Griffing, Lake, and Stevenson, 1877.

Jackson, Richard Plummer. *The Chronicles of Georgetown, D.C., from 1751–1878.* Washington, D.C.: R. O. Polkinhorn, 1878.

Jarrett, James H., L. Allison Wilmer, and George Vernon. *History and Roster of Maryland Volunteers, War of 1861–5 . . . by L. Allison Wilmer, J. H. Jarrett, Geo. W. F. Vernon.* Baltimore: Guggenheimer, Weil, 1899.

Johnston, Christopher. "Lowndes Family." *Maryland Historical Magazine* II (1907): 276.

Jones, Ray. *Harpers Ferry.* Gretna, La.: Pelican, 1992.

Jourdan, Elise Greenup. *Early Families of Southern Maryland,* vol. 7. Berwyn Heights, Md.: Heritage Books, 2007.

Keeler, Ralph. "Owen Brown's Escape from Harper's Ferry." *Atlantic Monthly,* March 1874.

Lesko, Kathleen M., Valerie Melissa Babb, and Carroll R. Gibbs. *Black Georgetown Remembered: A History of Its Black Community from the Founding of "The Town of George" in 1751 to the Present Day.* Washington, D.C.: Georgetown University Press, 1991.

Marx, Robert F. *Shipwrecks in America.* Mineola, N.Y.: Dover, 1987.

McGrigor, Mary. "Edmonstone of Duntreath Family History." http://tiny.cc/duntreath (accessed June 1, 2011).

McIlwraith, Thomas Forsyth, and Edward K. Muller. *North America: The Historical Geography of a Changing Continent.* Lanham, Md.: Rowman & Littlefield, 2001.

McLaws, Lafayette. *Official Records of the War of Rebellion.* Washington, D.C.: U.S. Government Printing Office, 1862.

McNeil, Priscilla. "Pretty Prospects: The History of a Land Grant." *Washington History* 14, no. 2 (2002–3): 6–25.

———. "Rock Creek Hundred: Land Conveyed for the Federal City." *Washington History* 3, no. 1 (1991).

Middleton, Arthur Pierce. *Tobacco Coast: A Maritime History of Chesapeake Bay in the Colonial Era.* Newport News, Va.: Mariners' Museum, 1953.

Minutes of the Annual Meetings of the Church of the Brethren: Containing All Available Minutes from 1778 to 1909. Elgin, Ill.: Brethren Publishing House, 1909.

Mitchell, Mary. "The Potomac Insurance Company of Georgetown, 1832–1841." *Records of the Columbia Historical Society* 69 (1969–70): 102–113.

Newman, Harry Wright. "John Turner of Anne Arundel County." *Maryland Genealogical Society Bulletin* 33, no. 2 (Spring 1922): 344–347.

Newton, John. *The Posthumous Works of the Late John Newton.* Philadelphia: W. W. Woodward, 1809.

Oates, Stephen B. *The Fires of Jubilee: Nat Turner's Fierce Rebellion.* New York: Harper & Row, 1975.

Peale, Charles Willson. *The Selected Papers of Charles Willson Peale and His Family,* vol. 1. Edited by Lillian B. Miller, Sidney Hart, and Toby A. Appel. New Haven: Yale University Press, 1983.

———. *The Selected Papers of Charles Willson Peale and His Family,* vol. 2. Edited by Lillian B. Miller, Sidney Hart, and David C. Ward. New Haven: Yale University Press, 1988.

———. *The Selected Papers of Charles Willson Peale and His Family,* vol. 3. Edited by Lillian B. Miller, David C. Ward, Sidney Hart, and Rose S. Emerick. New Haven: Yale University Press, 1991.

Pohl, Robert S., and John R. Wennersten. *Abraham Lincoln and the End of Slavery in the District of Columbia.* Washington, D.C.: Eastern Branch Press, 2009.

Poole, Martha Sprigg. "Early Rockville Taverns." *The Montgomery County Story* 1, no. 3 (1958): 1–6.

———. "Ninian Beall." *The Montgomery County Story* 3, no. 3 (1969): 1–9.

Portrait and Biographical Record of the Sixth Congressional District Maryland; Containing Portraits and Biographies of Many Well Known Citizens of the past and Present. Together with Portraits and Biographies of All the Presidents of the United States. New York: Chapman, 1895.

Rediker, Marcus. *The Slave Ship: A Human History.* New York: Viking, 2007.

Richardson, Cynthia. Interview with a Person over 50 Years of Age about the Highlights of the Times in Which He Lived. 1979. Unpublished manuscript.

Ricks, Mary Kay. *Escape on the Pearl: The Heroic Bid for Freedom on the Underground Railroad.* New York: William Morrow, 2007.

Riley, Robert Shean. *The Colonial Riley Families of the Tidewater Frontier*, vol. 1. Salt Lake City: Family History Library, 1999.

Russell, George Ely, and Donna Valley Russell. *The Ark and the Dove Adventurers.* Baltimore: Genealogical Publications, 2005.

Scharf, John Thomas. *History of Western Maryland*, vol. 1. Philadelphia: L. H. Everts, 1882.

Sellers, Charles Coleman. *Charles Willson Peale: A Biography.* New York: Charles Scribner's Sons, 1969.

———. "Charles Willson Peale and Yarrow Mamout." *The Pennsylvania Magazine of History and Biography*, 1947: 99–102.

"Sergeant Dorsey, Decatur." Congressional Medal of Honor Historical Society. http://tiny.cc/dorsey-decatur (accessed June 3, 2011).

Singewald, Joseph T. *The Iron Ores of Maryland, with an Account of the Iron Industry.* Baltimore: Johns Hopkins University Press, 1911.

Smith, Joseph Henry, and Philip A. Crowl. *Court Records of Prince Georges County, Maryland, 1696–1699.* Washington, D.C.: American Historical Association, 1964.

Smith, M. R. *Harpers Ferry Armory and the New Technology: The Challenge of Change.* Ithaca, N.Y.: Cornell University Press, 1980.

Sollors, Werner, Caldwell Titcomb, and Thomas A. Underwood. *Blacks at Harvard: A Documentary History of African-American Experience at Harvard and Radcliffe.* New York: New York University Press, 1993.

"Stearns, Ozora Pierson." Biographical Directory of the United States Congress. http://tiny.cc/ozora (accessed June 3, 2011).

Stoner, Paula. "Claggett Farm, WA-III-055." Maryland Inventory of Historic Properties. http://www.mdihp.net (accessed June 7, 2011).

———. "Crampton-Mullendore Farm, WA-III-008." Maryland Inventory of Historic Properties. http://www.mdihp.net (accessed June 7, 2011).

———. "King Cole, Grim Farm, Edwards Farm, WA-III-010." Maryland Inventory of Historic Properties. http://www.mdihp.net (accessed June 7, 2011).

———. "Magnolia Plantation, WA-III-014." Maryland Inventory of Historic Properties. http://www.mdihp.net (accessed June 7, 2011).

———. "19th Century Brick Farmhouse, WA-III-011." Maryland Inventory of Historic Properties. http://www.mdihp.net (accessed June 7, 2011).

Thompson, Henry F. "Maryland at the End of the Seventeenth Century." *Maryland Historical Magazine* II (1907): 163–171.

Thompson, Michael D. "The Iron Industry in Western Maryland." Unpublished manuscript.

Trans-Atlantic Slave Trade. http://www.slavevoyages.org (accessed May 25, 2011).

Unrau, Harlan D., *Historic Resource Study: Chesapeake & Ohio Canal.* Hagerstown, Md.: U.S. Department of the Interior, National Park Service, C&O National Historical Park, 2007.

"Virginia Hollerith." Interview by Mary Jo Deering. Barnard-Talcott Hollerith Family Papers, Special Collections Research Center, George Washington University.

Walston, Mark. "Slave Housing in Montgomery County." *The Montgomery County Story* 27, no. 3 (1984): 111–126.

Warden, David Bailles. *A Chorographical and Statistical Description of the District of Columbia Seat of the General Government of the United States.* Paris: Smith, 1816.

Washington, George. *George Washington Papers at the Library of Congress, 1741–1799.* Edited by Donald Jackson and Dorothy Twohig. Charlottesville: University of Virginia Press, 1976.

Wiencek, Henry. *An Imperfect God: George Washington, His Slaves, and the Creation of America.* New York: Farrar, Straus and Giroux, 2003.

Acknowledgments

While it is my voice telling this story, the facts were obviously lodged elsewhere. In addition to frequenting libraries, archives, and the like, I interviewed 109 people in person or by phone and dozens of others by email and by letter. I was humbled by all the people who gave freely of their time and expertise in this endeavor.

Librarians, archivists, academics, and experts were prime contributors. The collections at the Montgomery County Historical Society Library, which have been under the supervision of Patricia Andersen for years, were a godsend. Of particular use were the library's genealogical folders on county families and maps of the old land tracts, which are the work of volunteers. Sheila Cochran was one of them. She and others spent years preparing those maps, and it was from looking at these that I discovered that Aquilla Yarrow and Mary Turner were neighbors.

Another woman at the historical society, Eleanor Vaughn Cook, took an interest in Yarrow Mamout and the Beall and Johns family years before I did. Her unpublished manuscript was the first significant in-depth scholarly research on Yarrow Mamout.

Jerry McCoy, librarian for the Peabody Room at the Georgetown Library, introduced me to Yarrow. He also spearheaded the fundraising to restore the Simpson painting after it was rescued from a fire at the library. At the Frederick County Historical Society, Brigette Kamsler did a search for Nancy Hillman's grave and tipped me off to the entries in Jacob Englebrecht's diary about the Hillmans. John Frye at the Washington County Free Library was a constant font of knowledge of that county's history. He grew up not far from where Polly Yarrow lived, and his great-grandfather tended the road that went past her house and over Solomon's Gap. At the National Archives, archivist Robert Ellis was my guide and told me of the file on Nancy Hillman's lawsuit. Chris Haley was my contact at the Maryland State Archives in Annapolis.

Late in my research, Janet Stanley, librarian at the Smithsonian African American Art Museum, learned of my struggles in making sense of Yarrow Mamout's name. She found material in that library's collections and introduced me to Tierno Bah, who is from Futa Jallon, and to Ahmed Acrati, both of whom helped. Sid Hart at the National Portrait Gallery in Washington guided me on Charles Willson Peale. The collection of Peale's papers that was edited and published by the scholars at the Portrait Gallery turned out to be a Rosetta Stone that was one key to unlocking the story of Yarrow's life.

Terry Alford's book *Prince Among Slaves*, on Ayuba Suleiman Diallo, made me realize that Yarrow was not the only Muslim from Futa Jallon to come to Maryland, and it enabled me to speculate on how he was captured. Alford also gave encouragement to my research. Jean Russo, with the Maryland State Archives, kindly let me use her unpublished research on how many convicts, indentured servants, and slaves came to Maryland in the period that Yarrow did and helped me understand how the port of Annapolis functioned then. Kees de Mooy similarly gave me the benefit of research he had done on Christopher Lowndes and Bostwick, Lowndes's house in Bladensburg. Susan Pearl of the Prince George's County Historical Society, a writer in her own right, was always ready to share her knowledge of that county. After I located the extant bible of Shadrick Turner, Samuel Turner's brother, Susan photographed it and gave me copies of the pages with slave names. Writer and historian Eileen McGukian provided similar help for the history of Rockville. Richard Raymond, with the National Park Service at Harpers Ferry, which had acquired the Storer College facility, furnished me with a list of the college's graduates, showing the name Emma Turner, and did the research to determine if Aquilla Yarrow worked at the arsenal. Dean Herrin at the Catoctin Center for Regional Studies gave me copies of Freedman Bureau records for Colored School No. 6 that he had found at the National Archives.

When it came to locating Yarrow's grave at his house in Georgetown, Nancy Kassner, then archaeologist for the District of Columbia, kindly accompanied me to the scene and wisely advised that the ground should not be disturbed. William Kelso, an archaeologist with Preservation Virginia, responded to my email request for help with the bricks at Yarrow's house. Based on my photographs, he felt that the bricks were probably handmade and hence dated from Yarrow's time. Kevin Smullin Brown at the University of London, Sulayman Nyang at Howard University, Ahmed Acrati, and Tierno Bah all looked at photographs of Yarrow's signature as it appears in the Recorder of Deeds book and concluded it was Arabic. Theodore Hazen, an expert on colonial water mills, was invaluable in understanding those structures and how Samuel Beall might have used them.

Current and former residents of Pleasant Valley were exceedingly patient and gracious in taking phone calls and visits from me to get oral histories. William Mullenix was the first resident I met. His grandfather had passed on to him the story of Polly Yarrow being a midwife. Bill had soaked up this and other stories when he was a boy and said he wished he had paid better attention. Robert Bowers and I spent an hour one hot Saturday in August slashing through prickly vines along Yarrowsburg Road, trying to find headstones he remembered from his youth that were said to mark the graves of Polly Yarrow, her husband, and a boy. Mullenix's aunt, Dottie Tritapoe, was Yarrowsburg historian when I first went there. She advised me to drop by Mt. Moriah Baptist Church. There I met then-pastor Sherman Lambert. It was Lambert that in turn invited me to the church's reunion service in October 2005 where I first met Mrs. Gloria Ford Dennis and learned of the Turners. Church elder James Brown helped with church history and with oral histories of life for blacks in Pleasant Valley. Through the church, I met its oldest member, Mary Gross, as well as Isabel Johnson and Gloria Edmundson who gave oral histories. Rev. Jonathan Davis at the A.M.E. church in Knoxville helped me untangle that church's history and its connection to Rev. Robert Ford. Rev. Charles Holder and Dennis Hammond did the same for the history of St. Paul's Episcopal Church in the valley.

Sabine Fisher, who with her husband, Frederick, owns Alexander Grim's old house, took it upon herself to resolve the legend of slave graves on Yarrowsburg Road that led me to Robert Bowers. Regina Jones owns the old John Gray farm and spent an afternoon telling me stories and showing Civil War relics that treasure hunters had found on the land. Denen Mullendore owns Eli Crampton's old farm and said that the springhouse had probably been where Simon Turner and his family lived. Ruff and Susan Fant own Kelly's Purchase, Samuel Beall's old farm, and allowed me to tour the land and photograph the house. South Lynn and the late Harold Kessissian bought and restored the Kennedy Farm that John Brown had rented near Yarrowsburg. They gave me a tour and told me the history they have uncovered about it. Historian Jean Libby also mined the valley for oral histories that she shared. No discussion of Pleasant Valley today is complete without mentioning Gary Himes, who dispenses valley history, legends, and personalities from his store on Weverton Road.

Then there are the descendants. Although Gloria Dennis was the first of Simon Turner's descendants that I met, my main contact was with her sister Cynthia Richardson. Mrs. Richardson's sisters Emily Willis and Denise Dungee helped too as, of course, did their cousin, Alice Truiett. Mrs. Truiett is Robert Turner Ford's daughter. Elie Crampton's lineal descendant is Charles Gardenhour. He loaned me Mollie Crampton's autograph book, letters, and an envelope with a lock of her bright red hair. Ed Adams was a Crampton descendant who did a family genealogy and who led me to Gardenhour. The Beall descendants were Jim Beall of Portland and his father Robert C. Beall. They are not descended from the Bealls that owned Yarrow, though. They trace themselves back to a collateral ancestor. Elwood Stith in Southampton County, Virginia, helped with the Nat Turner story. James Bateson, a Lowndes descendant, shared his research on slave ships.

Several other people deserve note. I used the late Brice Clagett's exhaustive genealogy of his family and got help from him before his death. Margaret Cheney is the current owner of Yarrow's lot and pointed out that the brick cellar may be original. John Heller owned the David Ross house in Baltimore County. His tour of the house revealed the surprisingly lavish lifestyle that Ross and others in Bladensburg enjoyed in early Maryland. Longtime Prince George's County resident James Rogers opened my eyes to the Bealls' connections to that county, tobacco, and Bladensburg. Gwendora Reese helped me understand how the small black communities in Montgomery County formed after tobacco wore out the soil and told me about Turner Town. I also want to note Michael Thompson and the careful research he did years ago on iron making in Western Maryland, which provided the basic understanding of Samuel Beall's move there in 1770.

Research is one part of a book such as this. Writing is another. Diane Broadhurst was the first to encourage me to write the Yarrow story, which she edited and published for the Montgomery County Historical Society's journal. Moreover, she gave me her research on Aquilla Yarrow and constantly and selflessly served as a sounding board for my own discoveries and miscues. Joel Chineson, then an editor with *Legal Times*, edited and published my second article on Yarrow, "The Mona Lisa of Georgetown." Tom Shroder at the *Washington Post Magazine* edited and published my third article, "The Man in the Knit Cap." And at the *Maryland History Magazine*, Patricia Anderson edited and published "Every Picture Tells a Story." Each of these editors helped shape how to tell this saga.

Additional editorial help and encouragement came from Jack Wennersten, who sought me out to tell me that I needed to write this book. My friend Rob Gunnison, a former newspaper reporter, edited the first manuscript. Ted Pulliam looked at drafts. Others did too but have asked not to be thanked by name. Serrin Ransom did the graphics for the book. She proved to me that a picture can be worth a thousand words if the picture is done right. I also want to recognize Will Cerbone and Fredric Nachbaur at Fordham University Press for seeing the merit in and publishing this work and my editor at the Press, Eric Newman, and my copy editor, Gregory McNamee, for their help. Last, I want to thank Ruth Mills for the enormous help and advice she provided on structure and flow that turned a manuscript into a book.

Index